JACQUES MARITAIN

Twentieth-Century Political Thinkers
General Editors: Kenneth L. Deutsch and Jean Bethke Elshtain

Raymond Aron: The Recovery of the Political
    by Brian C. Anderson, American Enterprise Institute
Jacques Maritain: The Philosopher in Society
    by James V. Schall, Georgetown University
Martin Buber: The Hidden Dialogue
    by Dan Avnon, Hebrew University of Jerusalem
John Dewey: America's Philosopher of Democracy
    David Fott, University of Nevada

JACQUES MARITAIN

The Philosopher in Society

JAMES V. SCHALL

ROWMAN & LITTLEFIELD PUBLISHERS, INC.
Lanham • Boulder • New York • Oxford

ROWMAN & LITTLEFIELD PUBLISHERS, INC.

Published in the United States of America
by Rowman & Littlefield Publishers, Inc.
4720 Boston Way, Lanham, Maryland 20706

12 Hid's Copse Road
Cummor Hill, Oxford OX2 9JJ, England

British Library Cataloguing in Publication Information Available

Library of Congress Cataloging-in-Publication Data

Schall, James V.
    Jacques Maritain : the philosopher in society / James V. Schall.
        p.   cm.
    Includes bibliographical references and index.
    ISBN 0-8476-8683-3 (alk. paper).—ISBN 0-8476-8684-1 (pbk. :
alk. paper)
    1. Maritain, Jacques, 1882–1973.   2. Political science—
Philosophy—History—20th century.   I. Title.
B2430-M34S43   1998
320'.092—dc21   97-24238
                                                                          CIP

ISBN 0-8476-8683-3
ISBN 0-8476-8684-1

Printed in the United States of America

♾ ™ The paper used in this publication meets the minimum requirements of
American National Standard for Information Sciences—Permanence of Paper
for Printed Library Materials, ANSI Z39.48–1984.

The philosopher in society witnesses to the supreme dignity of thought; he points to what is eternal in man, and stimulates our thirst for pure knowledge, for knowledge of those fundamentals—about the nature of things and the nature of the mind, and man himself, and God—which are superior to, and independent of anything we can make or produce or create—and to which all our practice is appendant, because we think before acting and nothing can limit the range of thought: our practical decisions depend on the stand we take on the ultimate questions that human thought is able to ask. That is why philosophical systems, which are directed toward no practical use and application . . . have such an impact on human history.

> —Jacques Maritain, Lecture at the Graduate School at Princeton University, 2 January 1953, in *On the Use of Philosophy: Three Essays* (New York: Atheneum, 1965), 7.

Nous avons dit . . . que tout grand système moral est en réalité un effort pour demander à l'homme, d'une manière ou d'une autre et à un degré ou un autre, de dépasser en quelque façon sa condition naturelle.

> —Jacques Maritain, *La Philosophie Morale,* (1960), in *Oeuvres Complètes* (Fribourg, Suisse: Éditions Universitaires, 1982), vol. 11, 1034.

The sorrows and hopes of our time undoubtedly stem from material causes, economic and technical forces which play an essential role in the course of human history, but even more profoundly they stem from the ideas, the drama in which the spirit is involved, the invisible forces which arise and develop in our minds and hearts. History is not a mechanical unfolding of events into the midst of which man is simply *placed* like a stranger. Human history is human in its very essence; it is the history of our own being. . . . Nothing is more important than the events which occur within that invisible universe which is the mind of man. And the light of that universe is knowledge.

> —Jacques Maritain, "On Human Knowledge," in *The Range of Reason* (New York: Charles Scribner's Sons, 1952), 3.

CONTENTS

ACKNOWLEDGMENTS

For the opportunity to pursue this study on Maritain, I am grateful to Professor Kenneth Deutsch for his invitation to include it in the Rowman & Littlefield series on Twentieth Century Political Philosophers. Likewise, I wish to acknowledge the opportunity provided by a Sabbatical leave from Georgetown University and from its Department of Government. The generous assistance of a grant from The Earhart Foundation is most appreciated.

The text, with many helpful and incisive comments, was read by Professor Raymond Dennehy at the University of San Francisco, by Susan Orr, at the Department of Health and Human Services, by Professor David Yost at the Naval Post-Graduate School in Monterey, in California, by Stuart Rowland in Australia, and by Mrs. Tracey Rowland, a Commonwealth Scholar at Cambridge University in England. I am also grateful to the Rowman & Littlefield editors for their careful reading of the text. Any remaining errors or confusions, of course, remain mine.

I wish to thank the following publishers for permission to cite from their Maritain publications: 1) Magi Books of Albany, N.Y., from Maritain's *Notebooks*; 2) the University of Chicago Press from *Man and the State*; 3) Ignatius Press, reprinted from *Christianity and Democracy*, 1986, pp. 10, 25, 28, 37, 53–54, 56, 58, 66, and 172 © Ignatius Press, San Francisco. All rights reserved; reprinted with permission of Ignatius Press; 4) University of Notre Dame Press, from *Art and Scholasticism* and *The Social and Political Ideas of Jacques Maritain: Selected Readings*, and 5) Harper/Collins, London, from Charles Scribner's Sons, *Freedom in the Modern World*.

INTRODUCTION

The cover of the Doubleday Image edition of Jacques Maritain's *Existence and the Existent: An Essay on Christian Existentialism* carries a promotional sentence from a *New York Times* book review. The sentence reads: This book is "vividly presented by a philosopher unusually sensitive to the main currents of his times."[1] Maritain is presented as simply "a philosopher," which is always how he described himself. This identification is what makes Maritain of particular interest in recent political philosophy; he is a philosopher who also accounts for political things. In the lists of twentieth-century writers in "political philosophy," Jacques Maritain is first and always "a philosopher," someone who seeks to know what the human mind can understand about the whole, of what different things are, and of how they are related to one another.

Maritain wrote on both speculative and practical philosophy. He saw no valid intellectual reason for excluding revelation and its content from philosophic examination. He understood this effort to scrutinize the coherent relationship of revelation and reason to be a question of simple intellectual honesty. Nothing of *what is* can be excluded from our ken.

We also know much about his personal life. He is obviously a human being with a warm and tender heart. This is evident in the memoirs of both Maritain and his wife Raïssa, who, as he often acknowledges, plays a fundamental role in his intellectual life.[2]

Maritain is a model in modern political thought. He devotes much of his time to metaphysics, physics, psychology, mathematics, theology, and logic, as well as to the meaning of history. His range of interests is breathtaking. This wide background is reflected in every page that he writes about political things. He reminds us of the truth that, to know political things, it is not sufficient only to know political things. His political thought is not set apart by itself, but stands within an overarching intellectual whole. The political philosopher who is also a philosopher is not lost within the natural limits of his own discipline. He is aware of approaches and responses to issues that arise in political things but that are not ultimately resolved there. Maritain is a living lesson in liberal education, another subject of great interest to him.[3] His approach is unique and refreshing, albeit demanding, for most students of political reality. He makes them aware of the unsuspected reaches of the highest of the practical sciences, as Aristotle called politics.

In Maritain, consequently, we feel the call and attraction to the intellectual life as one that is rooted in a tradition. "Sometimes, we feel sorry for those who have never felt themselves inflamed over reading Plato or Plotinus," Maritain observed in a conference at Kolbsheim in July 1968. "It is the style today to deprecate 'Hellenic thought'. I am persuaded, however, that it has played a providential role and that, just as in what concerns faith and salvation, God has given to the People of Israel a supernaturally unique mission, so in that which concerns reason, the Greeks were given a unique, natural mission that we have the duty of recognizing."[4] Maritain's *An Introduction to Philosophy*, intelligible to any student of political things, spells out not merely the relation of Greek, Hebrew, and Christian thought to each other, but the significance of this thought as it relates to non-Greek and modern systems.[5] Reading Maritain, then, makes demands on the modern reader that he will not often encounter in other thinkers.[6] Maritain is an excellent guide to teach us to progress from political philosophy to philosophy itself.

Maritain's *Existence and the Existent* is a clear analysis of existentialism as seen in the light of Thomas Aquinas's philosophy of being and existence, a subject that Maritain considered in detail before the rise of existentialism after World War II. But what is interesting about the reviewer's sentence above cited is what it implicitly reveals about the presumed function or purpose of the philosopher, namely, that his worth is related not to his pursuit of truth but to his sensitivity to the "main currents of his times." Maritain, in this approach, is to be praised because he took these main currents seriously. However, no reason can be found in this recommendation why a positivist, a Hegelian, a liberal, a socialist, or a fool could not equally show sensitivity to the same main currents of his time. Maritain is praised by a *New York Times* reviewer for his trendiness, not for his insight into truth, which is really the aspect of him most worth studying.

Jacques Maritain, even though he knew them well, was not a follower of the main philosophical currents of his time but rather of the thirteenth-century philosopher and theologian, Thomas Aquinas. Maritain, of course, could be most amused by what people thought of his philosophy. At the luncheon in New York on 9 January 1943, for example, on the occasion of his sixtieth birthday, when the volume of *The Thomist* dedicated to him was presented, Maritain recounted the following story:

> It is about my Thomism that I would like to say some words. An elderly lady, whom I venerate, speaking of me to one of my friends . . . said, "He is a Catholic, you know, but of a particular sect, he is also a Thomist." *Mon Dieu!* Thomism is not obviously a sect such as Christian Science. It is simply the philosophy of Aristotle baptized by Saint Thomas Aquinas. That does not exactly indicate a revolutionary air, but it is not necessary to trust to appearances. It is a question of attaching oneself to principles of reason and to principles of faith in the most strict doctrinal synthesis in order to have the most liberal view and to confront, in the most daring manner possible, the problems of our time.[7]

This last sentence contains the essence of Maritain. He chooses not to exclude philosophy or revelation. He insists that both must be fairly examined. Their relationship is not negative, but beneficial to both. What he proposes, however, he knows to be "daring."

Thomas Aquinas took care to state clearly and accurately the positions against which he argued. Aquinas is famous for his ability to state the position *against* which he is arguing better than the one making the case *for* it. The philosophical tradition of taking one's opponents' arguments seriously, no doubt, goes back to Plato and Aristotle. Aquinas was, in the beginning, simply a good pupil. If Maritain was likewise a good pupil in this tradition, that he was sensitive "to the main currents of his time" does not yet tell us anything about what he thought of these currents, whether he thought specific currents true or erroneous, and why. It is this latter enterprise—his analysis of what he thinks true, and what false—that interests us about any philosopher, including Maritain.

Though sometimes given to using odd words like "gnoseological" or "practical-practical," Maritain always presents the reader with a coherent, generally clear statement of what he maintained. He knew modern thought, but he was not a "modern" as that word has come to be used to justify a philosopher's volitional independence of classical and revelational thought about being, about *what is*. Maritain belongs to a philosophic tradition that maintained that the core issues of philosophy are "perennial." Plato, Aristotle, Augustine, and Aquinas are always in the "present." To be sensitive to one's own time is at best challenging and at worst historicist, but in any case a necessary, if insufficient, background for philosophy itself.

The Rowman & Littlefield series on political philosophers in the twentieth century recognizes that we are in as much need of a reflective understanding of reality as we are of acknowledging that there is a reality to understand in the first place. Man is both a rational animal and a political animal. Because he is rational, he can be political. Because he is political, he can be more of what he ought to be than he can be alone. But since he has free will, he can choose to be less rational, less noble than he ought to choose to be. Man when he is good, Aristotle has said, is the best of the animals; but when he is bad, he is far worse than any other animal. Such sobering words seem fitting in looking back at the twentieth century. We do need to understand our past, not merely know that we have lived through it. A past that is not understood cannot be properly preserved. And we can choose both not to understand and not to preserve.

Great figures of the twentieth century such as Alexander Solzhenitsyn remind us, not always to our liking, that the twentieth was the bloodiest of all the centuries during which man has been seeking to know himself, that unique mission on which Socrates sent him some twenty-four hundreds of years ago. We continue to be surprised at this truth about our mercilessness to ourselves, particularly because we thought that the eighteenth and nineteenth centuries were centuries of necessary "progress," that is, centuries during which we had found ways to avoid the ancient sins and errors of our kind—wars, poverty, injustice. We presumed that in the twentieth century and beyond, "democracy," now called the "best regime," is safe among us even if we neglect its philosophic and moral roots.

Leo Strauss, in an oft-cited remark, said that we would be lucky to be alive during the same time in which one or two of the greatest thinkers of our kind were alive.[8] Even were we to be alive during this time, moreover, the chances of our recognizing such a great thinker would be very slim. We need not be overly skeptical on this score. But, it seems, great thinkers come and go. In the 1930s, at the University of Chicago, something called "the Great Books" was invented. Studying these great books seemed like a good idea for the next half century until someone deconstructed the agreed canon of what these books were, until we began to doubt if we could learn anything from these or any books. We began to doubt, indeed, if we could know anything at all.

Doubting whether we could know anything at all, of course, was nothing new. The Greeks knew about this questioning of our knowing faculties, as did the medieval scholastic thinkers. Descartes, whom, as a Frenchman, Maritain knew well, even elevated doubting to the very heart of modern philosophy. However, the exercise of testing whether we could in fact doubt all things was what grounded the beginning of all thought. The analysis and refutation of skepticism remain the initial philosophic acts. To "know" that all things are doubtful is to know that something is not doubtful. Absolute doubt is an act of unexamined credulity, not of reason. When something in its denial is thus implicitly and essentially affirmed in the very statement of the denial, it follows that universal skepticism is itself untrue, untenable in the very statement of itself. The faculty of reason, paradoxically, functions quite normally even when it is used against itself. To continue in doubt becomes by that very fact an act of will, not reason. Consequently, if some one thing could be thought, perhaps something else could be thought. What this book will propose is a series of things worth thinking about because they have been coherently and intelligently thought about by a particular philosopher against the background of a modernity that has suspected that it need not take the claims of metaphysics and revelation seriously.

In any case, as Strauss also intimated, in reading any canon of great books, it becomes clear that the great thinkers contradict not only each other, but sometimes themselves. The principle of contradiction remains the central theoretic tool of reason, something directly involved in every thought and action that comes from us. Thus, if the variety of great books was the only judgment we had, we would be unable to know which of these books were the greatest, that is, which ones were true.[9] Seeking to discover and love what is true has been traditionally called philosophy. Philosophy implies, in the light of the contradictions found in the great books, that we have to rely upon ourselves, not claiming more for ourselves than we can deliver, but not claiming that the contradictions of the great philosophers exempt us from any effort to reach conclusions. As was suggested in Book Six of *The Republic*, philosophy stands outside the opinions of the city. In relying on ourselves, we do not rely, as much contemporary culture seems to assume, on our subjective feelings but on an order of reason, an order that is to be found in reality as reflected in our souls.

Nietzsche died in 1900, the first year of the twentieth century. With no little irony, he more than Marx, more than Mill or Darwin, turned out to be the best intellectual guide to what would happen during that century. Modern philosophy, so it assumed, thought classical philosophy and Christian revelation out of existence, all the while implicitly depending on them. Nietzsche chastised the weaklings as he called them, the philosophers, the politicians, and yes, the theologians of modernity, who were afraid or unwilling to live with what they themselves had come to think or believe about reality.

Eric Voegelin, a philosopher of great character, also has remarked that the origin of modern ideology could be located in this same weakness of faith in Christians that Nietzsche had noticed.[10] Modern political systems were the result of efforts to relocate the ideas of salvation and happiness from their transcendent origins to movements in this world dedicated to realizing these ideas by political or economic, not religious or philosophic, means. The result of this mislocation was to place an emphasis on social and political things that they could not bear. When we thought we were doing politics, we were often in fact doing a kind of theology. When the ideological alternatives to the projects of faith began themselves to fail, however, what arose was a marked tendency to employ power, now devoid of any rational control, rather than admit that anything was fundamentally wrong with our institutions and ways of life in the first place. Intelligence itself, it was thought, had already forfeited any claim to be of assistance to actual life. Nietzsche's famous "God is dead" and "will to power" are only the most well-known statements of this despair of ever finding some coherent explanation of the world that would be sufficient to bear human life. The "will to power" in fact seeks to establish an order and a justification for its use on the hypothesis that an explanation from God is not possible.

What seems to be most needed and valuable is a guide, a way to clarify things. I am going to present the French philosopher Jacques Maritain as this guide. No doubt we can find many good guides. I do not present Maritain as having no problems. I will indicate them when necessary. Maritain was particularly adept, however, at understanding the importance of thinking itself, thinking about things, understanding where they belonged in the order of reality, thinking about thinking itself. Whether Maritain should be called a "great" thinker in the sense of Plato or Aristotle need not be judged here. He certainly would not have so classified himself, but then neither would Plato or Aristotle. It was Aristotle, after all, who told us to be a friend of Socrates and a friend of Plato, but always more a friend of truth. Someone can be great because he built on the greatness of someone else, who lived before him. The fact is that Maritain thought his way through intellectual disciplines and practical realities in the light of the order that came to be argued in Aristotle and especially Aquinas.

The Rowman & Littlefield series on twentieth-century political philosophers will present analyses of a number of worthy thinkers—liberal, socialist, conservative, or some falling into a combination of the same. Maritain deserves attention because he argued to and through political philosophy from a consistent, articulated metaphysics and theology. Maritain was open in a way that was unique among twentieth-century political thinkers. To be sure, his pupil and friend Yves Simon made a similar argument. Between Strauss or Voegelin or Arendt and Maritain there is much similarity of purpose and analysis of problems. It is characteristic of much modern thinking to expect that arguments that arise from revelation should be downplayed or not presented at all. Moreover, among political philosophers, the influx of ideas from metaphysics or art or history will seem, if not exactly alien, at least not necessary. For Maritain, this inflow is normal.

Maritain himself was a man of wide-ranging interests. He studied biology in Germany; he studied philosophy under Henri Bergson at the *Collège de France*; he explored St. Thomas under several Dominican thinkers. He knew Georges Roualt, the painter; Léon Bloy, the novelist; Charles Péguy, the poet; Charles Journet, the theologian; Arthur Lourié, the composer. His own grandfather, Jules Fauvre, had been a prime minister in the Third Republic in France. Maritain was as familiar with mystical theology as with social philosophy. He never hesitated to present the context from which he thought. He did not expect agreement, but he did expect an openness of mind and a comprehension of purpose. He was a Catholic philosopher who wrote as much for the non-Catholic and the nonphilosopher as he did for those who agreed with his positions. He served those willing to know, whatever their background.

To introduce the particular flavor of Maritain's personality and openness of mind, two passages are of particular significance. Maritain harbored no secret doctrine or hidden political or intellectual agenda. What he thought was true and ought to be done are always clearly stated and argued, within the corpus of his works. What makes him unique in contemporary political philosophy is that Maritain makes available the fullness of discussion that is required to encounter political, divine, and human things. Maritain understood that his being a philosopher did not close him off from other realities that incite the human enterprise and become a part of the objective evidence of philosophy itself.

The first passage is from a brief personal memoir of Maritain entitled "Confession of Faith." The frankness of this passage, its honest clarity about his own stand, is one of the pillars of Maritain's thought. "As a child I was brought up in 'Liberal Protestantism,' " he wrote in 1941.

> Later on I became acquainted with the different phases of secularized thought. The scientist and phenomenist philosophy of my teachers at the Sorbonne made me despair of reason. At one time I thought I might be able to find complete certitude in the sciences, and Felix Le Dantec thought that my fiancée (Raïssa Oumançoff) and I would become followers of his biological materialism. The best thing I owe to my studies at that time is that they led me to meet, in the School of Sciences, the woman who since has always, happily for me, been at my side in a perfect and blessed communion. Bergson was the first to answer our deep desire for metaphysical truth—he liberated in us the sense of the absolute.[11]

We note here already the many levels of Maritain's own experience—his French Protestant origins, his scientific training, the influence of his wife, and his earnest search for truth.

"Before being captured by St. Thomas Aquinas, I underwent some great influences, those of Charles Péguy, Bergson, and Léon Bloy," Maritain's memoir continues,

A year after we met Bloy, my wife and I were baptized Catholics (11 June 1906). . . . It was after my conversion to Catholicism that I came to know St. Thomas. I had voyaged passionately through all doctrines of modern philosophers and had found in them nothing but disappointment and grandiose uncertainty. What I now experienced was like an illumination of reason. My vocation as a philosopher became perfectly clear to me.[12]

What is important about this passage is its affirmation that Maritain considered himself to be primarily a philosopher, someone who both loved and pursued the truth. Philosophy did include the passionate voyage "through all doctrines of modern philosophers," but it also included St. Thomas as a central element in this voyage. We have in Maritain, in other words, a unique union of classic, medieval, and modern thought. This union is itself a pursuit of truth and a critical analysis of the instruments within us by which we can and ought to seek and find truth, insofar as this is possible to finite, human, yet redeemed rational beings.

The second passage concerns what Maritain expected of his listener or reader. On 3 April 1943, Maritain gave a lecture entitled, "World Trial: Its Meaning for the Future," before the thirty-eighth Council of the Union of American Hebrew Congregations. "I am deeply appreciative of the honor which is granted to me . . . and I sincerely thank the Union for its kind invitation to open the present symposium," Maritain began.

I have been asked to speak as a Catholic, about our common topic *The Healing of Humanity*. To tell the truth, I feel rather frightened at the magnitude of such a subject. I shall nevertheless try to treat it with simplicity, that is to say, with full awareness of and resignation to my inadequacy. I trust that in freely expressing my own views I do not run the risk of hurting the conscience of anyone in the audience.[13]

Maritain here, as in all his works, reveals himself as a sincere and humble man. His modesty is not false; his humility is an honest humility.

What is significant about the passage cited above, to conclude this introduction to Maritain's thought, is something that constitutes the presupposition of this book in presenting him as a political philosopher. It is entirely proper and honorable for him to make his own arguments clearly and completely. He neither wants nor has to hide what he himself holds as a Catholic and a philosopher. Here are democracy, toleration, and ecumenism at their best. No doubt, audiences and individuals exist before whom it is prudent to worry about hurting the feelings of the fragile or inciting the animosity of the biased.

But as in 1943, the audiences and readers before whom we can present our deepest thoughts will be the ones who allow us to state what we in fact hold to be true and why we hold it. The pursuit of truth, whether by a philosopher, a Protestant, a scientist, a Hebrew, or whomever, at least demands this freedom, this invitation "to speak as a Catholic," to make arguments as persuasively and as freely as one can. To know political things, after beginning with Machiavelli's legacy in the first chapter, we need to realize, as Maritain shows us in the second and third chapters, how they relate to artistic and philosophic things. Maritain's legacy to students of political philosophy is both to "enflame them to the love of Plato or Plotinus," of Aristotle and Aquinas, and also to teach them the truth in all things on which the cities and empires of men rise and fall, things of experience and of history, of reason and of revelation.

Notes

1. Jacques Maritain, *Existence and the Existent: An Essay on Christian Existentialism*, trans. Lewis Galantiere and Gerald B. Phelan (Garden City, N. Y.: Doubleday Image, 1957).

2. See Jacques Maritain, *Notebooks*, trans. Joseph W. Evans (Albany, N.Y.: Magi Books, 1984); Raïssa Maritain, *Raïssa's Journal*, presented by Jacques Maritain (Albany, N. Y.: Magi Books, 1974).

3. See Jacques Maritain, *Education at the Crossroads* (New Haven: Yale University Press, 1943); *The Education of Man: The Educational Philosophy of Jacques Maritain*, ed. Donald and Idella Gallagher (Garden City, N. Y.: Doubleday, 1962).

4. Jacques Maritain, "Réflexions sur le savoir théologique," in vol. 13 of *Oeuvres Complètes* (Fribourg Suisse: Éditions Universitaires/Paris: Éditions Saint-Paul, 1992), 861. Henceforth, this French edition of Maritain's *Opera Omnia* will be cited as *OCM*. Unless otherwise indicated, all translations are by the author.

5. Jacques Maritain, *An Introduction to Philosophy*, trans. E. I. Watkin (London: Sheed & Ward, 1946).

6. For a useful secondary source, see *Understanding Maritain: Philosopher and Friend*, ed. Deal W. Hudson and Matthew J. Mancini (Macon, Ga.: Mercer University Press, 1987).

7. Jacques Maritain, "À Mes Amis de New York," *OCM*, vol. 8, 797–8. The Maritain volume of *The Thomist* 5 (January 1943) was also published in book form by Sheed & Ward, 1943.

8. Leo Strauss, *Liberalism: Ancient and Modern* (Ithaca, N. Y.: Cornell University Press, 1968), 3.

9. Ibid. See also Frederick D. Wilhelmsen, "The Great Books: Enemies of Wisdom," *Modern Age* 31 (Summer/Fall 1987): 323–31.

10. Eric Voegelin, *Science, Politics and Gnosticism* (Chicago: Gateway, 1968), 108–114.

11. Jacques Maritain, "Confession of Faith," *The Social and Political Philosophy of Jacques Maritain: Selected Readings,* ed. Joseph W. Evans and Leo R. Ward (Notre Dame: University of Notre Dame Press, 1976), 331. Maritain notes the importance of his wife Raïssa in his own intellectual work in this document. This influence is underscored by a letter of Olivier Lacombe, after Raïssa's death, to Jacques Maritain, dated 25 July 1963: "She collaborated with you constantly. Nothing of your abundant work was published that she did not follow at its different stages of elaboration, and up to the last; and you attached the greatest value to her vigilant and penetrating judgment." "Une Lettre d'O. L.," *OCM*, vol. 15, 504.

12. Ibid. Chap. 3 will take up the question of Maritain's philosophic vocation and its relation to other ways of life, particularly to political philosophy.

13. Jacques Maritain, "World Trial: Its Meaning for the Future," *OCM*, vol. 8, 828.

1

JUSTICE, BRAINS, AND STRENGTH: MACHIAVELLI AND MODERNITY IN POLITICAL PHILOSOPHY

> But there is one prayer that I address to God—it is that never should Jacques be called to an action that is, in practice, political. He has created a political philosophy, the only one constituted to struggle against that of Machiavelli, who is universally followed up to the present moment by men of State, and we see the results! Of that "anti-Machiavellianism" that I propose, why would not the new men of action be inspired by it?
>
> —Raïssa Maritain, *"Trois Notes de Raïssa sur Jacques"*[1]

> Machiavellianism comes from the incessant victories gained by evil means in the political achievements of mankind, and from the idea that if a prince or a nation respects justice, he or it is doomed to enslavement by other princes or nations trusting only in power, violence, and lawless greed. The answer is, first, that *one can respect justice and have brains at the same time, and manage to be strong*; . . . second, that in reality Machiavellianism does not succeed. For the power of evil is only, in reality, the power of corruption—the squandering and dissipation of the substance and energy of Being and of Good.
>
> —Jacques Maritain, *Man and the State*[2]

I.

In a famous essay, "What Is Political Philosophy?" Leo Strauss wrote that "the founder of modern political philosophy is Machiavelli. He tried to effect, and he did effect, a break with the whole tradition of political philosophy."[3] What was the character of this break? This "turn-

1

ing point" in political philosophy was later addressed by Charles N. R. McCoy, who had argued that first in the series of intellectual reversals that have taken place within modern political philosophy began with a reversal within the practical intellect as understood by Aristotle. This reversal was engineered by Machiavelli, who inverted the priority of art and political prudence.[4] Maritain likewise understood the importance of this reversal of art over political prudence as the guiding principle in actual political action.[5]

Machiavellianism, with its strange, but strong, appeal to the human soul, caught Maritain's attention. His reflections on Machiavelli place him squarely within the philosophic debate about the place of politics in intellectual affairs. Strauss had remarked that consideration of the best regime was the closest that political philosophy came to philosophy itself. By beginning with Maritain's deliberations on Machiavellianism, on the worst regime, as it were, we see better why he dealt with political things as he did. He needed to argue the case against the worst regime not merely within political philosophy but within its more subtle origins in philosophy itself.

Maritain had a genius for drawing out the implications of philosophic positions, something that particularly distinguishes his contribution to political philosophy. The subject of politics is human freedom in the public choices for good or evil of the rational being who is finite and mortal. This freedom is displayed in men's organized actions to know and achieve what is, or is called, good. This subject matter is necessarily obscured by the intricate uniqueness of each particular choice and action. The fact is, however, we can know what we are about. We understand that the effort to illuminate our actions is an essential enterprise of man, the political being who thinks about *what he is*. If politics is the "art of persuasion," it is also the reflective examination of the truth of what in fact persuades and of the observed consequences of what we have been persuaded to do.

Maritain's essay, "The End of Machiavellianism," was published in 1942, against the background of the totalitarian systems of World War II.[6] He considered Machiavellianism, rooted in Western thought itself, to be the central intellectual cause behind that terrible war. He worried about whether the democracies had not in fact embraced many of its principles.[7] "The End of Machiavellianism" is precisely an essay in political philosophy. It coherently examines and challenges the dubious claim that all political action, to be successful, must follow Machiavelli's principles.

To examine the end of Machiavellianism, Maritain spells out both why it might be attractive and whether, in its own terms, it succeeds. Anyone who has taught *The Prince* or *The Discourses* recognizes that Machiavelli does, at least initially, attract students, rather than repel them, as we might at first expect. He captivates readers for what at first sight appears to be a noble reason. He boldly claims to cut through the supposedly turgid arguments of the classical political philosophers who are said only to care about fuzzy "ideal" things, not reality.[8] Machiavelli, as he tells it, penetrates to what actually goes on in any polity. Students readily affirm that what Machiavelli is claiming seems, from their own unexamined experience, to be the situation.

Machiavelli explains what is really going on beneath the surface in all civil societies. It is not especially pretty. Machiavelli is thus systematic, even "scientific," and intensely beguiling. To avoid his charm is difficult. He fascinates us by forthrightly justifying that which the philosophers said could never be justified. He "liberates" politics from the "restrictions" of morality. He gives politics a freedom to accomplish things quickly and efficiently. Machiavelli, it is held, sets aside any troubling ethical questions that were said to have hindered effective political action.

Maritain does not downplay the appeal of Machiavelli. Essentially, what concerns Maritain is whether Machiavelli's system is true and, if not, how to go about examining his claims? Machiavelli informs us that he is specifically controverting the classical opinions about what man ought to do. Basically, Machiavelli himself is debating with Socrates, who maintains that it is never right to do wrong, that nothing can harm the good man, and that death is not the worst evil. Further rejecting any transcendent "republic," Machiavelli is also debating with Christ and Augustine about the Kingdom of God and its location.[9]

II.

In responding to Machiavelli, what is particularly interesting in Maritain is the acknowledged latitude that he grants to good and ethical politicians in employing dangerous and forceful means in the actual world, many of which would often be called unscrupulous by ordinary people.[10] A major cause of Machiavellianism, Maritain argues, is a "hypermoralism" that righteously prevents responsible politicians from employing strong or legitimately coercive means against the Machiavellians themselves.[11] At first, Maritain seems to be something of a "crypto-Machiavellian." But it is his care in sorting out the relevant principles that makes his thought so pertinent.

The name "political realism" has been applied to three classical thinkers—Thucydides, Augustine, and Machiavelli. Nothing can be found in Machiavelli's description of what human beings do "do," however, that cannot also be found in Plato, Aristotle, Thucydides, Cicero, Augustine, or Aquinas. The basic spirit of Machiavelli's claim is already laid out by Thrasymachus in Book One of *The Republic*. However, Machiavelli's "political realism" is different from that of the classical writers or that discussed by Maritain. Political philosophy must identify this difference.

Maritain speaks of "Machiavellianism" and not merely of Machiavelli. Likewise, he distinguishes between "moderate" and "absolute" Machiavellianism.[12] Maritain argues that "moderate" Machiavellianism—a selective, cautious use of evil means—inevitably leads to absolute Machiavellianism—their unrestricted use.[13] Machiavellianism itself, moreover, as a political philosophy, eventually leads to a form of Hegelianism that becomes a metaphysics. That is, it turns into an explanation of what is and what must be, a form of what-is-done must be what-is-rightly-done. The initial "realist" observation is shared by both Augustine and Machiavelli; namely, we often see politicians doing evil things. The frequency of politicians doing evil things, however, is not the essence of Machiavellian political realism. No classical philosopher has the slightest difficulty in recognizing that evil things are often found in historic political experience. Christianity begins with the fact of human sin. Machiavelli himself is not a moral philosopher who called evil good. In advocating the use of evil actions, he knows they are evil, though also, he thinks, necessary.

Before Machiavelli, however, the politicians who did evil things still "had a bad conscience—to the extent that they had a conscience." This bad conscience meant that within the politician's soul, there still lurked shame for what he did. "This [sense of shame] prevented the crimes in question from becoming a rule, and provided governed people with a limping accommodation between good and evil, which, in broad outline, made their oppressed lives, after all, liveable."[14] To suffer under a tyrant who is aware that what he does is wrong means that the moral dignity and common bond of what is right are still operative, however unfortunate the circumstances. What makes more modern tyranny "unlivable" is the calling of its deeds simply good or necessary.

The essence of Machiavellianism, then, is not that politicians do evil things. Nor is it the attempt to abolish the existential distinction of good and evil, the "beyond good and evil" of a Nietsche, though this abolition would follow logically in the history of philosophy after Machiavelli's initiative. The essence of Machiavellianism, at the beginning of modern political philosophy, applies primarily to the politician. His "politics," unlike classical politics, is not connected with his individual ethics or with ethics itself. He separates them into different spheres. The new politician is not to be bound in his actions by the same rules that bind the rest of men. The Machiavellian prince or politician, as it were, wants the people to be good. He would like to be loved by them. However, he cannot rely on this love, so in fact he prefers to be feared by them.

Maritain sees Machiavelli as a teacher of princes and politicians, an "unarmed prophet," who explains to rulers how to rule with clear conscience, how to be evil when they think it "wise" for a political end. In this sense, on his own terms, Machiavelli is largely a successful teacher because even democratic professors and politicians embrace his principles of rule as valid at crucial moments. The evil of Machiavellianism is manifested in the blameless conscience that it gives to the prince or to the legislator doing evil deeds, along with the lack of hope in ethical principles that it leaves in those subject to these same princes, legislators, judges, or presidents.

"After Machiavelli, not only the princes and conquerors of the *cinquecento*, but the great leaders and makers of modern states and modern history," Maritain continues,

> in employing injustice for establishing order, and every kind of useful evil for satisfying their will to power, will have a clear conscience and feel that they accomplish their duty as political heads. Suppose they are not merely skeptical in moral matters, and have some religious and ethical conviction in connection with man's personal behavior, then

they will be obliged, in connection with the field of politics, to put
aside these convictions or personal morality on the altar of the political
good.[15]

The Machiavellian prince thus displays a kind of worldly asceticism
whereby he girds himself to do evil, however bad it looks, in the name
of his end, which is that of the state itself, the *raison d'état*.

Machiavellianism is a theory of what the politician is permitted for
his end as politician. Maritain's own rejection of Machiavellianism presupposes, consequently, an account of politics as an ethical discipline that
can explain all of political reality, including the Machiavellian deeds, or
their supposed necessity, without simultaneously exempting the politician from the bonds of good and evil. Maritain presents an ethical alternative to Machiavellianism that does not shy away from or deny the
situations that seem to make Machiavellianism inevitable to many politicians.

In the title "The End of Machiavellianism," Maritain does not
mean only that this system results in moral corruption for all who participate in it. He also understands that the Machiavellian's chosen means
are justified by a purpose, a new "good," as it were, that replaces the
hierarchy of political ends found in the classical writers and based on
human happiness and nature. This new "good" is *success in remaining in
power.* The prince or president who uses "good" means (that is, classi-
cally moral means) and loses power is, by this standard, a bad ruler. But
the prince or president who uses "bad" means and loses power is, likewise, a bad ruler. In either case, the moral atmosphere of the polis is
corrupted because what is objectively "right" is not the criterion of rule
in the polity.

"For not only do we owe to Machiavelli our having become aware
and conscious of the immorality displayed, in fact, by the mass of political men," Maritain writes in coming to the essence of Machiavellianism
itself,

but by the same stroke he taught us that this very immorality is the
very law of politics. Here is that Machiavellian perversion of politics
which was linked, in fact, with the Machiavellian *prise de conscience* of
average political behavior in mankind. The historic responsibility of

Machiavelli consists in having *accepted*, recognized, endorsed as normal the fact of political immorality, and in having stated that good politics, politics conformable to its true nature and to its genuine aims, is by essence nonmoral politics.[16]

Thus, even when a modern Machiavellian prince or president uses what are by classical standards good means, he is not acting morally in the classical sense. The corruption of political ethics begins with the establishment of a sphere in which the prince, as prince, is exempt from standards of classical right. Machiavelli has, in effect, provided for two moralities, each independent of the other.

III.

Maritain next asks why Machiavellian "realism" is attractive. Maritain is quite aware of Aquinas's principle that no evil is embraced except under the guise of something good or reasonable. Machiavelli proposes a clear solution to ancient problems. He seems amazed that no one ever thought of it before. The trouble is that, in fact, almost everyone thought of it before, beginning with Plato himself, and they rejected it. Maritain observes, however, that Machiavelli's own moral science, on examination, lacks certain fundamental principles. Machiavelli too handily calls evil what in fact may be an honest and delicate effort to act morally in dealing with very difficult matters.

In bypassing the complexity of moral life for the simplification of the prince bound to no principle of good, Machiavelli obscured the real drama of political life. Maritain himself is surprisingly realistic about what goes on in political life. Why surprisingly? Because Maritain wrestles with political morality even in the most complicated of cases, the ethics of "a regressive or barbarous society," as he called it in *Man and the State*.[17] But in doing so, he never allows the principle that the end justifies the means to become operative. Even the concentration camp, the worst case, is not a completely immoral environment. Honorable men have lived and died there, seeking to observe the rules of right action.

What Machiavelli impulsively calls "vice and evil," certain deeds he claims to be contrary to "virtue and morality," can in fact, on examination, be something else entirely, Maritain remarks. Such behavior that seems to Machiavelli to be merely the deeds of evil men in power may be "only the authentically moral behavior of a just man engaged in the complexities of human life and of true ethics."[18] Maritain shows a little sympathy for Machiavelli here by suggesting that he embraced the extreme positions that he did because of his own lack of insight into what was "realistically" going on in political life. Machiavelli, for all his supposed insight, was not especially perceptive and saw only moral evil where he was sometimes witnessing moral deliberation about which was a lesser evil. Maritain amusingly hints that Machiavelli lacked some refinement of realism itself.

An accurate theological account of The Fall remains for Maritain the proper background of his political analysis—that is, human nature is wounded but not corrupted or in itself evil. This inner good in each human being is what gives the drama of human action its depth and urgency, what gives history its purpose. Even though men do many evil things, human nature is not as such bad or evil, as Machiavelli thought. Maritain gives examples of what he means by not too easily granting Machiavelli's premises:

> For instance, justice itself may call for relentless energy—which is neither vengeance nor cruelty—against wicked and false-hearted enemies. Or the toleration of some existing evil—if there is no furthering of or cooperation with the same—may be required for avoiding a greater evil or for slowing down and progressively reducing this very evil. Even dissimulation is not always bad faith or knavery. It would not be moral, but foolish, to open one's heart and inner thoughts to every dull or mischievous fellow. *Stupidity is never moral; it is a vice.*[19]

This passage is remarkably nuanced. It reflects the spirit of the introductory citation of this chapter in which Maritain argued that it is possible to have *justice, brains and strength,* all three.

The principle of the toleration of the lesser evil, though often difficult to comprehend, is ethically grounded. Maritain's exasperated remark, *"stupidity is never moral,"* reflects his impatience with two types: (1) with the Machiavellian politician who does not even seek to find the distinctions of good and evil in the objective order, and (2) with the hypermoralist whose scrupulousness about not wanting to stain himself, through inaction, results in turning the world over to the absolute Machiavellians. Maritain, thus, forces us back to the more classical realisms of Aristotle and Augustine, who know what evil is but who do not approve it, who know what pains it takes to combine morality with protecting the good of all against evil rulers, against men who do need to be dealt with.

At this point in his argument, to which we shall return in chapter 2, Maritain indicates that the basic theoretical error of Machiavelli is the confusion of art with prudence. This is a momentous confusion, particularly for politics. Maritain, it should be pointed out, is a major thinker in the field of art and poetry.[20] He is a commentator on the classical understanding of art that found its roots in Aristotle's *Poetics*. Essentially, Machiavelli makes the prince an artist. This move allows him to conceive the prince after the model of an artist dealing with artistic material. If we give the politician the freedom over the people that is intrinsic to the artist over his material, it means that we have altered the subject matter of politics, that is, individual human persons freely acting to achieve their own good, a good that transcends and thus limits the activities of the prince. As a result, the prince has no obligation to the ruled but only to his own concept of what he wants to achieve. He is free from the restrictions imposed by the being of man. With the image of God removed from the subjects of rule, the prince need not treat the essential being of the ruled as limiting his actions or purposes.[21]

Maritain notes the instability of Machiavellian individuals and states. Since "success" in rule is the criterion of the discipline, the theory is incoherent when princes fail. The essence of Maritain's analysis of Machiavelli is his insistence that Machiavellianism as a principle of rule thrives by its illusion of "immediate success."[22] The emphasis is on the "immediate," not long-term success, where the failure appears. Maritain maintains that Machiavellianism eats away the substance of political life and is itself the great enemy of its own success, of its own announced purpose. In this regard, particularly in the light of the curious and sudden manner in which communism itself finally fell, Maritain has a most interesting and perceptive footnote:

> Three years after these pages were written (they were first drafted in 1941 . . .) the world contemplated the inglorious fall of Mr. Benito Mussolini. The triumphs of this wretched disciple of absolute Machia-

vellianism (he wrote a Preface of an edition of *The Prince*) lasted twenty years. Hitlerist Machiavellianism had a similar fate. Sooner or later Communist Machiavellianism will have a similar fate.[23]

Maritain's whole argument about Machiavellianism's staying power is that, ultimately, it does not succeed. That is, he accepts Machiavelli's own terms of justification for his [Machiavelli's] system and inquires into the reasons why it might succeed in the short run but not in the long run.

In practice, what happens, Maritain observes, is that the elimination of "moral values in the brain of the political artist as such" does not demand the elimination of the moral values and principles in those who are to be ruled. The subjects of the prince's or president's rule retain religious or ethical principles that are contrary to the operative norms of the artistic, reigning prince. What happens in such a situation?

> It is impossible that the use . . . of a thoroughly immoral art of politics should not produce a progressive lowering and degeneration of moral values and moral beliefs in the common human life, a progressive disintegration of the inherited stock of stable structures and customs linked with those beliefs, and finally a progressive corruption of the ethical and social matter itself with which this supramoral politics deals. Thus, such an art wears away and destroys its very matter, and, by the same token, will disintegrate itself.[24]

In this sense, neither moderate nor absolute Machiavellians can protect themselves from the disorder of soul that by example they teach the ruled. Once the ruled themselves begin to imitate the rulers in a "democratic tyranny," the premises of a successful Machiavellian prince are undermined.

IV.

Maritain next examines the scope and substance of the properly political life, the denial of which constitutes the disorder of Machiavellianism. He discusses his position under the heading of the common good, the good of all, not only of the prince. "For Machiavelli the end of politics is power's conquest and maintenance—which is the work of art to be performed."[25] Staying in power suggests a finesse, an adroit using of whatever means are necessary to achieve the end of rule. To have stayed in power is successful politics. To lose power is unsuccessful. This is why Maritain in effect attacks Machiavelli on his own grounds when he insists that Machiavellian methods to stay in power do not succeed except for a relatively short time.

This consideration about success brings up the more profound question, coming from Maritain's own background, namely, then, why, if these means ultimately do not succeed, is there such a thing as Machiavellianism at all? This question leads Maritain to distinguish clearly the difference between the temporal common good of the polity and the final good of each member of the polity as a person. A civil state is not, in the order of being, a substance. It is not a "being" or a thing. It does not have a life and inner purpose of its own, but rather is made up of beings who do. This is why the state is both natural and limited. Its reality is in the category of relation, not substance.[26] The person as person is a "whole," as Maritain will often say, in what touches his ultimate end.

"According to the nature of things, the end of politics is the common good of a united people, which end is something concretely human, therefore something ethical."[27] The human being does not serve the end of politics, but the end of politics serves the highest end of the person. This position will require considerable explication because Maritain does not doubt that man is also by nature political. The question that we just touched on, that the earthly common good is itself terrestrial and is not itself immortal, retains an active force in Maritain's thought.

Behind this position lies the more profound problem of why God allows evil deeds, such as those of the prince, to happen in the first place (see chapter 9) and what happens to these actions sent into the world by disordered wills? When Maritain speaks of politics and political ethics, even when the human actors produce evil deeds, he is not asking the question that would be pertinent to Socrates, Christ, or any martyr who dies at the hands of the state. Personal ethics and political ethics, while related, have different ends. Once it is apparent how Maritain understands this distinction, all of his thinking about the evil of Machiavellianism becomes much clearer.

Let me cite here the pertinent passage in *Man and the State*. "Politics is a branch of Ethics, but a branch specifically distinct from the other branches of the same stem," Maritain writes.

> For human life has two ultimate ends, the one subordinate to the other: an ultimate end *in a given order*, which is the terrestrial common good, or the *bonum vitae civilis*; and an *absolute* ultimate end, which is the transcendent ultimate, eternal common good. And individual ethics takes into account the subordinate ultimate end, but *directly aims* at the absolute ultimate one; whereas political ethics takes into account the absolute ultimate end, but its *direct aim* is the subordinate ultimate end, the good of the rational nature in its temporal achievement.[28]

That this clarification of politics and ethics appears within a broader discussion of Machiavellianism is of great importance. Maritain recognizes that he must not merely account for the transcendent end of a Socrates or a Christ or a martyr, but he must also account for the result of those moral actions themselves that have occurred within the polity and have been justified by Machiavellian criteria.

The temporal common good is a legitimate and natural end, a good therefore not to be deemphasized or rejected. The temporal common good deserves the best efforts of men with "justice, brains, and strength." The three accusers and the Athenian jury are responsible for the death of Socrates. Pilate and several high priests were the ones directly responsible for the execution of Christ.[29] What Maritain wants to know in these political reflections is not the ultimate destiny of Socrates, Christ, or the martyrs, but what happens within the polities as a result of these woeful political choices? Does Machiavellianism succeed there? Maritain is not content with asking whether those defeated and executed by banal princes have an immortal destiny. To be sure, that is an important issue, as Plato has taught us, one properly treated in metaphysics, theology, and ethics. Rather, Maritain wants to know whether the evil acts of the prince are finally "successful" within the temporal order itself. His argument here does not concern transcendence as a kind of ultimate compensation for morality's failure in the political order but is about politics as we know politics.

Politics is the highest practical, not speculative, science for man as mortal man, as man who lives a certain number of years in some more or less well-organized polity and dies there. The sense of Maritain's essay on Machiavellianism is primarily directed to this political level, not to the transcendent level, the existence of which he does not deny. He knows it is necessary to comprehend precisely in what sense the human being is not wholly consumed by the polity. When Maritain argues that the actions of a Machiavellian prince are possibly successful in the short run but not the long run, he is not simply following Plato's argument in Book Ten of *The Republic* that posits endless punishment or reward for deeds unpunished or unrequited in some existing political order.

Thus, Maritain could point out in his essay "The Meaning of Contemporary Atheism" that "neither Christianity nor the Church has a mission to make men happy, their mission is to tell them the truth—not to bring about justice and freedom in the political society, but to give mankind salvation and eternal life."[30] Telling the truth that leads to eternal life in actual regimes, no doubt, not infrequently leads to death. That it might well do so is the teaching of both Socrates and Christ. Maritain sees that in such deaths we have examples of a kind of Machiavellian political success in the short run. What Maritain wants to know is, do these actions succeed on political grounds as those grounds retain their own criterion of human action?

"It is never allowed to do evil for any good whatsoever," Maritain sums up the Greek and Christian positions. When confronted with the possibility of positively choosing what is precisely evil, in a clear case with no confusions about lesser evils, to obtain good, we must simply reject the evil alternative. Martyrs, saints, and politicians from Socrates to Thomas More have had this choice given to them. Maritain recalls Christ's example of being offered the whole world if He would worship Satan, wherein Christ does not reason with the proposition, but simply rejects it—"Get thee behind me, Satan."[31] What is the character of this response? "Such is the answer that the human person, looking to his own destiny as a person, to his immortal soul, his ultimate end and everlasting life, to his God, gives to Politics when Politics offers him the kingdom of the world at the price of his soul."[32] The human person is ordained to something higher than politics, because of which he must ordain his life to this higher purpose.

When politics claims to be autonomous, without recognizing any higher human purpose, as it implicitly does in the Machiavellian propositions, it is not just another bad example of an abuse of power. It is a claim that it is a good to use evil means, that there is no higher or interrelated end. When spelled out, this claim leads modern political theory into a kind of substitute or ersatz metaphysics. The evil incorporated into politics as good is accepted as the real order of the world. On this hypothesis, the world should or could not have been otherwise. That it can and should be otherwise is always the hope implicit in a theory in which evil could be rejected.

What, then, is the "end" of Machiavellianism? Maritain insists that his is a discussion of political philosophy, of law and right. It is not a debate about whether evil and unjust deeds take place. "Machiavelli is a philosopher of politics, stating that by right good politics is supramoral or immoral politics and by essence must make use of evil. What I have discussed is his political philosophy. There will be no end to the occurrence of misdeeds and mistakes as long as humanity endures. To Machiavellianism there can and must be an end."[33] To achieve this ending of Machiavellianism as an operative principle in our political conscience, we must seek to know what is true, together with a clear idea of how many princes, presidents, and legislators do act. We need to know that this acting, claiming that to do evil is a valid political alternative, is "bad politics." To end Machiavellianism, we must cease to think that the conduct that is advocated in this system works without further corrupting politics itself.

V.

In concluding his essay, Maritain returns to his discussion of relative and absolute Machiavellianism. He argues that even "moderate" Machiavellianism—the selective use of evil means—does not stand by itself but serves to corrupt the social fabric of justice and its expectations. Even though it acknowledges that evil is generally wrong, it implies that its judiciously chosen evil will not corrupt or will corrupt less. Maritain recognizes the possibility that, rooted in Machiavellianism, the worst regimes come to power because the principles of their establishment are not resisted by good men. If Machiavellianism is resisted by presumably good men using immoral means, it becomes impossible to tell the difference between good and bad regimes. Maritain proposes as the alternative to a Machiavellian state a "democracy or the commonwealth of free men" that is "by definition a political regime of men, the spiritual basis of which is uniquely and exclusively law and right."[34] For Maritain, a "political" regime, without denying the actual fallen human condition, means one that is composed of rational and free men operating according to law, itself based in what is right.

Maritain does not exclusively look to a supernatural source to requite the actual political evils of Machiavellianism. The temporal results of evil actions will become manifest because of that to which they lead.

> Machiavellianism is an illusion, because it rests upon the power of evil, and because, from the metaphysical point of view, evil as such has no power as a cause of being; from the practical point of view, evil has no power as a cause of any lasting achievement. As to moral entities like peoples, states, and nations, which do not have any supratemporal destiny, it is within time that their deeds are sanctioned; it is upon earth that the entire charge of failure or nothingness, with which is charged every evil action committed by the whole or its heads, will normally be exhausted.[35]

Again, Maritain's central consideration about Machiavellianism is that it fails in its own temporal order, the very place wherein it seemed to achieve the most success. While there are key metaphysical and theological elements in Maritain, his essential response lies within the polity itself, within the framework provided by political philosophy.

This discussion of Machiavellianism can best conclude by recalling some reflections in *Man and the State* about dealing with the worst conditions, ones that seem to justify Machiavelli's view that the good will be destroyed if they only use good means in their defense. The whole of Maritain's tractate on Machiavelli, to be sure, is that we must only use just means, that unjust means will eventually, in the long run, destroy the moral fabric of any society that uses them. Maritain is not merely calling forth a transcendent but an inner or this-worldly judgment on Machiavellianism.

"The more perfect and ruthless become the techniques of oppression, universal mutual spying, forced labor, mass deportation and mass destruction peculiar to the totalitarian States, the more difficult any attempt to change or overcome from the outside those gigantic Machiavellian robots," Maritain writes.

> But they do not possess lasting inner force; their huge machinery of violence is a token of their inner human weakness. The breaking

down of human freedom and conscience, because it engenders everywhere fear and insecurity, is in itself a process of self-destruction for
the body politic. How long, then, can the power of a State endure
which becomes more and more of a giant as regards the external or
technical forces, and . . . a dwarf as regards the internal, human, actually vital forces? It will do during some generations the job it has been
assigned or permitted. I doubt that it can take root in the historical
duration of nations.[36]

This passage, one that seems quite remarkable in the light of twentieth-
century totalitarian regimes, illustrates the heart of his thesis in political
philosophy, namely, that unjust regimes may last for some time but that,
because of the nature of their actions, because evil has no creative power,
they will eventually lose their inner coherence.

In imagining the worst case, the barbarous society, say, the concentration camp, Maritain is logical enough to ask, could only passive or
purely evangelical or philosophic means be employed to escape such a
dire prospect? The situation humanly looks hopeless. Therefore, those
so caught must prepare to accept death as the only alternative. Are such
transcendent means the only actions justified by the circumstances?
Sometimes they are, no doubt. Maritain argues that as the level of society
itself lowers, it becomes less and less clear what is and what is not an
unjust action. But some political effort still is justified and worthwhile.
One of the most difficult and sad laws in moral life, Maritain writes, is
that

> according to which the application of moral rules immutable in them-
> selves takes lower and lower forms as the social environment declines.
> The moral law must never be given up, we must fasten on to it all the
> more as the social or political environment becomes more perverted
> or criminal. But the moral nature or specification, that moral *object* of
> the same physical acts, changes when the situation to which they per-
> tain becomes so different that the inner relation of the will to the
> thing done becomes itself typically different.[37]

What Maritain provides here is a summary of principles by which we
can reject the Machiavellian argument even in what is apparently the
most obvious case for its use.

Ultimately, Maritain deals with the positive argument against the

Machiavellian position that the end justifies the use of evil means for good ends. Evil must never be chosen. But this principle does not mean that "justice, strength, and brains" need to be lacking to men seeking the good in the worst situations. On the contrary, even in the worst situation, we can see how means, that, without examination, might appear to be evil, are in fact moral. Maritain has argued all along that, on the surface, the most persuasive argument for a Machiavellian position was a misreading of the actions of just men trying to prevent the very evil that Machiavellianism fosters. Maritain, with such emphasis, sees both Machiavellianism—the use of evil means as a legitimate tool of the politician—and hypermoralism—the refusal to do any action for fear of tainting one's conscience—to be two aspects of the same problem. Looked at in this way, he is realistically defending the principle of just and legitimate means in all political cases. In his political and ethical philosophy, Maritain takes into account all interrelated levels of political life from the worst to the best forms of rule.

Thus, in answer to Raïssa Maritain's wonder, cited at the head of this chapter, about why men of action do not attend to Maritain's analysis of the meaning of Machiavellianism, it is evidently because they do not go through the delicate effort to see that the long-range consequences of Machiavellianism are destructive of politics and morality itself. They refuse to see that the choice of Machiavellian means is not as necessary as it seems to the politician employing them. The last words of Maritain on Machiavellianism remain—*one can respect justice and have brains at the same time, and manage to be strong—stupidity is not a virtue.* Maritain, I think, provides a way to repair the Machiavellian break in political philosophy. The break still needs to be repaired, as the temptation to identify might and right, good and evil, occurs at some time or another in every heart, in every citizen, in every regime.

Notes

1. Raïssa Maritain, "*Trois Notes de Raïssa sur Jacques*," *OCM*, vol. 15, 851.
2. Jacques Maritain, *Man and the State* (Chicago: University of Chicago Press, 1951), 62–63. Maritain's main study is "The End of Machiavellianism," *The Social and Political Philosophy of Jacques Maritain: Selected Readings*, ed. Joseph W. Evans and Leo R. Ward (Notre Dame: University of Notre Dame Press,

1976), 292–325. This essay appeared in the *Review of Politics* 4 (January, 1942): 1–33, and later in *The Range of Reason* (New York: Charles Scribner's Sons, 1952), 134–64. It is found in *OCM*, vol. 8, 307–55.

3. Leo Strauss, "What Is Political Philosophy?" *What Is Political Philosophy? and Other Studies* (Glencoe, Ill.: The Free Press, 1959), 40.

4. Charles N. R. McCoy, "Machiavelli and the New Politics: The Primacy of Art," in *The Structure of Political Thought* (New York: McGraw-Hill, 1963), 157–79. I have traced the meaning and nature of these reversals in *Reason, Revelation, and the Foundations of Political Philosophy* (Baton Rouge: Louisiana State University Press, 1987).

5. Maritain, "The End of Machiavellianism," 298–301.

6. Maritain, ibid.

7. Further comments on Machiavellianism are found in Maritain, *Man and the State*, 58–62.

8. In classical philosophy and Christianity, what is real and what is most real are not things somehow "added" to sensible reality, nor are they simply abstract beings of the mind, but things that really are and are most eminently.

9. See James V. Schall, S. J., "Augustine and Machiavelli," *Perspectives in Political Science* 25 (Summer 1996): 117–23.

10. "As to the means of Christian politics . . . I would say: first, that those means should always be just, not excluding force, but subordinating it; second, that a hypermoralism demanding that these means be not only good in themselves but pharisaically pure—I mean free of the contact with the impurities of human history which would stain them from without—this hypermoralism is as contrary to a true political ethics as is a Machiavellian cynicism; third, the seemingly irresistible power of the weapons of violence, of deceit and infamy, employed today by men who have discovered that the absolute rejection of all moral rule opens the way to a kind of omnipotence and a paradise of force, obliges Christians more than ever to fix their attention on the hierarchy of means." Jacques Maritain, *Scholasticism and Politics* (Garden City, N. Y.: Doubleday Image, 1960), 210. See Raymond Aron on Maritain, "French Thought in Exile: Jacques Maritain and the Quarrel over Machiavellianism," in *In Defense of Political Reason*, ed. Daniel J. Mahoney (Lanham, MD.: Rowman & Littlefield, 1994), 53–66.

11. Maritain, "The End of Machiavellianism," 323–25; *Man and the State*, 62–63.

12. Maritain, "The End of Machiavellianism," 300–01. Moderate Machiavellians listed are Henry VIII, Elizabeth, Mazarin, Richelieu, Frederick, Catherine the Great, and Talleyrand. Absolute Machiavellians are those who rule twentieth-century totalitarian systems, such as Stalin and Hitler.

13. It might be remarked that the cases of Lincoln, Churchill, Franklin Roosevelt, and de Gaulle did not prove that this was inevitably done.

14. Ibid., 293.

15. Ibid.

16. Ibid., 294.

17. Maritain, *Man and the State*, 71–75.

18. Maritain, "The End of Machiavellianism," 296–97.

19. Ibid., 297.

20. Jacques Maritain, *Art and Scholasticism and the Frontiers of Poetry* (Notre Dame: University of Notre Dame Press, 1974); *Creative Intuition in Art and Poetry* (The A. W. Mellon Lectures in the Fine Arts; New York: Meridian, 1955).

21. Maritain, "The End of Machiavellianism," 298–301.

22. Ibid., 308.

23. Ibid., n. 9, 308–09. It seems worthwhile to cite Maritain's previous footnote n. 8 in this context: " 'Hitler told me he had read and reread *The Prince* of the Great Florentine. To his mind, the book is indispensable to every political man. For a long time it did not leave Hitler's side. The reading of these unequaled pages, he said, was like a cleansing of the mind. It had disencumbered him from plenty of false ideas and prejudices. It is only after having read *The Prince* that Hitler understood what politics really is.' Hermann Rauschning, *Hitler m'a dit*, (*The Voice of Destruction*, 1940)," ibid., 304.

24. Ibid., 300.

25. Ibid., 301.

26. For a further discussion of this point, see James V. Schall, "The Reality of Society according to St. Thomas," in *The Politics of Heaven and Hell: Christian Themes from Classical, Medieval, and Modern Political Philosophy* (Lanham, Md.: University Press of America, 1984), 235–51.

27. Maritain, "The End of Machiavellianism," 301.

28. Maritain, *Man and the State*, 62.

29. See James V. Schall, "The Death of Christ and the Death of Socrates," in *At the Limits of Political Philosophy: From "Brilliant Errors" to Things of Uncommon Importance* (Washington, D. C.: The Catholic University of America Press, 1996), 123–44.

30. Jacques Maritain, "The Meaning of Contemporary Atheism," in *The Social and Political Philosophy of Jacques Maritain: Selected Texts*, 206.

31. Maritain, "The End of Machiavellianism," 305.

32. Ibid.

33. Ibid., 323.

34. Ibid., 325.

35. Ibid., 323.

36. Maritain, *Man and the State*, 58.

37. Ibid., 73.

2

ON THE RELATION BETWEEN ART AND POLITICS

The question of the importance of the subject in painting has been adequately solved only in the terms used by great painters of the twentieth century. Most of them have not bothered with subjects important in themselves because of their significance or their natural beauty, but all the more have they laid stress on the most subtle quality of that which they depicted—linking it not only to a peculiarly refined technique but to the presence of that very soul of all the arts, that invisible and sovereignly operative poetry, which is essentially to be found not in some "subject" external to the painter, but in the emotion that engenders the whole, the entire work, matter and form alike.

—Raïssa Maritain, *We Have Been Friends Together*[1]

For in a way [the artist] is not of this world, being, from the moment that he works for beauty, on the path which leads upright souls to God and manifests to them the invisible things by the visible. However rare may be at such a time those who will not want to please the Beast and to turn with the wind, it is in them, by the very fact that they will exercise a *disinterested* activity, that the human race will live.

—Jacques Maritain, *Art and Scholasticism.*[2]

I.

In reflecting on the difference between poetry and other art, Jacques Maritain inserts an amusing remark that alerts us to the intellectual "work" involved in understanding, clearly and properly, even something visible like a painting. "The previous considerations [on art and

21

poetry] help us, probably, to realize," Maritain writes with self-effacing humor, "how philosophy succeeds in making difficult issues a little more obscure."[3] The irony of making already difficult issues not less, but more, "obscure" should remind us that it is often better for something to be "obscure" than for it not to be known at all. A little light at dusk is better for seeing than no light at all at midnight. Often the best a philosopher can do is begin to make things otherwise completely unknown become at least obscure, with the intention that someone, probably not himself, will continue to clarify what is worthy of the human intelligence at its best and of the topic at hand.

I do not begin with these words about obscurity to suggest that Maritain's works on art and politics are examples of a particularly cryptic style on his part. Though he was a precise Frenchman in his own language, he also, during his some quarter-century sojourn in the United States, wrote in English. His English and the translations of his works are generally accurate and comprehensible by the ordinarily attentive reader who is willing, at the same time, to think through with him the important and wide-ranging human and theoretical subjects Maritain treated.[4] His work on art and poetry is, as the essay on Machiavelli discussed in the previous chapter, quite lucid and insightful. Maritain is a philosopher who makes a considerable effort to understand art and, in understanding it, to see how it is related to things, like politics, that might be confused with its ethos and procedures. Already—and there is no way to be prepared for this in advance—we are alerted to the tremendous implications of our subject matter when we come across for the first time Maritain's recollection of St. Thomas's wondrous remark that "the being of all things derives from the divine Beauty."[5]

In Book Ten of *The Republic*, Socrates recalls the "old quarrel between poetry and philosophy" (607b). I want to consider this famous passage in the light of Maritain's remark, initially mentioned in the previous chapter, that the root cause of Machiavelli's error in politics was his assigning to the politician a task that is properly the work of an artist.[6] This famous "old quarrel" between poetry and philosophy, furthermore, is exacerbated by the fact that we likewise find in classical thought a similar quarrel between poetry and politics and between politics and philosophy, almost as if to say that sorting out what is proper to each is a first step in thinking correctly about philosophy, politics, poetry, or the unity of human existence.[7] When one or the other discipline absorbs the other two, we know we are in intellectual trouble.

Initially, this "old quarrel" had to do with the admitted charm and beauty of Homer and ultimately of poetry or music in comparison either with philosophy, which, at least at first sight, seems dry or with politics, which seems sordid. Nor can we forget that the principal accuser of Socrates at his trial was the relatively young poet, Meletus, just as Anytos, the craftsman and businessman, was the one whose political weight, thrown in later in the proceedings, assured the condemnation of Socrates, the philosopher, in a legal trial. That this controversy between the philosopher and the poet was presented before and decided by the political vote of a democracy convinced the anguished young Plato that philosophy had to flee the city, any existing city, if it were to survive and keep its integrity. There can be no doubt that in Plato's Academy, where philosophy fled, the city that it erected was preserved largely by the beauty of Plato's own philosophic poetry.

Meletus, poet and politician, never ceases to strike the modern student as a strange and unexpected figure to play such a significant role in Socrates's trial and death. Art, students think, is relatively harmless, there is nothing dangerous about it. Yet the whole corpus of Plato's works teaches us to be more circumspect about the validity of this opinion.[8] Nevertheless, the polity, for its own sake, needs the poets to sing of its constitution and its ways of life, of its order of justice, of its glory, if only to habituate its citizens to the actual regime and to justify itself before the rising generations and before the nations. All polities have foundation myths explaining their order of regime in terms they take to be noble. All polities build monuments and compose songs to praise those whom they judge worthy of acclaim, those who exemplify the "virtues" on which the polity considers itself to rest. These honored public "virtues" are the very ones that philosophers like Plato sometimes, on examining them in terms of philosophy itself, call "vices," a pronouncement that, when known, upsets, even enrages, the politicians trying to rule.

Thus, the work of the philosopher, who critiques the way we live, becomes ominous if the politician should think that the philosopher is undermining the order of the existing polity. The politician does not, like the philosopher, ask in theory what men ought to do but what they "do" do. The particular virtues and vices that polities praise and blame in their members in fact gave Aristotle his grounds for classifying the three good regimes—monarchy, aristocracy, and polity—and the three bad forms—democracy, oligarchy, and tyranny. Statecraft reveals soul-craft, to recall Plato again. Aristotle wanted to explain to us the different kinds of regimes as they manifested the organized implications of the activities of different kinds of souls.

Socrates quite frankly acknowledges the attraction of Homer. There is no sense in denying it; he loves Homer. But Socrates understands that disorder in the polity comes initially through disorder in the souls of the potential philosophers, the sons of the political, economic, and social leaders, who are educated in the ways of the polity by their reading of this same fascinating Homer, the traditional book of the Greeks and the origin of their great glory. If the polity itself were disordered, the songs that sang its praises, however delightful to compose, recite, or listen to, would also be disordered. The poets were not philosophers, were not automatically exempt from the disorder around them. They were all too often at the command of the politicians. The gods and heros were found, in the accounts of the poets, to be doing evil things and being lauded for it. To do evil and yet to be praised for it is, however, the greatest of the disorders of soul in *The Republic*. Plato himself, understanding clearly the root of the problem, writes *The Republic* in the charming style that he does precisely to attract to philosophy those souls who were not philosophers but who would rule the actual city, who would sit in the courts some day in judgment of the philosopher for corrupting its order.

II.

Jacques Maritain devoted a good deal of attention to art in all its forms—the fine arts and the crafts, poetry and painting. He knew personally a number of poets, painters, novelists, and artists of his time—Rouault, Péguy, Gide, Mauriac, [Julian] Green, Satie. Maritain thought art a worthy and necessary subject of study and intellectual understanding, something that a thorough philosopher or politician accounted for. As a young man, on 10 April 1906, he wrote: "Philosophers play with fire (poets also). Nothing is so comical as a course at the Sorbonne, in which an enervated professor expounds his historical views to some dunces, and discusses David Hume as peacefully as Plato."[9] We need not doubt here that Maritain is writing of his own personal experience.

Philosophers and poets play with fire—these are not the words of a dunce or an enervated professor. No one, while understanding his words, can discuss Hume or Plato "peacefully." The worst thing about academia, for Maritain, was its lack of any reaction to the fire. Maritain wanted to do justice to art, to know where and how it fit into intellectual order, both because it was a worthy subject in itself and because, misunderstanding art, we would likewise misunderstand politics, philosophy, and revelation.

"It is a mortal error to expect from poetry the supersubstantial nourishment of man," Maritain writes in *The Frontiers of Poetry*.

> The search for the absolute, for perfect spiritual liberty, combined with the absence of any metaphysical and religious certitude, has, after Rimbaud, thrown many of our contemporaries into this error. They expect from poetry alone—in the midst of a despair whose sometimes tragic reality must not be overlooked—an improbable solution to the problem of their life, the possibility of an escape toward the superhuman.[10]

Notice, in this revealing passage about Maritain's analysis of art and poetry over against metaphysics and politics, in what the error consists.

Maritain does not doubt that there is a "supersubstantial nourishment" in the objective order, nor that we seek it in our highest, if not in all, our moments. Yet there is a "mortal" error. It is an error of the contemporary world, especially of the poets, whose lives do in a way bear on the "tragic reality" of those who seek this nourishment in the wrong places. "Perfect spiritual liberty" is not unlike the perfect liberty of Machiavelli's prince; it is rooted in the same problem, in the failure properly to understand art itself. There is, in other words, a quarrel between the philosopher and many of the poets about the proper understanding of poetry itself.

These artists seek certitude in "poetry alone." They seek there "the solution to the problem of life." Their search seems to be an escape "toward the superhuman." These words come from Maritain, a philosopher, who is himself most attuned to the "superhuman," to the contemplative, and who has no intention of discounting the validity and meaning of this search. These poets lack any "religious or metaphysical certitude." It is precisely this lack that causes them to look to poetry to do something it is incapable of doing and to neglect or misunderstand the noble thing that it does do. Yet it is not unusual for poets to look to their own souls and experience, when they do not also look to religion or metaphysics, to know themselves. Writing of certain trends in modern art, Maritain observed, with some sharpness, that "the creative power of the human spirit craved after pure creation—jealous, as it were, of God, Who was tactless enough to create before us."[11]

Maritain's position, however, as he shows in his lovely analysis of Dante in the last chapter of *Creative Intuition in Art and Poetry*, is that poets and musicians who do know this religious and metaphysical certitude are the ones who put our understanding of art in the right order.[12] They see it for what it is, something legitimate and with its own proper reality—"artistic creation does not copy God's creation, it continues it."[13] In this sense, Maritain will disagree with Plato. Maritain does not want the philosophers to rewrite the poems or to reconfigure the dances, even though he wants poets and dancers to be inspired by what inspired creation in the first place insofar as they can glimpse something of it. Maritain understands the poets themselves to create what is beautiful. They do this after the manner of human beings. They are creators having themselves been created.

Human artists do not create *ex nihilo*, but they do put into existence something beautiful that was not there before.

> Such is, in its longing for beauty, that pure creativity of the spirit, to the release of which the appetite basically tends, together with the intellect, in the vital dynamics of the fine arts. Here we do not have a demand for the satisfying of a particular need in human life (as in crafts). We are beyond the realm of the useful. The need is not extraneous to the intellect; it is one with the intellect. We have a demand for the participation, through the object created, in something which is itself spiritual in nature. For beauty, which is of no use, is radiant with intelligence and is as transcendental and infinite as the universe of intellect.[14]

Artists do not take their commands from the state but from reality, from *what is* as seen in their creative intuition, itself a capacity to fashion something in itself beautiful, something never seen before. The divine Artist does intend the human artist to make beautiful things that are not themselves initially found among the beautiful things of nature. Art as such comes from a source that is not specifically political.

III.

Maritain's discussion of the medieval craftsman, however, is not without an eye to modernity, to a theory of art and artists that allows the artist making beautiful things to conceive of himself as creating his own autonomous world. Some modern artists, however, did view themselves to be using a power given to them to make something beautiful. But created beauty itself is also mindful of a transcendent beauty. The beautiful, humanly made thing points to a further, transcendent beauty. True beauty satisfies, pleases, and also unsettles because it does force us to wonder about what causes any beauty at all. "Things are not only what they are," Maritain writes in a lovely and memorable passage.

> They ceaselessly pass beyond themselves, and give more than they have, because from all sides they are permeated by the activating influx of the Prime Cause. They are better and worse than themselves, because being superabounds, and because nothingness attracts what comes from nothingness. Thus it is that they communicate with each other in an infinity of fashions and through an infinity of actions and contacts, sympathies and ruptures. I would think that this mutual communication in existence and in the spiritual flux from which existence proceeds, which is in things, as it were, the secret of creative sources, is perhaps in the last analysis what the poet receives and suffers, and grasps in the night of his own Self, or knows as unknown.[15]

Maritain insists that the makers of created beauty, as reflected in their poems and paintings themselves, recognize that there is a source, seemingly unknown, without which there would not be anything beautiful at all.

The medieval craftsman "did not work for the rich and the fashionable and for the merchants, but for the faithful; it was his mission to house their [the people's] prayers, to instruct their intelligence, to delight their souls and their eyes. Matchless epoch, in which an ingenious people was formed in beauty without even realizing it. Man created more beautiful things in those days, and he adored himself less."[16] Maritain is conscious that art in modernity, which he set out to explain and defend, could separate itself from reflection on the whole, from prudence in particular, and present itself as an alternative to God. Maritain's remark about creating more beautiful things by adoring one's own self less was intended to remind us that the ordinary or humble artist, not being full of himself, may see more to make and even make more beautiful things because he sees more in the first place, "in the spiritual flux from which existence proceeds."

Maritain consistently teaches that the artist's vocation is a proper one. He is to make things, beautiful things. "The need of the intellect to manifest externally what is grasped within itself in creative intuition, and to manifest it in beauty, is simply the essential thing in the fine arts."[17] The artist's artistic activity as such is "for its own sake" and not primarily something secondary to fostering some moral or political purpose, not that Maritain had any objection to making ordinary and useful things that have some specific purpose—tables and chairs—also beautiful. Rather, if moral or political or religious purposes were to shine through the work, this was because they were in the work as a result of what the artist put there in the pursuit of his making, a making that finds its own origin in his original insight or conception of what was to be made. A medieval cathedral, thus, might well have many didactic purposes within its very creative intuition, but the finished product itself is simply beautiful with an ordered beauty designed to reflect the mystery of all beauty.[18]

Art, though a practical virtue, is primarily an intellectual virtue. It includes the idea or understanding of what is to be made, the intelligibility that goes into the work, including all the mystery and insight that the artist sees in his intuition of what he wants to bring forth into the world. Since art is an acquired habit of a given human being, it includes experience, the practice by which the intellect is able to know what is worthy to make and actually knows how to make it. There is no formula for making a good and beautiful piece of art, but there is a knowledge at its very core, a knowledge or intuition that is first in the mind of the maker and from thence incorporated into the thing made. The truth of art, again, is when what is made does correspond with what the artist intended to make. There is a conformity of mind and reality, not of the divine mind with created things (which is called ontological truth) but of the mind of the artist with the beautiful thing made and put into the world. Once the beautiful thing is made and put into the world, it can then be encountered by other finite minds struck by what they did not know existed or by its depths.

IV.

Prudence, like art, is also called an "intellectual" virtue, the intellectual virtue of the moral or practical virtues. What does this mean? What is at stake is the delicate manner in which the human mind is stamped on human things other than mind, on the passions, the pleasures (temperance), the fears (courage), on our relations with others (justice). The virtues of courage, temperance, and justice deal directly with these capacities that need to be ruled. Prudence, the intellectual moral virtue, must also be present in every other virtue to give it precise intelligibility. It relates every virtue both to what it is to do in a particular action and, through that action, to the end of the human being himself. Prudence deals with our will in its search for our authentic good as it is manifested through what we do and through the circumstances of each particular case that comes up before us.

Here is how Maritain located prudence within his general discussion of ethics in his *Introduction to Philosophy*:

> Though ethics is as practical as any science in the strict sense can be, we must not therefore suppose that it is essentially practical (no science *vere et proprie dicta* is essentially practical), or that it is sufficient to make men behave rightly. It supplies, it is true, rules immediately applicable to particular cases, but it has no power to make us constantly apply them as we should in particular cases, in spite of the difficulties arising from our passions and the complexity of material circumstances. It remains, therefore, essentially speculative in its final object (*knowledge* of human acts) and in its procedure (the deduction of truths from their premises, not incitement to *action*) and is thus practical only in an improper sense. If man is to do the right thing in the order of action, moral science must be supplemented by the virtue of *prudence*, which, if we make use of it, makes us always *judge* correctly of the act we should perform, and *will* always that which we have thus judged to be right.[19]

Prudence is a habit, a way of constantly using our mind rightly. It stamps our imprint on each of our actions. It shows that the action comes from our choice. It relates to our becoming and being good human beings, to our choosing rightly in all we do.

Our effort here has been to establish just what is wrong with calling a politician an artist rather than a prudent man, which is what he should both be and be called. We cannot, for example, call a politician a good politician and a bad man at the same time without first having embraced Machiavellian principles that imply that human goodness is not what politics is really about. Maritain illustrates this principle with Aristotle's famous comparison between the good artist and the good politician. The good artist can err deliberately. He can show me how I paint something wrongly or sloppily by imitating what I do. When he does this instruction, that is, himself producing a sloppy work to teach me, he does not thereby become a bad painter. He does not lose his habit of painting well. When a politician deals with his subject matter, that is, the human lives of citizens, however, he cannot, even though they should already know what it is, deliberately show them what murder is by giving them an example. In murdering someone by way of example, the politician becomes a bad human being by the very demonstration. Implicit in making the politician an artist is the giving to him this artistic freedom over his subject matter, the citizens.

What makes the politician different from the artist is that on which the politician "works." The artist works on marble or canvas or musical notes. The composer can whistle a bad tune, for example, if only to show us what one is. The subject matter of politicians is human lives seeking their proper common end, as human persons, through the faculties that are specifically human, intellect and will. This seeking includes the human life of the politician himself in the acts and deeds he puts into the world that manifest his own character or soul. The precise freedom that the Machiavellian artist-politician claims is the freedom to treat his subject matter as if it were equivalent to the subject matter of the artist. This subject matter is conceived to be inert matter whose good is to be perfected by the artist's working on it through his own intuition about what is good for the polity.

If the politician can do the same thing to his subject matter as the artist to his, however, it means he is not limited by what the subjects of his rule are in themselves. He does not rule them after the manner of reason by which human beings are to rule themselves and others, that is, by persuasion in seeking rational ends through means conformed to *what man is*. If the politician is an artist, however, it implies that nothing in his subject matter transcends his own ruling purpose. The citizens are simply instruments. There can be no appeal of the subject matter, of human persons, to some criterion higher than the purpose of the successful politician achieving his own end, itself completely under his own control.

V.

Maritain has no trouble acknowledging that someone can do something wrong in practice and still recognize what is objectively right, at least to the degree that he has not acquired the habit opposite to the virtue. Maritain thus maintains that a bad man in his personal life might well maintain or uphold good moral principles when called on to explain general moral criteria to others. Thieves do not generally argue that stealing from their own goods is legitimate. What Maritain calls speculative-practical sciences and practical-practical sciences—rather awful words, no doubt—are designed to show how it is possible for a politician or moral scientist, who errs in his individual life, to affirm that, say, murder or adultery is wrong in principle, while, at the same time, in his own personal life indulging in such vices.[20] Such a thing may happen; everyone knows instances of it.

Generally speaking, murderers, liars, traitors, adulterers, and robbers, if they be politicians, try to justify such activities in the abstract as good for some polity. But if they actually do these things and claim them justified by political principle, their examples, unless accompanied by the kind of repentance that does in fact acknowledge the disorder, will indicate to everyone else that some exceptions to absolute norms are claimed by the politician. Everyone will see that the politician's political status is a claim to exempt him from the general moral rules. The "good" polity does not, in this Machiavellian sense, require the politician to be a good man. Goodness is said in fact to hinder him. His not being a good man allows him to perform acts that make him bad while calling himself a good politician. The polity is said to prosper because bad acts are for a "good" that does not include the moral good as a necessary component. This consequence is what Maritain sees to be the direct result of confusing art and prudence, of attributing artistic, not prudential, powers to the politician.

Maritain speaks of an "opposition" between art and prudence that is more obvious in the case of the fine arts because "of the very transcendence of their object."[21] What does he mean by this opposition that is increased by the transcendence of the object of the fine arts? Fine arts, for Maritain, are a relatively recent division not conforming to the medieval distinction between liberal and servile arts. One of Maritain's great contributions to the theory of art is his defense of modern art that is not, like craft art, mainly a beautifying of something already needed or useful, but is the creation of a new beautiful object in reality, something that arose out of an artist's own intuition. "The basic significance of modern art lies in this advance (away from emphasis on the ego to emphasis on the artist's creative intuition), and in the effort to discover and penetrate and set free the active mystery of poetic knowledge and poetic intuition."[22] Maritain has argued that the vocation of the artist and the existence of beautiful things are both necessary to the human spirit. However much we need politics, we also need art for what it is in itself. *Homo politicus* is incomplete without *homo faber* and vice versa.

Maritain maintains that, when properly sorted out (something that he has devoted his work on art to accomplish), the place of art and prudence, with their amicable relation to each other, can be properly identified. Nevertheless, a "transcendent object," such as that attributed rightly to the fine arts, claims an independence and a source that is not properly political. This openness to *what is* is likewise true of speculative intellect as it seeks simply to know. The very common good of which Maritain speaks so often and so well requires that art be itself in any well-ordered polity, that it be allowed to be what it is. In saying this, Maritain is not unmindful of Plato's worry about the political danger of the arts. But he does not see the solution of this danger to lie in the interference of the politician in the work of art.

"The Artist is subject, in the sphere of his art, to a kind of asceticism, which may require heroic sacrifices," Maritain explains,

> He must be thoroughly undeviating as regards the end of his art, perpetually on guard not only against the banal attraction of easy execution and success, but against a multitude of more subtle temptations,

and against the slightest relaxation of his interior effort, for *habitus* diminish with the mere cessation of their act, even more, with every relaxed art, every act which is not proportionate to their intensity. . . In the sphere of the making and from the point of view of the good of the work, he [the artist] must possess humility and magnanimity, prudence, integrity, fortitude, temperance, simplicity, ingenuousness. All these virtues which the saints possess *purely and simply*, and in the line of the supreme good, the artist must have *in a certain relation*, and in a line apart, extrahuman, if not inhuman.[23]

Notice here that Maritain is defending the all-consuming effort needed by the artist to embody his transcendent intuition into reality in the form of beautiful things made. He is also addressing himself to the artist in the line of his own soul's ability to see *what is*. The artist's "extrahuman" insight suggests not only an independence from politics in the pursuit of his own purpose, but also that what is to be beautiful if made in the fine arts itself is in line with the source and origin of all beauty. The fine artist is not an independent god, but a human being with a given capacity that he did not give himself. This capacity, when perfected with the habit of art, adds to creation in the line of the goodness of creation itself.

"The philosophers . . . say that his making activity is principally and above all an intellectual activity. Art is a virtue of the intellect, of the practical intellect, and may be termed the virtue proper to working reason," Maritain writes in "An Essay on Art."

> But then, you will say, if art is nothing other than an intellectual virtue of making, whence comes its dignity and its ascendancy among us? Why does this branch of our activity draw to it so much human sap? Why has one always and in all peoples admired the poet as much as the sage? It may be answered first that to create, to produce something intellectually, to make an object *rationally constructed*, is something very great in the world: for man this alone is already a way of imitating God. I am speaking here . . . of art as the virtue of the artisan.[24]

What the artisan does is something very great in the world; he rationally constructs and skillfully puts an object into existence. Art, as a virtue, is the perfection of his capacity to do this. "The creator of art is he who discovers a *new analogate* of what is beautiful, a new way in which the radiance of form can shine in matter."[25]

Evidently, God wanted more beauty in the world than His own initial creation of it. Though human artists do not create from nothing, as God does, and have no complete independence of what already is, still the power of God is shown more graphically by beings who are not God but who possess the capacity to bring forth what is beautiful in conjunction with what exists not of their own making. All beauty, including man-made beauty, points to that which is the origin of beauty itself. "Art is a creative virtue of the intellect, which tends to engender in beauty, and that it catches hold, in the created world, of the secret workings of nature in order produce its own work—a new creature— the consequence is that art continues in its own way the labor of divine creation," Maritain writes in *Creative Intuition in Art and Poetry.*[26]

VI.

Prudence, on the other hand, in contrast to art, is the use of our intellect to rule ourselves in the accomplishing of our proper human end. What does this mean?

> Prudence [including political prudence, the rule of the polity] perfects the intellect only presupposing that the will is straight in its own line as human appetite, that is to say, with regard to its own proper good, which is the good of the whole man: in reality it concerns itself only with determining the *means* in relation to such or such concrete human ends already willed, and therefore it presupposes that the appetite is rightly disposed with reference to these ends.[27]

If art looks to the thing made so that the mind's function is primarily directed to that end and means by which it is to be achieved, prudence does not "create" out of itself the end to be made. Prudence guides the intellect through discovering the proper means to accomplishing the end that the man has willed for himself on the basis of his understanding of *what he is* from nature. Prudence is oriented to the particular. It looks to each human action in its intelligibility, in what is found in that activity placed there by the doer.

Prudence, the intelligent guiding of the individual, the family, or the polity, to its proper human end, will differ according to the diversity of the objects ruled. The individual is to rule over himself, the parents to rule over themselves and their children, the rulers to rule over the polity. Neither the individual, family, nor polity make themselves to be what they are. What they are is from nature. Willing this end that they know from their intellects, they have to choose how to perfect each of these objects of rule. This is why, in prudence, the starting point is always the end chosen as the purpose of human actions that are designed to achieve this end. What this end is, properly speaking, is a matter for the intellect to present to the will to choose.

The point can be made clear if we examine the expression "good thief." In scripture, this incident means that a man who actually was a thief, on being punished for his thievery, acknowledged both the wrongness of thievery and the proper end toward which right living tends. The expression, "good thief," could also mean in other contexts, that someone who is a thief is also shrewd and clever at stealing things. This would mean that as a man, the individual is a morally bad human being, but he is adept, has the habit, that is, the vice, of stealing cunningly, easily, and skillfully. The man is worse because of his habit, just as he would be better if he had the virtue of justice. The prudent man is one who is able to know what his proper end is, choose it, and see, as they come along, the particular acts (means) that lead to it in practice. Prudence requires every day practice and an awareness of the right end of human living.

Political prudence as opposed to political artistry means that the politician knows the proper end of the citizens and of himself. He is not a different kind of a being from those he rules. It also means that he is able to see the means in particular that lead to their best end or the means that prevent bad habits or actions. The politician is limited by the good of each citizen—this is the ultimate root of the idea of a limited politics. He is not free to assist them in their vices or to assume that he can do whatever is necessary for him to maintain the polity. The relation of art and politics, in Maritain's presentation, is established when it is understood what each virtue is, what it does.

Behind the practical sciences and habits, and presupposed by them, are the speculative sciences. Neither Aristotle nor Maritain had any doubt that most people, most of the time, were mainly concerned with matters that would fall under the daily routine of the practical life, the moral virtues, art and craft, the keeping alive. But while the practical sciences are legitimate in themselves, they are not the highest sciences, but only the highest sciences relative to human life as it exists in this world. The being of man is itself good and worthy. Political science is the highest of the practical, not speculative sciences. The practical sciences, in other words, by being themselves, by doing what they are designed to do, make it possible for man to do something else, to do something that is traditionally called contemplation, something for its own sake. The very existence of art as itself a legitimate and worthy virtue and of its artifacts is, on the natural side, the most important element in keeping alive the realization that there is a transcendent purpose to human living itself, something that is more than human.

"Man cannot live a genuinely human life except by participating to some extent in the suprahuman life of the spirit, or of what is eternal in him," Maritain wrote in *The Responsibility of the Artist*.

> He needs all the more desperately the poets and poetry as they keep aloof from the sad business and standards of the rational animal's maintenance and guidance, and give testimony of the freedom of the spirit. It is precisely to the extent to which poetry is useless and disengaged that poetry is necessary, because it brings to man a vision of reality-beyond-reality, an experience of the secret meanings of things, an obscure insight into the universe of beauty, without which men could neither live, nor live morally.[28]

This passage is a particularly significant one as it makes a connection that runs throughout Maritain's works about the necessity of revelation and speculative reason even to live a normally moral life that can be explained with great accuracy by the philosophers but that is always lived in practice with great difficulty.

In conclusion, it is clear that Maritain's work on art, by emphasizing the worthwhileness of something created as beautiful, as an object of the artist's creative intuition, indirectly redounds on the ethical and political life as a reminder or guide to what is more worthwhile, to what is divine, as even Aristotle saw (1177b31). In keeping the poets and the musicians in the city, Maritain still gives them a Platonic purpose, one of living and living morally because of something that they behold as apparently "useless." Neither the artist nor the politician, however, is completely autonomous or independent of *what is*. Both are worthy, both are themselves, both are necessary for the city and for human perfection, but in being themselves, both point to something higher in the line of the good or the beauty for which each stands.

Eric Voegelin attributed the lapse into ideology in the twentieth century primarily to a practical loss of faith among Christians in the transcendent object of their belief and a subsequent effort to find an alternate end in this-worldly politics.[29] There was a lowering of sights, a turning away from the highest things. Maritain took a similar view:

> To turn away from Wisdom and Contemplation, and to aim lower than God, is for a Christian civilization the first cause of all disorder. It is in particular the cause of that ungodly divorce between Art and Prudence which one observed in times when Christians no longer have the strength to bear the integrity of their riches. That is doubtless why Prudence was sacrificed to Art at the time of the Italian Renaissance [Machiavelli], in a civilization which no longer tended to anything but humanist *Virtù*, and why Art was sacrificed to Prudence, in the nineteenth century, in "right-thinking" circles which no longer tended to anything but Respectability.[30]

Everyone needs to sort out the relationship between art and political prudence. Maritain's willingness to save the dignity of art by seeking to define exactly what it is and does is a service to political philosophy, whose tendency in modernity is to begin with Machiavelli's initial confusion, that of making the politician into an artist. Maritain's service to political philosophy thus appears, at first sight, in a surprising way. He understands that careful regard to the relationships within the classical practical sciences and virtues is necessary to save both art and politics.

NOTES

1. Raïssa Maritain, *We Have Been Friends Together*, trans. Julie Kernan (New York: Longmans, Green, and Company, 1943), 45.

2. Jacques Maritain, *Art and Scholasticism and The Frontiers of Poetry*, trans. Joseph W. Evans (Notre Dame: University of Notre Dame Press, 1974), 37.

3. Jacques Maritain, *Creative Intuition in Art and Poetry* (The A. W. Mellon Lectures; New York: Meridian, 1955), 133.

4. *The Collected Works of Jacques Maritain*, in 20 volumes, is now in the process of being published in English by the University of Notre Dame Press.

5. Maritain, *Art and Scholasticism*, 86.

6. See Charles N. R. McCoy, *The Structure of Political Thought* (New York: McGraw-Hill, 1963), 159–68.

7. See the book of Maritain's friend, Etienne Gilson, *The Unity of Philosophical Experience* (New York: Charles Scribner's Sons, 1937), on the relation of intellectual disciplines and ideas.

8. See James V. Schall, "The Death of Plato," *The American Scholar* 65 (Summer 1996): 401–16.

9. Jacques Maritain, *Notebooks*, trans. Joseph W. Evans (Albany, N. Y.: Magi Books, 1984), 29.

10. Maritain, *The Frontiers of Poetry*, 132.

11. Maritain, *Creative Intuition in Art and Poetry*, 56.

12. Ibid., 250–96.

13. Maritain, *Art and Scholasticism*, 60.

14. Maritain, *Creative Intuition in Art and Poetry*, 40–41.

15. Ibid., 92.

16. Maritain, *Art and Scholasticism*, 22.

17. Maritain, *Creative Intuition in Art and Poetry*, 41.

18. See Maritain's note on mystery and beauty in *Art and Scholasticism*, 28.

19. Jacques Maritain, *An Introduction to Philosophy* trans. E. I. Watkin (London: Sheed & Ward, 1946), 201–02.

20. See Maritain's chapters, "Art and Morality," *The Responsibility of the Artist*, 11–46; "Art and Morality," *Art and Scholasticism*, 70–74.

21. Maritain, *Art and Scholasticism*, 78.

22. Maritain, *Creative Intuition in Art and Poetry*, 151.

23. Maritain, *Art and Scholasticism*, 78.

24. Jacques Maritain, "An Essay on Art," in *Art and Scholasticism*, 85–86.

25. Maritain, *Art and Scholasticism*, 45.

26. Maritain, *Creative Intuition in Art and Poetry*, 50.

27. Maritain, *Art and Scholasticism*, 16.

28. Maritain, *The Responsibility of the Artist*, 85.

29. Eric Voegelin, *Science, Politics, and Gnosticism* (Chicago: Regnery-Gateway, 1968), 109.

30. Maritain, *Art and Scholasticism*, 81.

3

ON THE POLITICAL IMPORTANCE
OF THE PHILOSOPHIC LIFE

The vocation to wisdom and the vocation to political power are, then, separated. And from this separation, the question is posed of knowing which, the philosopher or the man of State, leads the life most worthy of envy. Let us say that each excels in his proper order, but in order to be faithful to the principles of Aristotle on the superiority of the contemplative life, let us also say that the order to which the philosopher excels is more elevated than that in which the man of State excels.

—Jacques Maritain, *"Aristotle," La Philosophie Morale*[1]

Nothing is more immediately necessary for our times than a sound political philosophy.

—Jacques Maritain, "The Philosopher in Society"[2]

I.

The classical question about which way of human life is the highest and why remains significant, perhaps more than we care to acknowledge. We are reluctant to admit that specific deeds, words, and lives can be noble. A "way" of life, a "vocation" in life, or a "calling," of course, recognizes that human beings live their lives in different ways, but this does not deny that there are good and better ways. Indeed, we also witness differing degrees of inhuman and evil ways of life. The very notion of a common good means that this diversity of worthy ways of life enables everyone to achieve his own good and to participate in the common good. No one could attain either of these goods if everyone had to do absolutely everything by himself. This human necessity and privilege of encouraging differing ways of life held together in common includes two things: first, that even the most insignificant human life is worthy, and second, that something really different and valid is found in the ways of life of the poet, the craftsman, the politician, and the philosopher. This difference can be philosophically identified and justified. The comparative ranking of ways of life does not lessen the positive worth of the lives spent in differing ways. The common good itself makes the differing ways of life possible and sees in their relation to each other both justice and something in the nature of a gift or sacrifice, rather than an envious downplaying or degrading comparison of one way of life to the advantage of another.

Maritain was aware of the dimensions of the problem. In "Action and Contemplation," from *Scholasticism and Politics*, he spells out, in Greek and Christian terms, how the issue of the best way of life is understood. He also related, in turn, both the lives of politics and art, discussed in the previous chapter, to the life of contemplation, to the philosophic life. Maritain writes:

> The great truth which the Greeks discovered . . . is the superiority of contemplation, as such, to action. As Aristotle puts it, life according to the intellect is better than merely human life. But the error follows. What did that assertion mean to them practically? It meant that mankind lives for the sake of a few intellectuals. There is a category of specialists—the philosophers—who lead a superhuman life, then in a lower category, destined to serve them, come those who lead the ordinary human life, the civil or political one; there are in turn those who lead a sub-human life, the life of work—that is, the slaves. The high truth of the superiority of contemplation was bound up with the contempt of work and the plague of slavery.[3]

What is to be noted here is that the Greek experience does not lead Maritain to deny the relative superiority of contemplation, the way of the philosopher, as such. Rather, it leads him to ask how or from what sources is the unacceptable conclusion about the other forms of life corrected, yet in a manner that does not deny the validity of the Greek insight about contemplation? The Greek view is precisely an "error," a philosophical error, that can, once understood, be corrected. This correction does not indicate, however, that no identifiable difference is discovered in the ways of life of the politician and the philosopher.

Maritain maintains that the intellectual impetus for this resolution, though ultimately capable of being argued also in philosophic terms, historically came from principles found in Christian revelation. There are four points to consider: (1) that "love is better than intelligence," (2) that philosophic contemplation looks first not to the perfection of the contemplator but to the object of contemplation, (3) that purposeful work, however difficult, is the imitation and extension of creation on the finite level, and (4) that contemplation is intended for everyone and that no one, conversely, can neglect the needs of the least of our kind.[4] None of these four points, on examination, denies any of the essentially positive points of the Greek idea about the superiority of contemplation to politics, poetry, or work. Intelligence is still the highest faculty that seeks truth for its own sake, though love penetrates through the knowledge of an object to what is loved in its real existence. Contemplation remains the delight and perfection of the knower. Work must have a positive purpose, it too does something needful and worthy of being done. Our spiritual and corporal life is not as restricted or as self-centered as would seem to be the case on the basis of the Greek error.

Greek principles, however, can be rethought within their own context to eliminate those errors that make some ways of life unworthy or merely instrumental to the highest life. At the same time, the defense of the highest life, the contemplative life, is likewise the defense of all other forms of life, including the political life. Without the philosophic life, no proper order of human things could be ascertained. Behind these considerations is the idea that neither human life nor creation itself needs to exist. Reality does not originate in the order of justice but more in the order of mercy and generosity, something that allows for a greatness and distinction in others, including God, that did not imply that we do not have a place for ourselves as we are. We do not need to become some other sort of beings besides ourselves to find a legitimate metaphysical place for our finite selves.

II.

Machiavelli's acid preference for the politician over the philosopher is often cited: "Many have imagined republics and principates that have never been seen or known in truth; because there is such a distance between how one lives and how one should live that he who lets go that which is done for that which ought to be done learns his ruin rather than his preservation."⁵ This was the first step within practical philosophy in overturning the order of classical and medieval thought, the modern preference of art to prudence as a guide in human things. Speculative philosophy, in this Machiavellian perspective, with obvious reference to Plato, appears to be largely irrelevant, even dangerous, to practical life. In Machiavelli's view, practical life could not be bound by what the mind discovered within its own activities about man's nature and purpose. The recovery of a proper place for the philosophic life as such is a major contribution of Maritain's examination of political things.

Likewise, with some soberness, we still remember Karl Marx's ringing Eleventh "Thesis on Feuerbach": "The philosophers have only *interpreted* the world, in various ways; the point, however, is to change it."⁶ But now that we have seen what they have wrought who would "change the world," a task normally assigned to the politicians, the way of philosophy seems capable of recovering its lost glory. Yet neither Machiavelli nor Marx was primarily a politician. Both were philosophers. Their views on politics stemmed from what they formulated in their minds, in their studies. Both were "unarmed prophets," to recall Machiavelli's famous phrase. Both remind us of the Plato, who saw that one part of the vocation of the philosopher is to educate the young politicians, or at least to render them benevolent to philosophy. Indeed, both Machiavelli and Marx held that if there was any justification of the philosophic vocation, it was to vindicate the things that the politician has to do to achieve his own ends.

The candidates for the highest way of life, however, are many—the way of the entrepreneur, the way of the politician, the way of the artist, the way of the saint, the way of the philosopher, the way of the ordinary person. Every philosophic system, in fact, contains implicitly or explicitly an account of what it considers to be the best way of life. Philosophic controversy is about the best way of life, about the highest things. Maritain remarks, as we saw in the previous chapter, that the very fact that Christ chose to follow the carpenter's trade of Joseph indicates to the Christian mind that the way of life of the ordinary trades is also a worthy one.⁷ This example of the carpenter's trade is an especially remarkable one because it necessarily recalls and contrasts the view among the Greeks, just touched on, that the life of the trades, by its very demands, is one that kept the craftsman from the highest things. It is a servile, not liberal, way of life; in other words, it is a life lived not for its own sake, but for accomplishing purely utilitarian purposes.

There is something to this Greek reluctance to exalt servile labor, of course. Repetitive, laborious work, by the sweat of one's brow, leaves time for little else. Aristotle's "statues of Daedalus" that weave cloth automatically foreshadow in some sense the technological revolution that replaced much of this drudgery. Maritain's effort to deal with art and craft, however, seeks to give a philosophic reason, indeed, a Greek philosophic reason, about why art and craft as ways of life are worthy ones. For other things to be what they are, however, philosophy needs to be what it is. The philosophic life is ultimately necessary to explain the worthiness of the nonphilosophic life. We can also notice that the influence of revelation on genuine philosophy is not to eliminate it. Rather, revelation clarifies, guides, and corrects by deepening philosophy itself through seeking to understand what is revealed.

Nevertheless, even though the lives of the artist and craftsman, the businessman and the lawyer—precisely the professions of those who accused Socrates—came to be considered worthy ways of life, instead of barely human ways, as they sometimes appeared to the Greeks, the question of the highest way of life remains because a variety of ways of life exist. As a philosopher, Maritain knows from Aristotle about the difference between the ways of life of the politician and the philosopher. *The Politics* and *The Metaphysics* are not the same book, but they are both legitimate books. Maritain knows that Aristotle separates the life of the politician and the life of the philosopher on the grounds that each has its proper place within an order that included both doing different things. The world, even the human world, was a cosmos, an order, not a chaos, a simple lack of order. Unlike the Plato of *The Republic*, Aristotle thinks that what the politician does is not what the philosopher does. Neither the politician nor the philosopher has the time to be the other. The danger that the disordered politician poses to the philosopher, however, is clear from the history of Socrates, the philosopher, in Athens. This danger explains why very often political philosophy, the explanation to the politician of the importance of what is not politics, must be secured before philosophy can be seriously undertaken in any city.

Political philosophy, therefore, is not so much about the structure of the polity, a question largely of prudence and therefore variable, as it is about the reason why the politician ought not, for his own or the city's peace, kill or silence the philosopher. Political philosophy is primarily a presentation of the arguments about why the philosopher ought to be allowed, even encouraged, to do whatever it is that he does, something not at all clear to everyone in the polity. The politician does not have time to be himself a philosopher if he is to do his own task. The politician's is a task of prudence, of knowing the particular things that ought to be done for ordering free citizens, each of whom has an orientation, usually through religion, to the highest things, things not directly subject to the rule of the polis. Neither is political philosophy a blanket justification for the philosopher to think whatever he wants on the basis of nothing other than his own undisciplined inclinations. Political philosophy defends the philosopher because, and only because, he is seriously interested in the truth of things. The prudent politician will always find his most dangerous enemy to be the aberrant philosopher, just as the most tyrannical ruler, even when the rule is by a democracy, would find his greatest adversary to be a Socrates.

As a Christian, Maritain is used to the distinction between the way of life of the philosopher and the way of life of the saint or the prophet. Indeed, it is the Christian idea that even the most humble can participate in the highest things that directly challenges the Greek idea about the exalted position of the philosopher. Both the philosopher and the saint or prophet, however, are in danger of being killed by the politician. Some philosophers are saints; most are not. Indeed, as Ralph McInerny pointed out of him, Maritain was a man who chose the way of life of philosophy and who also sought, with genuine earnestness and humility, to pursue sanctity. "I believe that it is out of this union of his intellectual life with the pursuit of sanctity that Maritain's lively sense of the variety, yet interrelatedness, of the uses of the mind arose."[8]

When asked, Maritain always referred to himself as a philosopher. This was his vocation, his way of life. He did not choose the life of a carpenter or chef or politician or businessman. But he was aware of the great tradition of Plato, St. Paul, and St. Augustine that warned of the pride and foolishness of the philosopher, which also would worry the perceptive politician vaguely aware that the origin of the most serious civil disorders is usually rooted in the heart of a philosopher somehow gone wrong. Maritain was concerned about this worry of the politician. He proposed a constitutional structure that had built into it habits and laws designed to counteract this danger arising from philosophic disorder.

III.

In *An Introduction to Philosophy*, Maritain defines philosophy itself as "the science which by the natural light of reason studies the first causes or highest principles of all things—[it] is, in other words, the science of things in their first causes, in so far as these belong to the natural order," a very careful definition indeed. He then adds: "The difficulty of such a science is proportionate to its elevation. That is why the philosopher, just because the object of his studies is the most sublime, should personally be the humblest of students, a humility, however, which should not prevent his defending, as it is his duty to do, the sovereign dignity of wisdom as the queen of the sciences."[9] Humility and truth are not the opposites of each other; pride—the taking our individual human selves to be the cause of everything else—and truth, however, are. Humility—acknowledging what we are—and truth—saying of *what it is* that it is—are necessary to each other. This moral firmness before the truth underscores the sense in which Socrates was humble. He knew that to do wrong was evil, as he remarked in *The Apology*. He would not doubt what he knew to be true, even as he acknowledged how much he did not know.

Leo Strauss, in a famous passage, calls political philosophy the "queen of the social sciences."[10] Maritain, as we just saw, calls philosophy itself "the queen of the sciences." Maritain, no doubt, acknowledges with Aristotle that political philosophy is the highest of the practical sciences, though he holds, with Aquinas, that theology as such is a higher science, itself a "queen" of all the sciences. At the same time, Maritain does not deny the superior dignity of philosophy within the human sciences because its object is simply *what is*. The validity of the philosophic vocation remains, is perhaps ever increased, in the light of revelation.

Yet though he took his own vocation as a philosopher seriously, Maritain always bore it with a touch of amusement. At the 1943 luncheon in New York, in his honor, on the occasion of his sixtieth birthday, he remarked, "Ordinarily, we find very many illusions, for and against, in appreciating an animal so bizarre as a philosopher."[11] And in one of his 1967 lectures at Kolbsheim, he showed some of the same whimsicality: "I begin with some preliminary observations. Indeed, the perspective of my reflections is that of the reading of a text by a Christian of any walk of life in search of intelligibility—even be he a slightly delirious old philosopher."[12] The search for "intelligibility" is again something that is of concern to more than the philosopher, while the philosopher needs to have an awareness of what he does not know, of his "being slightly delirious," as Maritain put it. Maritain was not in fact delirious, even slightly, in the technical sense of that word, but he did recognize that there was a certain exhilaration and delight in the philosophic life that might well seem odd to those who do not pursue it as devotedly as he did.

The question considered in this chapter is that of the political purpose of the philosophic vocation, a subject that needs constant attention by both politicians and by philosophers themselves. This way of life, if not understood correctly, can cause enormous damage in both practical and theoretical life. The point at issue is not, however, how much philosophy the politician himself needs to prevent him from becoming a tyrant, from becoming another Callicles. Socrates in fact does not deliberately involve himself in properly political things. He finds them rather uninteresting and often positively dangerous. In Plato's *Gorgias*, to recall, Callicles was the handsome, successful, decisive politician, who studied, even enjoyed, philosophy in his youth at college; but now that he is a practicing politician, he has put aside such boyish things as philosophy whenever it interferes with his necessary political decisions.

Maritain specifically addressed this topic of the relation of philosophy to society in a lecture given at Princeton in 1960, though it was a theme that we find frequently throughout his career, especially in the second "Conversation" in his early dialogue, *Theonas: Conversations with a Sage*.[13] The point I wish to emphasize here is that what makes Maritain unique and especially relevant on this topic is that he does not argue the purpose of the philosopher in political or societal life as if some intrinsic contradiction existed between the lives of the philosopher and the politician. He does not, like Plato in *The Republic*, combine them into one person. In his theory of democracy, Maritain provides for a legitimate place for all lives within the polity, provided that place allows for a discussion about what is worthy of respect in the first place, of the best life, of *what is.*

Moreover, Maritain accepts that a body of revelational teaching exists, itself directed to intellect and life, itself needing and profiting from philosophic attention, that does not derive directly from philosophy. Revelation is addressed to philosophy because it too seems to secure man's highest end. This revelational teaching promises the highest things also to the simple and faithful, not only to the philosophers and not solely as a result of the study of metaphysics. I stress this latter aspect of Maritain, his awareness of the worthiness of each life as seen in revelation, because it is within the context of valid but differing ways of life that he makes his argument for the essential and irreplaceable vocation of the philosopher. This is but another aspect of the Thomist principle that grace builds on nature and does not contradict, alter, or destroy it. If the contemplative or philosophic way of life is the naturally highest way, then its neglect, even within the context of revelation, which often supplies what philosophy lacks through faith, will have enormous consequences to society, consequences that themselves require philosophic attention.

In Maritain's *Essay on Christian Philosophy,* he takes special care to insist that revelation does not substitute for everything. Philosophy by being itself can in fact take account of what belongs to it by nature. "Within the realm of the real, created and uncreated, there exists a whole class of objects which are of their nature attainable . . . through the natural faculties of the human mind."[14] But philosophy ought not to close itself off in such a manner that it can only consider what the human mind itself could come up with by its own powers. To make this closure is "the modern project."[15] It reduces reality to the methods by which reality is itself studied. "They [rationalist philosophers] satisfied themselves that to philosophize properly, that is to say, according to the exigencies of reason, it is necessary to believe only in reason, in other words to be only a philosopher, existing only *qua* philsopher."[16]

Maritain points out that philosophers are and remain men, not just minds, not just philosophers, so that "where man departs philosophy can no longer remain."[17] He recognizes that it is a whole man who philosophizes, not just a mind. This same man is not in a pure state of nature, but in a fallen and redeemed state. Understanding these positions enables Maritain to retain the title of a philosopher capable of admitting for consideration evidence from whatever source when it is addressed to genuine philosophical questions formulated by the philosopher. "Philosophy seeks enlightenment about sensible objects from the natural sciences, what is to prevent it from learning of divine things from faith and theology?"[18] The answer is, of course, that nothing is to prevent it, provided the philosopher recognizes what he is doing so that he properly frames and considers what belongs to experience, what to philosophy, what to faith. When Aquinas, for instance, uses the word friendship in Greek and Latin to be the basis for explaining charity in revelation, he shows us how this relationship between faith and reason can be most fruitful.

What, then, remains for the philosopher to do? What is the societal importance of the philosopher, of the philosopher who is not a "pure philosopher" because he is aware of the advance in and importance to philosophy that results from its being addressed, indirectly at least, by revelation? The philosopher who conceives himself to exist only "*qua* philosopher," who deliberately excludes any consideration but the human mind enclosed within itself, is not the Aristotelian "pure" philosopher who was open to whatever the human mind could know insofar as it could know anything at all. There was a liberal openness to Aristotle's philosopher that Maritain recognizes and praises. Aristotle's "non" use of revelation is simply a matter of fact, not of principle. He does not "exclude" what he does not know. He is not in this sense like the modern philosopher. It was the vocation of St. Thomas, nevertheless, to show how this accurate reading of Aristotle showed that Aristotle, even when wrong, is not wrong on a matter of possible philosophic principle. His errors were always intellectually plausible, as are the revelational answers that would indicate a different possible meaning to his own philosophy.

As Theonas had said, there were things of which even Aristotle "had not the least suspicion."[19] Nonetheless, Maritain holds, even when these things that Aristotle did not know become intellectual stimuli, as in the thought of St. Thomas, philosophy still remains. "So far as Thomism in particular is concerned, first we must say that if it is a philosophy at all, it is so to the point that it is rational, not to the point that it is Christian."[20] That is, the Christian influence on philosophy is itself philosophic to the extent that it is itself subject to philosophic examination and seen to be related to genuine philosophic questions. These philosophic questions are initially fashioned by someone like Aristotle, who clearly was not Christian. These questions have in fact received no other adequate, that is, philosophically examined, response from any philosophy but that stimulated by revelational influences. And Maritain adds, "all great modern philosophies are 'Christian' philosophies, philosophies which without Christianity would not be what they are."[21] Maritain's point here is that the questions that had been traditionally treated in theology or spirituality or metaphysics suddenly came to be treated by philosophy alone without acknowledgment of their origins in revelation. Marxism's "classless society" has distinct origins in the Garden of Eden and its perfections, but placed at the end and not the beginning of history. The elevated expectations for human nature caused by revelation remained within modern philosophy even when the revelational means to consider these expectations were denied or were erroneously claimed to be capable of achievement by purely philosophical or political means.

IV.

In Maritain's essay "The Philosopher in Society," we find the explanation of his own vocation as a philosopher and why this vocation is, at the same time, central to political and cultural life. Maritain, even while defending the primacy of philosophic contemplation within philosophy, while devoting a considerable amount of his work to political philosophy, while acknowledging his own faith and the ordered intelligibility of its contents, remains in his own mind primarily a philosopher. To be a philosopher is the personal vocation, as we have seen, that he took seriously, humbly, and, at times, with some amusement. Maritain begins "The Philosopher in Society" by pointing out something that Leo Strauss also stressed, namely, that the difficulty with the great thinkers is that, ultimately, they contradict each other.[22] The study of the great thinkers thus is often a study that leads to skepticism, a study of error. Does not this intrinsic philosophic discord portend ill for the political order? What has philosophy to do with any existing polity? Why bother with philosophy, in short, if it leads to lack of concord, if it cannot really deal with the normal problems of most men? In the face of such questions, Maritain insists on the integrity and dignity of philosophy, although it often reveals disagreement. Even in his later years, after he had joined a religious community in France, Maritain considered himself to be a philosopher.

Maritain is the first to think that it is religion, not philosophy, that renders most cities governable, to the degree that they are governable in this life. He holds this because he thinks that revelation is able, by means of original sin, to understand the worst in man. Yet, the essential goodness of human nature as created by God is not denied. Revelation is also able to direct itself to those who are not themselves philosophers, the majority of mankind, in terms of the real final end of actual men in this historical dispensation. But Maritain does not think that philosophy ought to be something other than itself. "No one will grant that philosophy should suffer duress: neither the non-Christian, in whose eyes faith would impose restraints on philosophy and obstruct its view; nor the Christian, for whom faith does not restrain philosophy but strengthens it and helps it to improve its vision."[23] Revelation is not the equivalent of the old idea that those who are not philosophers must be ruled by myth or faith because they cannot understand the philosopher. Revelation also addresses the philosopher in his own unanswered questions precisely because of the prior relation of the philosopher to revelation through *what is*; the experience of revelation itself strengthens and improves philosophy's vision and man's conduct.

Maritain, after defining a philosopher as "a man in search of wisdom," brings up the question of the usefulness of philosophy in this manner:

> Unfortunately, there is no such thing as *the* philosopher; this dignified abstraction exists only in our minds. There are philosophers; and the philosophers, as soon as they philosophize, are, or seem to be, in disagreement on everything, even in the first principles of philosophy. Each one goes his own way. They question every matter of common assent, and their answers are conflicting. What can be expected from them for the good of society?[24]

This passage poses in classic form the problem of the political purpose of philosophy. The multitude of wise men, the philosophers, do not agree with each other. The ordinary citizen and politician cannot but take this disagreement as a sign of relativism.

Maritain, for his part, is not deluded about the dangers posed by the philosophers, especially the most famous and the best of them.

> Historians bestow the honor of having been the "fathers of the modern world" upon two men, the first of whom was a great dreamer and a poor philosopher, namely, Jean-Jacques Rousseau; the second, a poor dreamer and a great philosopher, namely, Hegel. And Hegel has involved the modern world in still more far-reaching and still more deadly errors than Rousseau did.[25]

Not only do the philosophers not agree, but some disagreements are positively dangerous. Maritain does not mean that these men as individuals were necessarily capable of mayhem but rather that their ideas exist in such a way that they will influence others, no doubt after their own time, in a way that will undermine moral life and the proper relation of the political order to itself and to revelation.

Maritain recognizes also that a philosopher can be great without being right. The philosophers indicate what the human mind is thinking. An accurate knowledge of philosophic thought is vital for mankind, even when this thought is wrong, indeed, especially when it is wrong. "It is better for human society to have Hegelian errors with Hegel than to have Hegelian errors without Hegel—I mean hidden and diffuse errors rampant throughout the social body, which are Hegelian in type but anonymous and unrecognizable."[26] Maritain thus understands the variety of philosophers and their disagreements as a sign of the human search for something worthy for its own sake. It is the one enterprise that has no further "use," that is for its own sake, not for something else. Philosophic disagreement cannot be disguised or rejected simply because it is disagreement. Philosophy, in its effort to claim truth before the forum of mind, is simply what the human intellect at its highest does. Philosophy is not a means to something else but a search for "the very reason for living—and suffering and hoping."[27]

V.

In his famous "Democratic Charter," in *Man and the State*, Maritain, acutely aware of intellectual disagreements, is found seeking, perhaps unsuccessfully but still with a certain intellectual bravery, to protect the realm of philosophical disagreement. He is certain that philosophic agreement could not be politically mandated. Nor does he want skepticism to seem intellectually justified because of the disagreement of the philosophers. He allows genuine philosophic controversy to go on in its own "beyond politics" realm without political interference. To guarantee this freedom, he proposes a list of rights or principles according to which men could agree to live together politically in peace but without insisting on agreement about the principles that establish these norms or standards of living. Maritain's hope is that this practical agreement could take place before intellectual questions were resolved. This practical intellectual process by which these common rights and principles are justified would not have to be uniform at the political level. The hope is that the same practical conclusions can be explained in different ways. Still, Maritain admits that the reasonings behind practical agreements would have to withstand philosophic examination at the speculative level.[28] Maritain, in other words, seeks to protect both politics and philosophy, in their own orders.

Maritain's proposals about the Democratic Charter, it is to be noted here, are the other side of what he is arguing about the use of philosophy in society. Far from being signs of the human mind's incapacity to know the truth, these intellectual disagreements rather are, at their highest levels, evidence of its search in freedom for truth. "Philosophy is essentially a disinterested activity, directed toward truth loved for its own sake, not utilitarian activity for the sake of power over things."[29] In the light of this latter comment, it might be added, the debates in political philosophy with Machiavelli, Hobbes, the utilitarians, Marx, Nietzsche, Heidegger, and the recent deconstructionists are themselves first of all philosophic debates about propositions that claim to be true and therefore not primarily about power as such. The idea that philosophy or politics is about power rather than truth or the good is itself a part of the philosophic argument about truth and good. It is part of the philosophic realm that exists for its own sake and ultimately can exist at no other level.

Thus, Maritain takes care to protect a realm of discourse, of conversation, that can take place in freedom and include all the great philosophers, even when they contradict each other. He wants everything in this realm to be in the open, to be capable of philosophic examination.

He wants to be able to see most clearly, as he says, what, say, Hegel said, because this reveals better than anything else what is the actual condition of human analysis and thought. In protecting the conditions of philosophic freedom, Maritain recognizes that the great philosophic quest continues. Arguments could take centuries and eras. Things that were established or known in one place or time could be forgotten or rejected. Philosophy is singularly independent of time, and its insights remain within the discipline, within the contemplative life, even when temporarily rejected. "Philosophy is a science, and . . . it attains certain knowledge," Maritain writes.

> By this we would not be understood to claim that philosophy provides certain solutions for *every* question that can be asked within its domain. On many points the philosopher must be content with probable solutions, either because the question goes beyond the actual scope of his science . . . or because of its nature it admits only a probable answer, for example, the application of moral rules in individual cases. But this element of mere probability is accidental to science as such. And philosophy yields a greater number of certain conclusions, and of those many more perfect, namely, the conclusions of metaphysics, than any other purely human science.[30]

Clearly, Maritain does not think that the disagreements of the philosophers as an empirical fact obviate that philosophy is a science with its own norms and procedures that abide over time. This is why the study of Plato and Aristotle, Augustine and Aquinas, of Maritain himself, is still a contemporary study.

Maritain does not doubt that the great controversies that overturn or establish order in society first take place in the hearts and minds of the philosophers, the dons, before they ever reach public attention. The philosophic enterprise, battled out in the heat of politics, loses track of that almost endless time it needs to examine differing positions. Nevertheless, in the tradition of St. Thomas, we can expect something of the truth in any philosophic system, no matter how erroneous that system may be. "If we try to do justice to the philosophic systems against which we take our most determined stand," Maritain writes, "we shall seek to discover both the intuition which they involve and the place we must grant them from our own point of view."[31]

What is the duty of the philosopher to society? "A philosopher may set aside his philosophic pursuit and become a man of politics. But what of a philosopher who remains simply a philosopher, and acts only as a philosopher?"[32] Clearly, Maritain is one who thinks that the more noble decision is the latter, to remain a philosopher. This remaining a philosopher does not mean silence in public, but, as we recall from Socrates or Christ, it may entail sacrifice before the state because of philosophy, of truth. "The philosopher must bear witness by expressing his thoughts and telling the truth as he sees it. This may have repercussions in the domain of politics; it is not, in itself, a political action—it is simply applied philosophy."[33] Maritain holds that the philosophic vocation is important for society because we need to know the truth of the ideas that stand behind all civil order. "The foundations of a society of free men," he writes, "are essentially moral."[34] Without the rational defense of these very foundations, a society of free men would not be possible. This is how Maritain envisaged his own philosophic vocation of the philosopher as such.

About philosophic disagreements and their political importance, Maritain is clear. "The fact that philosophical discussion seems to consist of deaf men's quarrels is not reassuring for civilization."[35] Philosophers manifest the vanities and weaknesses of other men, perhaps in an acute form. Yet in principle, they can "cooperate." The disagreeing philosophers could not in honesty maintain that their systems were in agreement if in fact they are not. But in the realm of philosophic discourse, everything remains open, the contemplative order remains in force. However, "there is not toleration between systems—a system cannot *tolerate* another system, because systems are abstract sets of ideas and have only intellectual existence, where the will to tolerate or not to tolerate has no point," Maritain reminds us. "But there can be justice, intellectual justice, between philosophical systems."[36] Men tolerate other men, not systems. It is this area in which intellectual justice could be freely maintained that Maritain sees to be the arena in which the philosopher lives.

Maritain's final statement of the importance of philosophy in society is, I think, one of great force and beauty. "If philosophy is one of the forces which contributes to the movement of history and the changes that occur in the world," he writes,

> it is because philosophy, in its primary task, which is the metaphysical penetration of being, is intent only on discovering and contemplating

what is the truth of certain matters which have importance in themselves and for themselves, independently of what happens in the world, and which, precisely for that reason, exert an essential influence in the world.[37]

This is why truth is prior to action that depends on it.

At first, the actual life of the world is dominated by religion and politics, both of which have their proper place in philosophic reasoning. The political importance of the less visible philosophic life, as Maritain understands it, "its essential influence in the world," is that ideas and systems of thought be tested. They are to be subject to examination before and through the "metaphysical penetration of being" that looks to and stands for the truth of things. He acknowledges the importance of craftsmen, artists, politicians, and, yes, saints. But as he lived it, his is also the vocation of the philosopher, not the"pure philosopher," but the philosopher who knows about revelation and about modern philosophy, about Machiavelli, Luther, Rousseau, Hegel, and Nietzsche, about Plato, Aristotle, Augustine, and Aquinas. He continues to stand on the side of human reason, testing what it could know and what could be known. Without such philosophic vocation, all other ways of life, even the life of faith, stand under the political danger of the philosopher "*qua* philosopher," of the man whose intellect has no other object but itself.

NOTES

1. Jacques Maritain, *La Philosophie Morale, OCM*, vol. 11, 315.
2. Jacques Maritain, "The Philosopher in Society," *On the Use of Philosophy: Three Essays* (New York: Atheneum, 1965), 13.
3. Jacques Maritain, *Scholasticism and Politics* (Garden City, N. Y.: Doubleday, Image, 1960), 165.
4. Ibid., 165–68.
5. Nicolò Machiavelli, *The Prince*, ed. Leo S. de Alvarez (Irving, Texas: University of Dallas Press, 1980), 93.
6. Karl Marx, "Theses on Feuerbach," *The Marx-Engels Reader*, ed. Robert C. Tucker (New York: Norton, 1972), 109.
7. Maritain, *Art and Scholasticism*, 20–21.
8. Ralph McInerny, *Art and Prudence: Studies in the Thoughts of Jacques Maritain* (Notre Dame: University of Notre Dame Press, 1988), 2.

9. Jacques Maritain, *An Introduction to Philosophy*, trans. E. I. Watkin (London: Sheed & Ward, 1946) 80–81.

10. Leo Strauss, *The City and Man* (Chicago: University of Chicago Press, 1964), 1.

11. Jacques Maritain, "*À Mes Amis de New York*," *OCM*, vol. 8, 797.

12. Jacques Maritain, "*Faisons-lui une aide semblable à lui*," *OCM*, vol. 13, 679.

13. Jacques Maritain, *Theonas: Conversations with a Sage*, trans. F. J. Sheed (New York: Sheed & Ward, 1933), 15–26. Theonas is the imaginary hero of the dialogue, the believing wise man.

14. Jacques Maritain, *An Essay on Christian Philosophy*, trans. Edward H. Flannery (New York: Philosophical Library, 1955), 14.

15. The phrase is from Leo Strauss, *The City and Man*, 3–4.

16. Ibid., 16. Strauss would have found the idea of a Christian philosophy unintelligible, but he did not allow that philosophy or theology could exclude each other. See Susan Orr, *Jerusalem and Athens: Reason and Revelation in the Works of Leo Strauss* (Lanham, Md.: Rowman & Littlefield, 1995).

17. Ibid.

18. Ibid., 22.

19. Maritain, *Theonas*, 25.

20. Maritain, *An Essay on Christian Philosophy*, 30.

21. Ibid., 32.

22. "The greatest minds do not tell us the same things regarding the most important themes; the community of the greatest minds is rent by discord." Leo Strauss, "What Is Liberal Education?" in *Liberalism: Ancient and Modern* (Ithaca, N. Y.: Cornell University Press, 1989), 3–4.

23. Maritain, *An Essay on Christian Philosophy*, 36.

24. Jacques Maritain, *On the Use of Philosophy: Three Essays* (New York: Atheneum, 1965), 3.

25. Ibid., 3–4.

26. Ibid., 4.

27. Ibid., 7.

28. Jacques Maritain, *Man and the State* (Chicago: University of Chicago Press, 1966), 108–46.

29. Maritain, "The Philosopher in Society," 7.

30. Jacques Maritain, *An Introduction to Philosophy*, trans. E. I. Watkin (London: Sheed & Ward, 1946), 81–82.

31. Jacques Maritain, "Truth and Human Fellowship," *On the Use of Philosophy*, 28.

32. Maritain, "The Philosopher in Society," 14.

33. Ibid.

34. Ibid., 12.
35. Maritain, "Truth and Human Fellowship," 25.
36. Ibid., 28.
37. Maritain, "The Philosopher in Society," 8.

4

ON DEFINING POLITICAL THINGS

> There is no more thankless task than trying rationally to distinguish and to circumscribe—in other words, trying to raise to a scientific or philosophical level—common notions that have arisen from contingent practical needs of human history and are laden with social, cultural, and historical connotations as ambiguous as they are fertile, and which nevertheless envelop a core of intelligible meaning.
>
> —Jacques Maritain, *Man and the State*[1]

> If philosophy enables the human intellect to apprehend with absolute certainty the highest and most profound realities of the natural order, it cannot therefore claim to exhaust those realities by making them known to the utmost extent of their intelligibility. From this point of view science does not destroy the *mystery* of things, that in them which is still unknown and unfathomed, but on the contrary recognises and delimits it; even what it knows it never knows completely. The wise man knows all things, inasmuch as he knows them in their ultimate causes, but he does not know, is infinitely removed from knowing, everything about everything.
>
> —Jacques Maritain, *An Introduction to Philosophy*[2]

I.

What is striking in reading Maritain is the frequency and care that he takes to clarify, to point to what he is speaking about. He expects the reader to understand him; but he knows that to accomplish mutual comprehension, he must explain exactly what he means in the light of what ideas and words signify in themselves and in context. He does think, moreover, that it is possible for human beings to understand one another, even across languages and cultures. The exercise of intelligence and of its communication is not futile. "We only fully know a thing," Maritain explained in his *Major Logic*, "if we know that which grounds it in being and in intelligibility: these causes then, and these principles, for the principles of the being of a thing are also the principles of its intelligibility. *To know* a thing, then, implies that we know its cause."[3] To know something means to find what category of reality, substance or accident, it is in, then to find its cause. Political things are no exception to this effort of understanding.

Maritain is likewise aware that words in every language are central tools by which we understand things, by which we explain reality to ourselves and to others. They are a symbol that refers to reality. Words, no doubt, can change their emphases or even meanings, not merely across languages, but within the same language over time. With attention, we can follow the course and direction of this change when it happens. Maritain understands univocal, equivocal, and analogous concepts and words. That is, some words or concepts are used in exactly the same way, some words have the same spellings but not at all the same meanings, and some meanings are somewhat the same, but somewhat different in a given understanding or usage. We have to make the effort to grasp these differing concepts and meanings of words and the reality to which they refer. Maritain does not think this an impossible enterprise, but it is one that needs care and attention, step by step, in knowing what we talk about or do.

In the essay entitled "To Exist with the People," in *The Range of Reason*, for instance, the first subheading is, "Class, Race, People." These notions, Maritain explains, "affect the consciousness and political debates of our day."[4] We need to state what they mean or how we mean them. The word "people" in this essay gives a good idea of how Maritain approaches the definitions of political things. He remarks first of all that "people" can refer to one of two things: (1) a whole people, or (2) "the lower levels of society." Generally, the idea that people have of themselves is different from either of these definitions. If we look at this latter definition, that is, the people considered as the lower levels of society, most people would in fact see themselves as more human, more loosely bound together than the more sociological term, "lower levels of society," would indicate. In one sense, the people means the nonprivileged classes, but positively, the word comes to mean "a moral community centered on labor"—farmers, workers, and those associated with hard or manual labor. This understanding is not unrelated to Maritain's study of art and craft as elevated through the Christian emphasis on the dignity of the carpenter, of work as such (see chapter 2). Maritain uses the term "moral" community of this lower level of society because, to be complete, the word "people" must include a deliberately recognized consciousness that comes from living the hard life of work and the suffering that goes with it.[5] The real people in this sense are those who work and suffer.

But Maritain is not content with the implications of the definition thus far. He thinks that the modern notion of the word "people" includes religious overtones. It contains the implications of the Beatitude that the poor are "blessed"; their status has almost a mystical overtone to it. The notion of the communion of saints, of the blessed poor, has been, in part, transferred from the spiritual to the temporal order. In this sense, it becomes a social–ethical idea, not exactly the old Roman idea of a *populus* or *plebs*, but still indicative of the poor, working people who have a special consciousness and are especially loved by God. The working poor, in turn, came to be replaced by the destitute, by those who had nothing, as the privileged definition of the people. The people were the proletariat or the exploited. In the Marxist system, class, an economic notion, became identified with the proletariat, the working poor who had nothing. The proletariat were said to be the people. But neither the categories of class or race predominated over that of the people. It was the word "people" that won out as the preferred word to all the other divisions and groups in society, such as class, race, or nation; it implies an "awareness of a developing personality, the necessary condition for the future birth of a personalistic democracy."[6]

Maritain's essay ends with the two interrelated concepts, people and personalistic democracy, that reappear in his seminal work, *Man and the State*, in a more comprehensive form. The first two chapters of *Man and the State*, the substance of which book was given as part of the Walgreen Lecture Series at the University of Chicago in 1949, contain Maritain's most famous endeavor to define and explain political words, ideas, and realities. He is aware, of course, that the term "state" is a particularly modern word finding no exact correspondence in classical political thought. Indeed, the term, state, could have meanings and connotations that Maritain wants to have nothing to do with, ideas of absolutism and limitless power. On the other hand, he endeavors to save the term, state, and to outline a legitimate usage for it within a more complete and coherent system of political analysis.

These two chapters are models of expository inquiry that should precede and eventually become instruments of any political teaching and of political understanding. These chapters constitute some of the most instructive passages in the whole corpus of Maritain's writings. The very fact that Maritain did not entitle the book merely *The State* but *Man and the State* indicates the importance of understanding politics both as an expression of itself and as an aspect of what it is to be a man, a human being, in the full sense, a sense that will include, as Maritain always notices, more than politics, more even than philosophy. Maritain's political philosophy is ever a remarkably open one, constantly refreshed by a hard look at the reality he is talking about. He refrains from simply concocting political ideas from his head.

These two chapters are fifty-three pages long. By far the longest treatment of these various political concepts, which takes up the whole second chapter of twenty-five pages, is devoted to sovereignty. This idea, Maritain thinks, has a noble history but still is an idea that has no useful place in political things. To understand just why Maritain reacts so strongly against the idea of sovereignty in politics, the theological history of which concept he takes great pains to sketch, we must follow Maritain's first chapter in which he spells out what he means by the basic political terms—community, society, nation, body politic, state, and people. Anyone can, of course, read these relatively brief pages in an hour or so. To reread them takes considerably longer. They are pages that require pondering along with other ideas that we commonly come across in Maritain, such as that of the person or of the common good. Many of Maritain's works, of course, will repeat or reanalyze these very terms. He spent his long lifetime with most of them. But generally, Maritain explains clearly enough what he means by these political terms. They are not arbitrary terms or definitions. They belong to something, identify something, something real that is encountered in human experience that, following our natural desire to know *all that is*, must be dealt with, identified, explained, understood in its causes.

Man's political realities are ones that fall into a special category of being. States, societies, communities—these are not like trees or rabbits that we come across on our afternoon walks. Yet we encounter states, societies, and communities all the time. We recognize them as very fa-

miliar, once they are pointed out or reflected on, such as jury duty arising from civil society. These realities exist because, and only because,
human beings and whatever causes human beings exist. They are a part
of our human reality, an aspect of what human beings are, however
much they might also reflect what caused human beings to be what they
are. Realities like society, state, nation, or city fall not in the category of
substance, like trees or human beings themselves, but into the category
of relation, of how we stand to each other in our activities and in our
habits. Even though a state may have monuments and buildings that
manifest its presence, a state itself it is not a building or a monument.
Yet we know when we cross a national border, for instance, from Italy
into France, that we have passed into another way of doing things, a
different spirit and reality, a different set of relationships according to
which people act. The actions that people direct towards one another
relate them to each other in a different way, a Brazilian or a Swedish
way, even when they are doing something very familiar like eating or
drinking or penalizing a traffic violator.

Maritain's first chapter, moreover, is not entitled, as is his book,
Man and the State, but rather "The People and the State." In his other
philosophic works, Maritain has given great attention to the subject of
the ontological, moral, and theological status of man, to *what he is*.[7]
Political things, as it were, only begin when we have reflected on human
things and seen what, as persons, they do. We have seen from the essay
in the *Range of Reason* that the term "people" was the one that historically came to include not merely all the classes and races and all the
individuals, no matter how poor or destitute, but it became the basis of
"personalistic democracy," that is to say, a people is composed of individual human beings who are persons, each of whom, as such, has an
end, a purpose that transcends politics but does not deny its reality, but
rather relies on it. Much of Maritain's most fruitful work has to do
with reconciling and coordinating the demands of man's transcendent
personal goals with the same man's practical goals of this life. Although,
if not properly understood, an opposition can exist between these things,
between man and state, Maritain's effort to define what he is talking
about is largely governed by the idea that there need not be an intrinsic
opposition between the differing aspects of the fullness of the human life
that appears and flourishes in the polity.

II

Amusingly, Maritain remarks about the effort to explain how political notions are understood that "everybody is the more at ease in using them [political terms] as he does not know exactly what they mean."[8] This "ease" in confusion, of course, will never do for a philosopher. Maritain considers it to be both a virtue and an obligation to state "exactly what he means." His philosophical background, moreover, is apparent in his ability to achieve this desired exactness that he thinks incumbent on him as a philosopher. He is aware, no doubt, that any exactness is itself precarious, particularly when dealing with variable individual things. "Such [political] concepts are nomadic, not fixed; they are shifting and fluid. Now they are used synonymously, now in opposition to one another."[9] It is of course necessary to observe and record such changes in political terms. But beneath this changingness there is a stability in what we mean and what we indicate, a stability that can preserve intellectual integrity and the philosophical enterprise of understanding political things, in the reality they have. Aristotle had said that we should not expect more certitude of a science than the methods of that science can bring forth, something that was especially relevant to political things whose propositions stated in their generality hold "for the most part," but not always (1094b20–27). How particular circumstances affected principles in their application is part of the ethical tradition to which Maritain belongs.

The three political terms that are most necessary "for a sound political philosophy to try to sort out" are "Nation, Body Politic (or Political Society), and State." Even though these words are often used interchangeably, there is a great danger in identifying or confusing what really are separate things if we understand the realities to which the words point. And lest we think that Maritain's exercise in definition is merely that, an exercise, he adds, "the austerity of my analysis may perhaps be excused . . . on account of the importance of the principles in political philosophy it may make us aware of."[10] That is, the very exercise of defining political terms, an exercise that may seem at first "austere" or dry, cannot help but make us aware of the principles in political philosophy that they spell out. In other words, Maritain's analysis is educative of the mind seeking to know the principles and the order of political things as they appear and exist in themselves as flowing out of human persons in their interactions and relationships.

Maritain's first step is to distinguish community from society, words often used interchangeably. This distinction is made first because it forms the basis of the other political definitions that Maritain discusses. Both community and society are "ethicosocial and truly human" terms; they are not biological terms. Both terms involve the use of reason, the properly distinctive human power. The realities that Maritain deals with all depend on and flow out of the faculties of both reason and will that set man apart in the universe of other things. A community, for its part, is based on a fact. This fact, say, the members of the same tribe or nation, is not itself the product of reason. The fact is recognized by reason. However, as a result of this fact, certain things follow that are acknowledged by reason and will. That I am born and live in the mountains or on a farm is a fact. All those similarly born and living in the mountains or on the farm will as a result have a certain feeling and consciousness of a way of life, of things to be done, of tradition, all of which arise out of this common fact that is the occasion of their community.

A society, on the other hand, is strictly based on a purpose or an end to be accomplished. This end and the means to attain it are products of human reason. Most societies are voluntary and need not exist, but do exist because some human purpose is thought worthy of accomplishment by organizing members. Thus, "a business firm, a labor union, a scientific association are societies as much as is the body politic. Regional, ethnic, linguistic groups, social classes are communities."[11] In the community, the memory, the feeling, the sense of belonging to the group are primary. In the society, what is most important is the purpose, the rational order of the enterprise or organization by which the acting human beings in the group achieve their end.

Maritain calls both the family and the political society natural societies, not communities. He recognizes that both institutions have a long history of development and a particular consciousness, but essentially both are products of reason as to what they are and the purpose of their organization. Around societies of reasonable purpose there also come to exist communities of feeling and loyalty. For example, ball teams as such, with regard to their end and rules of play, are almost purely rational societies, but in the support of fans and followers they form communities. Maritain does not think, however, that community is something irrational as such. The fact around which a community is formed is itself perfectly intelligible and objective, a fact, a good that can be desired. Nothing inhuman or irrational is involved in recognizing a fact. Societies, moreover, can and normally should give rise to community, to tradition and familiarity. But a community never develops into a society, though it be the natural soil from which society originates. A society always involves taking conscious and deliberate effort to achieve some purpose and to organize the members of the group to achieve that purpose.[12]

Armed with this distinction between community and society, Maritain proceeds, as a first step in any societal analysis, to indicate what the group under discussion or analysis is in its basic form. Is it rooted in a fact or is it rooted in a purpose or goal? Thus, Maritain asks to which of these categories does the "nation" belong? "Now the nation is a community, not a society."[13] We recall that most modern states are called precisely "nation-states," as if this combination of words indicates something particularly important in identifying what the contemporary political organization is. Somehow, to call it simply a nation or simply a state is not an accurate description of the complexity of the societal unit. It is not always easy to come to terms with the idea of a nation, "perhaps the most complex and complete community engendered by civilized life."[14] In the twentieth century, considerable struggle exists about whether class or nation is the more enduring and accurate description of the basis of human organization. Whenever it comes to a head, Maritain observes, the nation generally proves to be the deeper and more enduring concept, but he also thought that the concept of the nation itself needs considerable clarification.

The origin of the word "nation" comes from a Latin word meaning "to be born." Hence, nation means those of a common birth. Notice that this birth will be the "fact" that will ground the community that is the nation. But the fact needs to become conscious and a cause of feelings and associations that involve reflection and reason. Not every or even most facts of common birth result in a community called a nation. Maritain does not think that the word nation as such is a bad thing, but it can be and has been used in a dangerous fashion in the twentieth century, particularly when it is confused with state. Much of the history of the twentieth century, including the colonial history, has to do with the unfortunate placing of the nation over the state as the criterion of organization, or the reason for breaking up a state into its national or linguistic components. This latter fact is one of the reasons why Maritain must deal with nation, as well as race and class, with such care.

Listen to how Maritain describes the nation.

> It is something ethicosocial: a human community based on the fact of birth and lineage, yet with all the moral connotations of those terms: birth to the life of reason and the activities of civilization, lineage in familial traditions, social and political formation, cultural heritage, common conception and manners, historical recollections, sufferings, claims, hopes, prejudices, and resentments. An ethnic community . . . can be defined as a *community of patterns of feelings*, rooted in the physical soil of the origins of the groups as well as in the moral soil of history, it becomes a nation when this factual situation enters the sphere of self-awareness, in other words, when the ethnic group *becomes conscious* of the fact that it constitutes a community of patterns of feeling . . . and possesses its own unity and individuality, its own will to endure in existence.[15]

Clearly, human nature needs something more than family and body politic to express its whole reality. The area of community and voluntary society yields a wide scope to institutions that are not bodies politic yet have a legitimate place in them. Moreover, it is quite conceivable to have members of the same nation being citizens of differing bodies politic, something that modern immigration patterns have made both possible and frequent.

What specifically concerns Maritain about the nation that claims to be a state is not the value and worth of differing birth or origins but of using this criterion alone to define membership in a body politic. Even when a country uses birth as the principal criterion of citizenship, this citizenship itself is already defined in terms of constitutional order, itself a product of rational understanding.

> The State, when it has been identified with the nation, or even with the Race, and when the fever of the instincts of the earth has thus invaded its own blood—the State has had its will to power exasperated, it has presumed to impose by force of law the so-called type and genius of the Nation, thus becoming a cultural, ideological, caesaropapist, totalitarian State. At the same time, that totalitarian State has

degenerated by losing the sense of the objective order of justice and law.[16]

Maritain's point is that the good qualities of community need the order of something other than itself to remain what they are. The aberration of both state and nation is the use of communitarian feelings and traditions, good in themselves, as substitutes for the objective of justice and law that are rationally defined by the society.

III.

In following Maritain's scheme of definitions, what will seem confusing at first sight is his distinction between the body politic and the state, both of which belong on the side of society, not community. Normally, we would be tempted to contrast the community that is the nation with the state. Maritain's intention is not to get rid of the nation or the communities of ethnic or cultural feelings and traditions that spontaneously arise among diverse people. This diversity is itself part of that good that the civil society or body politic is designed to protect and foster. Maritain seeks rather to explain the exact dimensions of Aristotle's principle that man is by nature a political animal. That is to say, for man to be what he is by nature, he must set up through the use of his reason an organized set of laws and relationships within which *what man is* can reach its fulfillment, its flourishing.

The essential step in this analysis is to relate the body politic and the state. Both state and body politic fall into the category of society. They indicate an organized relation of law and reasoned habit concerning how citizens act towards one another. Both body politic and state have a rational purpose or end; the end of the state is for the good of the body politic. Maritain calls the body politic a natural society, by which he does not mean that it grows on trees, but that is rationally necessary to complete *what man is*. The body politic is necessary if man decides and chooses to become complete man, to complete all his practical potentialities. It is intelligent for him, in union with others of his kind, to see the need for and actually to set up a society. Thus, the body politic comes forth in time, moreover, it can be more or less well designed and executed. Body politic, not state, is Maritain's basic political unit; it is the whole of those belonging to a given polity.

Yet, following Aristotle, the political side of man is not the highest thing in him as a person, even though everyone needs the body politic, which engages him in a common good with others during his lifetime. Within the body politic, someone or somebody within it must be designated to look specifically to its reasonable good. This instrumentality within the body politic is called, specifically, the state. To put it briefly, Maritain holds that the state is the topmost part of the whole that is the body politic. They are related as part to whole, not as two entirely different wholes or as two equal parts of one whole. The very validity of the state derives from an argument, itself rational and intelligible, about the need for authority (chapter 7).

"The State is only that part of the body politic especially concerned with the maintenance of law, the promotion of the common welfare and public order, and the administration of public affairs," Maritain writes. "The State is the *part* which specializes in the interests of the *whole*. It is not a man or a body of men, it is a set of institutions combined into a topmost machine: this kind of work of art has been built by man and uses human brains and energies and is nothing without man, but it constitutes a superior embodiment of reason."[17] When Maritain affirms here that the state is a "kind of work of art," however, he is not suddenly embracing Machiavelli's primacy of art over prudence. He is rather noting the particular configuration that, under the control of reason, each different state takes in its historical formation. Each will look quite different and yet still be a state under the essential definition. Presidents, monarchs, prime ministers, senates, courts, cabinets, all can be woven into the structure of a state in different ways with varying degrees of success and emphasis. No one set of institutions or laws works for all people; indeed the very variety of differing ways to constitute the state is one of the signs of active reason capable of achieving the same purpose in differing ways. At the level of the common good of the world, a wide variety of differing bodies politic and state arrangements is a positive good.

Moreover, when Maritain remarks that the state "uses human brains" and that it is "nothing without man," he means to distinguish the actual individuals in seats or offices of the state, however constituted, from the state looked upon as a designed series of offices and laws. He will call these actual people the administration or sometimes the government they can come and go without the body politic or state essentially changing if they rule "according to law." Over time, different administrations can and do occupy the same offices of state. By virtue of differing parties or ruling philosophies (often called governments), they can govern the same state with differing emphases, under the same constitutional law. When by virtue of a revolution or radical change of political structure, that includes new religion, philosophy, and purpose, so that the configuration of the state is not the same, we must speak of another state as having taken the place of the former one. Aristotle had already noticed this, and it is a common occurrence in history.

Clearly, the key concept for Maritain is not the state but the body politic, together with the nuances that the notion of the people add to it. The state and body politic then are manifestations of society, "even society in its highest or 'perfect' form."[18] The notion of a highest or perfect society does not mean an unlimited or transcendent group or organization. It means a society that includes after its own purposes other communities and institutions while acknowledging their ends. It includes them not by absorbing them, but by providing a framework in which they can better be what they already are. The whole is the body politic, itself composed of citizens who are persons first, the state is the topmost part of the whole, the part that makes the most necessary and basic decisions about what is good for the whole. The voluntary societies, persons, and communities within the state are, to be what they are, about their own business. They cannot look at what is good for everyone, a good that is not apart from everyone but includes everyone. "*Political society*, required by nature and achieved by reason, is the most perfect of temporal societies. It is a concrete and wholly human reality, tending to a concretely and wholly human good—the common good."[19] As a philosopher, Maritain recognizes the reality and good of this humanly organized body politic and state. This is a real good, a temporal good, that acknowledges that the human persons who are members of the body politic in their individual destiny transcend the temporal order.

The whole that is political society required by nature does not mean that its necessity or value lies outside of reason. Rather, it means that man, reflecting with the reason given in his own human nature on *what man is*, understands that this organization (body politic) is necessary if *that which man is* is to come about, if he is to be what he ought to be. So reason here understands both the end and establishes the means or order in which this end is "achieved." What is to be noted too is that the state is called specifically not an eternal society but a *temporal* society. That is, it has to do with man as he exists in time, in his human or mortal condition. The body politic is composed of changing members some of whom, at all times, are coming into existence or leaving it. Maritain, in the sentence cited near the end of the previous paragraph, repeats the words "concrete and wholly human" twice, once applying to reality and once to common good. He does this to emphasize the sphere of competence of the body politic and state. This competence is not a matter of abstract ideas and principles alone but these ideas and principles as applied and working themselves out for an end, a good, that is the purpose of actual human beings in differing states and differing stages of mortal life.

Man belongs to the state with his "entire" being but not with all that is in him. This is why Maritain insisted on calling the state an instrument of the body politic in achieving its common good. It is neither the common good itself nor the body politic. As an agency, the state is filled with persons, in Maritain's technical use of that term, who give it life and make it work (government, administration) not for themselves but for a common good. The state's rationale, its reason for existing, is not itself. To put it another way, when the state adequately performs its task as agent, only then do the most important things for human persons take place easily and on a large scale, things that lead us directly beyond the state, and even beyond the body politic. If the state and body politic look to justice for their "existence," as Maritain maintains, they look to "friendship" for their completion and higher form; they look to something, in other words, that leads to more than the political life, not denying that the political life, while it can greatly hinder these purposes, can also make them more easily attainable (chapter 8).

Maritain is clear that recognizing the danger of the modern state as it historically developed need not make him to be seen as completely "anti-state." His realism is always refreshing.

> We may dislike the State machinery; I do not like it. Yet many things we do not like are necessary, not only in fact, but by right. On the one hand, the primary reason for which men, united in a political

society, need the State, is the order of justice. On the other hand, social justice is the crucial need of modern society. As the result, the primary duty of the modern State is the enforcement of social justice.[20]

But the primary duty of the state is not to be the need or purpose of the body politic that is served through the state's attention to social justice but not exhausted by it. As the topmost agency of the body politic, the state's organizational purpose is to look after the framework that makes everything else possible and, as much as it can, to be proportionally fair. The state serves an instrumental purpose. Maritain says bluntly that he dislikes state machinery even though there is a valid need and its existence can be intellectually elaborated and examined. In honesty, he acknowledges the problems and difficulties upon which the good things, the realities of human life, are often built.

In the argument between a weak and strong state apparatus or agency, Maritain holds that room exists for a strong state, provided it remains what it is, a defined, limited agency. He does not think that a weak state necessarily guarantees freedom or the flourishing of the activities beyond politics. "The fact remains that the State has skill and competence in administrative, legal, and political matters, but is inevitably dull and awkward—and, as a result, easily oppressive and injudicious—in all other fields."[21] With his insistence on justice and friendship, on the protection and fostering of voluntary societies, and on his awareness of the dangers of the state apparatus, Maritain clearly maintains attitudes that contemporary conservatism would appreciate. His almost simultaneous insistence that the same state have enough authority and power to do its functions does not make him a liberal or socialist, but rather, as he says himself, an Aristotelian and a Thomist. That is, he thinks that human reason in a positive sense can understand what is due to it "by nature." In pursuing man's purpose by his skill, craft, and inventiveness, it is possible to form institutions of the state to foster social justice in the body politic. In its very operations, the state and body politic form the basis of goods that point to and make possible more goods than those proper to the state itself.

Maritain provides a way of considering the state that limits it by defining it and placing it in its own proper and intelligible order. The first and most necessary step in any process, including the political process, is knowing what we are dealing with and how accurately we must describe what it is. Maritain's precise usage of the word, state, will no doubt be unfamiliar to normal language that does not easily distinguish the state and the body politic or the state, community, and administration. However, what he is getting at is clear. He provides a standard against which we can consider both what a state is and its performance.

> The common good of the body politic demands a network of authority and power in political society, and therefore a special agency endowed with uppermost power, for the sake of justice and law. The State is that uppermost agency. But the state is neither a whole nor a subject of right, or a person. It is part of the body politic and, as such, inferior to the body politic as a whole, subordinate to it and at the service of the common good. The common good of the political society is the final aim of the State, and comes before the immediate aim of the State, which is the maintenance of the common good.[22]

When Maritain observes that the state is neither a whole, a subject of right that is not itself a person, he reminds us that the only whole that is a subject of right is the human person, not societies or communities of any sort. Maritain's political philosophy is designed to keep clear what depends on what. The state is thus an agency, inferior to the body politic, at the service not of itself but of the common good. The state is limited by its purpose.

IV.

Maritain's very detailed concern about sovereignty arises from his effort to limit the state. In this discussion, he deals with the political theories mainly of Bodin, Hobbes, and Rousseau. These thinkers understood sovereignty to mean that political power or authority arose outside of and over the people. It did not come from the people, nor was it always to be controlled by them. Perhaps it is useful to reflect here that the state in modern theory has in many ways become a substitute for divinity, at least conceptually. Nothing is allowed to stand over and to limit the state. This understanding of state power is really the origin of Maritain's polemic against using the concept of sovereignty. The word sovereignty, no doubt, does have a perfectly good and proper meaning when it is applied to God, though even there it makes a difference how

God is understood, particularly if He is understood as purely arbitrary will, as seems to have been the case with William of Occam, a position that undermines the stability of all reality. When this notion of God as pure, arbitrary will is applied to political things, we get Hobbes's Leviathan, Rousseau's General Will, and Bodin's Sovereignty, mortal gods and wills that are responsible neither to nature nor to God nor to the people.

Thus, the reason Maritain takes such careful aim at sovereignty is the hope that by explaining what it means in its historical context, it would be obvious why it is not a good political idea, certainly not one to describe the state or the people. This concept (of sovereignty) "is intrinsically wrong and is bound to mislead us if we keep on using it."[23] In Bodin's theory, the people give their power to their sovereign. He rules over them; he transcends the political whole, something that, in Maritain's argument, ought never to happen because political authority rises from the people, the body politic, and does not descend from above them.

In medieval theory, Maritain recalls, the ruler always exercises his authority as a vicar of the people. This derivation signifies that political authority is derived from them and what they are, ontologically, as individual persons. Medieval political theory is never absolutist, as is the early modern theory that has adopted the idea of sovereignty. This idea that all authority is exercised in the name of and in behalf of the people is lost with Bodin and those who follow him. The political sovereign takes on a kind of being or personhood of his own that does not derive from the people.[24] Thus, in the development of the idea of the sovereign, it came to mean "a property which is absolute and indivisible, which cannot be participated in and admits of no degrees and which belongs to the Sovereign independently of the political whole, as a right of its own."[25]

Maritain adds that Rousseau's democratic people yield their wills to one will. At first sight, this mechanism might seem to solve the problem of authority arising from the people, but what results is really the same concept as Hobbes's Leviathan. The only difference is that the collective people creating a General Will takes the place of the sovereign Leviathan but retains exactly the same powers. The state has complete, independent, and autonomous power over and above the people.

Rousseau . . . injected in nascent modern democracies a notion of Sovereignty which was destructive of democracy, and pointed toward the totalitarian State; because, instead of getting clear of the separate and transcendent power of the absolute kings, he carried, on the contrary, that spurious power of the absolute kings to the point of an unheard-of absolutism, in order to make a present of it to the people.[26]

The notion of sovereignty that is "destructive of democracy" arises from a theoretical misunderstanding of the origin and source of political order, whether in monarchies or popular governments. Giving absolute power to a democratic people is dangerous, perhaps more dangerous, than giving it to a Leviathan-type monarch. The "present" given by sovereignty to the people, in Maritain's analysis, is their own voluntary and complete subjugation. Maritain's concern with the idea of sovereignty and what it implies, then, is nothing less than an intellectual exercise in political philosophy designed to show where seemingly noble and lofty ideas could lead when not properly analyzed and clarified.

The alternative to sovereignty, then, is a proper understanding of the body politic and the state. The body politic governs itself with full authority regarding external affairs (but see chapter 11), that is, other bodies politic. It also governs itself with regard to its inner authority; that is, it rules itself through the constitutional structures set up by a people and limited by them to what it is. The state, as the topmost agency of the body politic, ought not to be overshadowed by other voluntary bodies when it comes to the essential elements of justice, law, and order. But the state is still an instrument of the body politic, not its replacement.[27] Maritain's analysis of sovereignty is designed to understand the sources of modern absolutism, even in a democracy. His analysis of community and society, body politic, state, and people is a high-level intellectual analysis, fundamental to the task of understanding political things. Maritain seeks to explain the right order so that by comparison disorder can be seen.

The "thankless task" of looking at political things, of defining them and the realities they stand for, remains a fundamental exercise of any political philosophy. Maritain's excursus on political definitions possesses the clear advantage of systematically working its way through the political words and their existential meanings. In one sense, this endeavor is a polemic against twentieth-century tyranny and its origins and, by extension, of any form of tyranny, however it arises out of the same moral and intellectual roots. In another sense, it is an introductory logic that patiently works its way through the often complex, though intelligible, realities that constitute an organized people and their relationships. Maritain wants to protect in their personhood the actual people themselves whose destiny and vitality transcend the state but not to deny the state a proper and central role in human thriving. Maritain understands that the mind, when used correctly, is the central protector of organized human beings, of the multitude of persons who compose the people thus organized in a body politic with a topmost agency we know as the state.

NOTES

1. Jacques Maritain, *Man and the State* (Chicago: University of Chicago Press, 1956), 1.
2. Jacques Maritain, *An Introduction to Philosophy*, trans. E. I. Watkin (London: Sheed & Ward, 1946), 107.
3. Jacques Maritain, *Grand Logique*, *OCM*, vol. 2, 686–87.
4. Jacques Maritain, "To Exist with People," *The Range of Reason* (New York: Charles Scribner's Sons, 1952), 122.
5. Ibid., 122.
6. Ibid., 123–24.
7. See Jacques Maritain, *The Person and the Common Good*, trans. John J. Fitzgerald (New York: Charles Scribner's Sons, 1947), "The Human Person and Society," *Scholasticism and Politics*, trans. edited by Mortimer J. Adler (Garden City, N. Y.: Doubleday, Image, 1960), 61–90; "The Common Good," *The Rights of Man and Natural Law*, trans. Doris C. Anson (San Francisco: Ignatius Press, 1986), 93–96.
8. Maritain, *Man and the State*, 1.
9. Ibid.
10. Ibid., 2.
11. Ibid., 3.
12. Ibid., 4.
13. Ibid.
14. Ibid., 4–5.
15. Ibid., 5.
16. Ibid., 7.
17. Ibid., 12.
18. Ibid., 9.

19. Ibid., 10.
20. Ibid., 20.
21. Ibid., 21.
22. Ibid., 23–24.
23. Ibid., 29.
24. Ibid., 34–35.
25. Ibid., 38.
26. Ibid., 45.
27. Ibid., 50–51.

5

THE NATURAL LAW–NATURAL RIGHT DILEMMA

If it is true that the rights of men have their foundation in the natural law, which is, at the same time, the source of both duties and rights—these two notions, moreover, being correlative—it appears that a declaration of rights ought normally be completed by a declaration of the duties and the responsibilities of men towards the communities of which they are part, notably toward the family society, the civil society, and the international community.

—Jacques Maritain, "*Sur la Philosophie des Droits de L'Homme*"[1]

Any kind of thing existing in nature, a plant, a dog, a horse, has its own natural law, that is, the *normalcy of its functioning*, the proper way in which, by reason of its specific structure and specific ends, it 'should' achieve fullness of being either in its growth or in its behavior.

—Jacques Maritain, *Man and the State*[2]

I.

Maritain's most brief and easily understood description of natural law is "the normalcy of functioning." With some diversion, to assist a class to see and to recall the meaning of Maritain's initial definition, I usually give some version of the following example, one that pedagogically seems—to me, at least—to be unavoidably memorable even to the most intellectually modest of students. I intend the example for a case when someone will ask a student for a preliminary definition of natural law that he can intelligibly explain. In classic Aristotelian tradition, recall, we understand a principle best when we see it in a pertinent example, even while realizing that the example is not itself the principle but its manifestation.

My example, which follows, can have dozens of formulations: "Suppose you are walking down the street one morning, and you notice a man coming toward you. As he gets closer, you observe something quite odd. The man seems to be accompanied by a duck, who is waddling along on a leash beside the man." At this point, one can be sure that the students are listening, albeit quizzically. "As you walk by the man, you greet him with your own cheery 'good morning.' What happens, however, is that, not the man, but the duck answers your greeting with its own clearly articulated, 'good day, sir.' "

The average class immediately laughs at this silly account. They look at the professor as if he were either a great wit or, more likely, slightly deranged. Next, I ask the class if there is anything wrong with the scene? Usually, some good student, to help out, will explain that ducks do not talk—an answer that already contains the principle that is at issue. If I persist a bit, someone will speculate about a ventriloquist, in which case, however, the duck does not in fact talk, so no real problem exists except the skill of the ventriloquist. On the other hand, by hypothesis, if the duck really does talk, I suggest, the talking critter is not a duck at all but some unusual form of rational animal. This example turns out to be a none too subtle way of recalling for the class Aristotle's definition of man as the animal with speech, which is itself a consequence of the essential definition that man is a rational animal.

Most students get the point that a duck talking is not its "normalcy of functioning," again to use Maritain's words that I want the students to remember, possibly with the help of the talking duck. If the duck had merely quacked, however, no one would have been particularly surprised. But when a human mind comes across something outside the normalcy of functioning commonly observed in the being it encounters, it knows that, for one reason or another, something outside that being's intrinsic "natural law" is taking place. This something must be accounted for as an event happening contrary to, or outside the scope of, the nature of the thing encountered, be it a duck or whatever.

The example that Maritain himself uses to make this same point is the piano. "All pianos . . . whatever their particular type and in whatever spot they may be," Maritain observes, "have as their end the production of certain attuned sounds. If they don't produce these sounds, they must be tuned or discarded as worthless."³ The piano has its own "natural law" that determines what it looks like, how it sounds, and the relation of its parts to the whole. The piano itself is the product of a craft, according to which the craftsman, knowing the purpose of the piano, produces an artifact according to the form or idea of its purpose that he has in his mind. He next needs to figure out how this purpose is to be effectively embodied in wood and metal to produce the appropriate sounds we know to come from a piano and not a violin. Usually, few students have any trouble in grasping the point of the duck talking or the piano in need of tuning. We expect the duck to quack and waddle. We expect that when someone, accomplished in playing this instrument, sits down at the piano, all of its parts fit together so that the desired sounds issue forth from it when it is actually well played.

The next step is to inquire, using the same analogy, whether human beings, for all their individual variety, have a "normal" functioning. Thomas Aquinas says that the basic natural law for human beings can be stated quite briefly, namely, "to act reasonably" (I–II, 94, 4). But do we not know a fair number of people, the vast majority perhaps, who do not act reasonably? Are they not human? Yet we notice that everyone who "acts unreasonably" will, when challenged, give some sort of a "reason" why he does what he does. It seems that the fact itself of acting unreasonably is not what strikes us most. Rather, what we note is the *reason* given for such evidently aberrant action. The given reason does not just sit there, as it were, but is itself situated before and directed to a higher standard of reason. It is open to examination. Not just any explanation will do. And this given reason can be tested by nothing but reason itself.

The laws of noncontradiction, causality, and evidence are there, indifferent to time or place, to examine and weigh the reasons given for any action. In a sense, the whole world is present and capable of examining the given reasons once they are adequately formulated by those who perform the action. The reason we give for what we claim to be reasonable does not stand by itself. It stands by the measure of man's nature, by *what he is*. Some actions and the reasons given for them are obviously quite contrary to what it is to be human—Maritain suggests as an example the proposition that "genocide is a fine policy."⁴ Man's "normalcy of functioning" seems to be indicated by his dogged persistence in giving reasons, good or bad, for what he does on the basis of his understanding of *what he is*. *What man is*, of course, is not something initially formed or created by man himself but something he receives from whatever causes reality, including his own reality, to be in the first place. That some original cause or nature stands behind the given being of man is what enables him to say, as he does and must, that some things are simply against *what man is*. In saying this, man speaks as if there were a standard to which he can appeal against reasons given for human actions that are unreasonable as judged by some known criterion. Without this supposition, there really can be no criticism of wrong ways of doing things.

II.

This natural law of "acting reasonably" is what distinguishes the human animal in creation. He possesses a power that other physical beings do not have, but one that other spiritual beings do have. As the classical writers put it, man is the highest of the beings composed of matter and the lowest of the spiritual beings; he is the *microcosmos*, the being who contains in himself all the levels of being. The human being is to rule himself and his actions towards what is not himself according to his highest powers or faculties. Unlike the piano or the duck, man has the capacity to accept or reject the reasonableness of his own given being. This capacity is what gives him his moral autonomy, what makes him responsible for what he does. He has the freedom to accept or reject his own nature, but only on the condition that he can give a reason for his choice; he never escapes this latter condition.

The question must be asked about why this standard of his acting is precisely a "law" when its essential contents are not initially established by human reason and will but are only discovered by them? Aquinas held that the ultimate origin of the natural law of anything, including human beings, is the eternal law of God. The natural law is the eternal law looked at not from the side of God, but from the side of the creature having been shaped by that (eternal) law (I–II, 91, 2). What appears as naturally right begins to take on the character of something commanded when it is realized that human beings, as they are, need not exist and do not cause themselves.

Aquinas meant by this relationship between eternal and natural law that the basic law of human beings is not something they give themselves, but something that is given to them not arbitrarily but for a purpose. By reflection, looking back on ourselves, which is what the power of reason can do, we see that our "normalcy of functioning" includes our reason and its hierarchical, ruling relation to everything else in us. Indeed, human beings are the only beings in physical creation with this capacity, to which all the other capacities in them are likewise ordained in one way or another. The human being is not a kind of disparate pile or conglomeration of differing powers and capacities, but a coherent order of many different parts, all related to each other. The human eye is an eye, but it sees as an instrument of intelligence. The whole is greater than the parts. The whole is known by reason. Through reason, guided by the will as the power to do something in the world and in oneself, the human person, that in which both reason and will are located, acts in the world. In knowing the world, the human being knows himself by knowing something not himself. Ultimately, this power of knowledge means that the human person, by being what it is, can, through knowledge, be all else that it is not. The mind is *capax omnium*, capable of being or knowing all things. Paradoxically, the "normalcy of functioning" of the human being includes the activity of reason by which all that which is not the human being becomes his after the manner of knowing. In simply knowing something is, the human being changes himself, not the world.

Maritain is a careful reader of St. Thomas. The most important consequence of the relation between the eternal law—that is, the order of reality in the mind of God—and the natural law—that is, this same eternal law looked at from the side of the created reality—is that the natural law, according to which each being acts in the way that it does, has an intelligent origin. What is at issue here, as Maritain understands, is the capacity of the rational being, in spite of this intelligent origin, to reject itself, or to propose itself as another kind of being at variance with its natural law as a manifestation of the eternal law. Maritain seeks to prevent, at least in theory, the human will from claiming, as in fact it does claim in modern philosophy, absolute autonomy over what it is and does, over human nature itself.

Maritain's statement of what is involved is as follows. "But that liberty presupposes nature, what does this mean for us? It means that ethics presupposes metaphysics and speculative philosophy, or that the right usage of our liberty presupposes the knowledge of *that which is*, and of the supreme laws of being. Metaphysics is a necessary condition of morals."[5] The statement of this priority of eternal law over natural law and of metaphysics over ethics lies at the foundation of Maritain's discussion of the relation of natural law and natural right, an issue that has become more, not less, controverted since he originally wrote on these matters.[6] The issue is: Is natural right related to or independent of natural law, which itself is seen as an expression of eternal law of the intelligent being?

The importance of the issue can be seen initially in two ways. If the "normalcy of functioning" is a proper statement of the natural law of something, this should mean, logically, that the natural law of mankind in particular is this: Most actual human beings frequently lie, cheat, and steal. Therefore, that is their nature expressed in their functioning. Many human beings in fact commonly do such disorderly things. Must this frequency not imply their actual nature? Why is not the criterion of what is reasonable simply what man does in historical circumstances, something we can record and even quantify? No doubt this problem is a variant in ethics of the Machiavellian thesis in politics.

However, when man is defined as the "reasonable" being, the criterion of this reasonableness is not solely what he does do, but what he ought to do. That is, metaphysically, he is a certain kind of being whose law is discovered through the self-reflective use of his reason. Neither his being nor his reason as a faculty is a reality that man gives himself in the first place. His being as such is not something that he creates from nothing by himself. What he manifests in commonly recurring actions, opposed to the order of what he ought to do, is not his nature or his natural law, but the purposeful misuse of his nature and his natural law by himself.

The second side of the issue of natural law comes into view as an aspect of modern "rights" theory, that legacy from Hobbes and Locke that has so much dominated modern and contemporary political philosophy. Maritain seeks to find a way to bridge the natural law–natural rights relationship so that he can explain, defend, and legitimize the usefulness of both natural law and natural right in a consistent understanding. He is quite aware that the classic Christian discussion about how human beings ought to act is formulated in terms of natural law and of divine positive law, as each relates to eternal law. That is, natural law has an origin, a source, outside of itself. Divine positive law (revelation) is not contrary to natural law, but neither is it the same thing. Revelation seems to be addressed both to certain difficulties in observing natural law and to clarifying the ultimate purposes for which the actual human race exists (I–II. 91, 4).

The emphasis in natural law theory is not, as in modern rights' theory, on what is "due" to us from others, but on what we owe to someone else, including God. Thus, say, murder is against the Fifth Commandment (divine positive law) or against the ethical or natural-law proposition that it is unjust to take the life of another innocent human being. Right conduct is stated in terms of what one ought or ought not to do in various situations and relationships. Clearly, if everyone has a duty not to murder me, and everyone obeys the law expressing this duty, I will not in fact be murdered. I will not be safe because I have a "right" to life but because every one else has and observes a duty to recognize what I am. It could thus be said that there is an objective rightness (*jus*, in St. Thomas's term) that exists in my relationship to everyone else. I am not a bundle of rights but a certain kind of being because of which others have duties and obligations in their differing relationships with me. The natural law and those objective "rights" (*jura*) that protect the individual person from the injustices of others constitute the basis of a person's own freedom and independence insofar as that is recognized by others in their actions.

Another, more common, understanding of "rights," however, exists in modern thought. This new rights' theory has caused and still causes considerable difficulty in human affairs and somehow justifies what is against the natural law. In this view, rights are not objective but subjective. They are rooted not in nature but in will. Will has no limit but itself. Natural right is what the will "wills." This is its content. Its only restriction is not reason self-reflecting on its given human nature. Rather, it is another will as unlimited as itself. Thus, if whatever is willed is right because it is willed, and only because it is willed, then there arises a certain parallel between law and right. In a sense, there can be no conflict between right and law, for whatever is willed is right because it is willed. The strongest will, the public will, takes precedence. The natural-law tradition envisions and provides for a possible conflict between what is willed and what is right. What is right, what is just, takes priority over what is willed. This is what Maritain implies when he says that metaphysics has priority over ethics. This is the origin of Augustine's position, repeated by Aquinas, that an unjust law is no law.

III.

What Maritain proposes to do in his discussions of natural law and natural or human rights is to suggest a way to coordinate modern rights' talk, seen to be in fact the most popular and well-known way of describing what a human being is, with natural law principles. The human being is a being with definite, defined, indeed, unalienable, rights owed to him or open to him. At the same time, Maritain does not want the word "rights," in terms of content, of what they are, to depend on a purely voluntaristic conception. This effort to save a legitimate place for using rights as a basis of common public discourse must be carefully related to the earlier discussion about the normalcy of human activities. Thus, when this "normalcy" is made to include those actions that are wrong by natural law standards but that are, at the same time, widespread and common in practice, implicitly willed, in other words, the resulting "rights" become the opposite of natural law.

Maritain has to develop a discourse about natural law as a statement of what is right or reasonable, even when men in practice do not do what is right and reasonable, that is, when they proceed to call this deviation a "right." He has to show how man's nature in "acting reasonably" requires him, by the same reason, to reject the many things counter to reason that people often do. The revelational way of dealing with this situation is to say that Christ came to save sinners, to teach repentance, not to establish their sins as a "right."

Maritain expands the list of rights, though in a manner he believes follows from Aquinas's ways of "changing" natural law either by making something more clear or deciding among legitimate alternatives (I–II, 97, 1–4).[7] Thus, he has to show that his own quite extensive list of rights—so extensive that it often confuses rights with legislation—is related to the natural law so that the listed rights indicate the duties of others to those claiming the rights. Much social legislation for Maritain seems to fall into this category. Rights ought not to be merely possible things that it would be nice to have or demand. The increasing number of rights seems finally to minimize prudence on the part of the people and legislators. Making everything a right can imperil freedom and further empower the state as the primary, if not the only, agent to bring such rights about.[8] But Maritain also has to find some way to deny that rights are, whatever they are, merely expressions of will limited by nothing but itself.

In a real sense, Maritain has lost the battle today since rights are increasingly and almost exclusively considered to be expressions of private or political will. We find that many of the things that are now described as "natural" or "human" rights are in fact against the natural law or the proper duties of man toward his neighbor. Abortion is the most obvious example of this. Natural law and natural rights come to be not two aspects of the same reality, but conflicting understandings of *what man is*. Maritain's definition of natural law as the normalcy of something's functioning remains in place as his briefest and most easily remembered statement, one which, when spelled out, explains what it means to be reasonable even when most people act, in many instances, against reason. Human rights in most contexts today do not mean what in justice is owed to others, but what a human being is permitted to do by his own will or by the law, whatever the law is. Clearly, this latter understanding is not Maritain's view.

Nonetheless, Maritain's effort to save rights from the voluntarist premises that they acquired in modern political thought is successful, in the sense that what he argues is coherent and consistent. In making duties the essential element of any rights discourse, Maritain prevents rights from standing openly by themselves as statements of subjective will. Very few people, however, understand that natural right means and must mean the objective duty that we have to what is right (*jus*), to what is due to another. Rights are not usually seen to be themselves discovered by reason looking at human nature as the expression of eternal law within each being. Natural right is not simply a reflection of what the human will wants, no matter what it wants. It is a reflection of the eternal law as it exists within each actual person deciding how it shall be with regard to itself, given what it is given to be.

IV.

Though he sees the possibility, Maritain does not anticipate that those with whom he is to discourse on natural rights would come to deny, in their effort not to admit any binding reason to natural law, the very validity of reason itself. This denial, expressed in terms of modern natural rights, is, however, the only real alternative someone has who denies natural law itself. The reason natural law assumes such importance for Maritain is because he takes it to be an objective and neutral way of talking about and understanding human activity on a philosophic basis that directly implies no revelational content. Aristotle, in the Middle Ages, had already served as the philosophic ground for Arab-Christian-Jewish philosophic discussion. St. Paul himself had told the Romans that they had reason that could have told them that certain activities, some of which have recently reappeared as "rights," were not reasonable, were not permitted (Romans, 1:20–32). Natural law is a historic, ongoing philosophic discussion that is not conceived to be primarily an exchange about the facts of revelation, though revelation from its own sources does deal with many of the same issues that natural law did. In fact, revelation is seen by Maritain to be something that confirms and develops what the natural law itself had already discovered.

Thus, in a world filled with a multiplicity of cultures and philosophies, Maritain thinks that natural law can provide a common ground of discourse apart from whatever similarities to it might lie in revelation. Maritain's moral or Democratic Charter, his list of basic standards or principles that a people has to agree on if any society is to cohere, is shrewd enough and realistic enough to acknowledge that even this common discourse of natural law would not serve everyone. Maritain's pragmatic theory of common agreement on certain actions (however the explanation of them is theoretically justified) recognizes that a common methodology of argument or intellectual background is not in fact accepted by everyone. This diversity at the theoretical level is a fact of the public order. Natural law, however, is the best and most historic context of any common effort at discourse. Maritain never hesitates to affirm that it is necessary to attempt such discourse. He knows that the real differences are found in the theoretic order. He realizes that practical agreement is precarious without theoretical agreement—little solid ethics without metaphysics. But he also understands that this theoretical discourse has to take place in an area of intellectual freedom itself and be oriented to finding and living the truth without coercion or political pressure (chapter 3).

Maritain is, in fact, amusingly impatient with those common critics who would simply deny out of hand the reality of a human nature expressive of the "normalcy of functioning" of a thing—its natural law—while, at the same time, in practice, to recall the case of the piano or the duck, they affirm it all the time.

> Since I have not space here to discuss nonsense (you can always find very intelligent philosophers to defend it most brilliantly), I am taking it for granted that you admit that there is a human nature and that this human nature is the same in all men. I am taking it for granted that you also admit that man is a being gifted with intelligence, and who, as such, acts with an understanding of what he is doing, and therefore with the power to determine for himself the ends which he pursues.[9]

The piano does not ask itself whether it is a piano and put into effect that internal order that makes it be a piano or a good piano. Man, on the other hand, is in the position of refusing to accept *what he is* and of refusing to be good in *what he is*. Yet when he does either of these things, denies *what he is* or acts contrary to *what he is*, he always does so by proposing reasons to justify what he does. He thereby opens himself to an examination about whether his alternate proposals are reasonable, just as a self-reflective piano that chooses constantly to play off–key, would have to explain why its offkeyedness is more reasonable than when compared to a piano that chooses for itself to play on key.

Maritain puts this comparison in his own words:

> But since man is endowed with intelligence and determines his own ends, it is up to him to put himself in tune with the ends necessarily demanded by his nature. This means that there is, by very virtue of human nature, *an order or a disposition which human reason can discover and according to which the human will must act in order to attune itself to the necessary ends of the human being. The unwritten law, or natural law, is nothing more than that.*[10]

It should be noted that when Maritain remarks that man has intelligence and by this intelligence determines his own ends, he is not saying that any end, because chosen, is therefore reasonable, even if we can give reasons for it. He does imply that even in willing wrong ends, we give a reason for our acts, the very fact of which indicates that we are using our reason. We implicitly open ourselves up to and abide by its standards, but we are free to reject a standard and give controvertible reasons for it.

V.

Maritain's most important contribution to the natural-law tradition is his distinction between the natural law as it is in itself and as it is known by us. The former, he maintains, remains always the same, the latter changes with our increasing knowledge of what is implied by it. What this distinction means is that we are not to be surprised by the long history of natural-law discussion, its periods of growth and decline. The human being's own understanding of his own law, insofar as his knowing is a result of self-reflection, experience, and good will, will take the same sort of time and effort as it has taken human beings to know about other forms of knowledge—how to build bridges, for instance.

Maritain holds that many of the problems that have arisen in the history of natural law came from neglect of this distinction between what the natural law is and our knowledge of it. "The law and the knowledge of the law are two different things. The man who does not know the law (so long as this ignorance itself does not spring from some failing) is not responsible before the law. And knowing that there is a law does not necessarily mean knowing what the law is."[11] Maritain develops this distinction in his treatment of natural law in *Man and the State*, wherein he uses the rather complicated Greek-based expressions the "ontological" and the "gnoseological" elements in natural law to indicate the reality of the natural law itself, its status in being, in contrast with our knowledge of it.[12]

Maritain generally speaks of natural law in the context of his discussion of the rights of man. From both the American and French revolutions, this mode of speaking has become a basic language in modern political thought. Maritain finds worrisome, as I have already indicated, that people might agree that there are certain acknowledged rights that everyone assents to, but that they can not agree in the way to defend or explain philosophically why such rights are valid. "Here we are confronted by the paradox that rational justifications are *indispensable* and at the same time *powerless* to create agreement among men."[13] Maritain

never underestimates either the importance of this very philosophic justification or its difficulty.

One might conclude from this seeming impasse to a legitimate intellectual skepticism about this very topic. What is remarkable about
Maritain as a philosopher is that he proposes a way to allow for this
disagreement at the level of common principle without the same disagreement being allowed in practice to destroy the public peace (chapter
3). He insists that rational justification is indispensable, as is fair debate
about the highest things, but neither can be imposed or arrived at by
any method other than a philosophical method. Hence, Maritain wants
all the arguments, right or wrong, to be proposed and to be known in
the intellectual order, to be treated squarely and fairly in freedom. He
never backs away from this position. He never ceases to be, in other
words, a philosopher who realizes that the ultimate struggles affecting
civilization and virtue take place at the theoretical level of understanding
what man is in the light of truth itself.

VI.

When it comes to the "gnoseological" side of natural law, to the
side of its being known, Maritain argues that this knowledge is a slow
and difficult growth to come by, make clear, and articulate in its content.
He does not think that this slowness should be surprising any more than
we should be surprised at the amount of time in human history it took
to develop the computer or the heart transplant. Maritain is aware that
the historical record can itself become a claim on what ought to be done
with no further criticism from philosophy or other sources allowed to
challenge its validity. Behind his concern for distinguishing ontological
and gnoseological natural law is the realization that the natural law, as an
understanding of *what man is*, needs to pass from metaphysics to ethics
and politics. If metaphysics comes before ethics as its guide and norm,
theoretical knowledge still has to be seen also as a guide in concrete
circumstances.

Notice how Maritain puts the issue: "Thus we arrive at the second
basic element to be recognized in natural law, namely natural law *as
known*, and thus as measuring in actual fact human practical reason, which
is the measure of human acts."[14] Practical reason means using our minds

to do or make something. It means using ourselves rightly because we know what we are. The "measure" of our acts means both what it is we do and how what we do relates to what we are. Reasonable beings have to know both what they are in each particular act that flows out of them and choose what they are. They always remain free to choose against themselves, against their own "normalcy of functioning," even if they know it. But they are not free *not* to give reasons why they do so. These given reasons are open to being compared with a measure, a standard, that does not permit them simply to stand untested by themselves.

Does everyone unavoidably start with any practical knowledge or measure? "The only practical knowledge all men have naturally and infallibly in common as a self-evident principle, intellectually perceived by virtue of the concepts involved, is that we must do good and avoid evil. This is the preamble and the principle of natural law; it is not the law itself. Natural law is the ensemble of things to do and not to do which follows from it in a *necessary manner*."[15] The things to do and not to do whereby we are called good or evil are the "measures" of each of our activities. That the recognized and operative principle of doing good and avoiding evil is present in us and recognized by us is seen when we give a reason to explain why what we do is all right. Cain could give a reason why he killed his brother Abel. That he gave a reason proved not that his reason was right, but that he appealed to reason itself. This very fact made his given reason subject to being itself measured in terms of good reason or bad reason.

Maritain thus argues that the natural law itself includes "the ensemble of things to do and not to do that followed" from the first principle of doing good and avoiding evil "in a necessary manner." He means both that the clear understanding of many of these good and bad things would take time to become known and that in fact everyone wrestles with the problem in each of his acts. It is here that Maritain brings in Aquinas's notion of knowledge by "inclination" or "connaturality."[16] He understands by this connatural knowledge that, from experience, we often see that certain measures of good or evil are known in a kind of implicit way, a way that is a real knowledge but not necessarily a clear philosophically stated knowledge. Normal people do not do certain things because they are wrong. They understand, without quite being able to state why in accurate terms, that some proposed act when sized up, is wrong, so they do not do it. Maritain wants to say that the reason they do not do something they might have done is because they reason connaturally, by inclination, to the proper conclusion. Yet when asked, they will not be able to give with precision a completely convincing reason in formal terms, but they know what they did was right (or wrong).

What about the obvious historical and experiential fact that so many people do all sorts of irrational and evil things? Maritain observes that we do not defend the natural law by denying this fact of reality that wrong things are frequently done. But he maintains that this factual wrongdoing is not an argument against what he maintains about natural law. Maritian's response is worth recalling.

> Montaigne maliciously remarked that, among certain peoples incest and thievery were considered virtuous acts. Pascal was scandalized by this. All this proves nothing against natural law, any more than a mistake in addition proves anything against arithmetic, or the mistakes of certain primitive peoples, for whom the stars were holes in the tent which covered the world, prove anything against astronomy.[17]

It took thousands of years of recorded history before someone developed the multiplication tables. From this delay, it does not follow that two times two equaling four was not true before the explicit knowledge of this truth became generally known. Maritain does not see why moral and ethical knowledge does not follow the same path. Before the multiplication table, many people knew what to do with two and two. Before the development of explicit conclusions of the natural law, men knew by inclination that it is wrong to kill the innocent.

The emphasis on human rights growing out of the natural-law background is something Maritain sees as a great advance in understanding, but not a growth in what the law is in itself. Human rights are, within the natural-law tradition, one possible philosophic or literary way to express the content of the necessary conclusions from the principle of doing good and avoiding evil, of what good and evil mean in this or that circumstance. It is healthy and according to human nature that we seek to make more clear, more explicit, things that at first seem vague. It is better, then, to know what murder is and its various degrees of responsibility than merely to know that it is wrong to do evil or harm to someone. Thus, the not doing evil implies a duty towards the lives of others. It could also mean that someone's duty to another can be expressed as the other's "right" to that duty. Someone's duty to act justly is someone else's "right" to that proper action. This does not mean that duties and rights are necessarily always coextensive. We may have duties, the highest ones, in mercy or charity that cannot and ought not to be reduced to rights. Human relationships reduced only to observing "rights" can easily produce a very impersonal and antagonistic society.

VII.

Whether Maritain is correct in this judgment about the proper understanding of rights and duties can be debated on the practical side. Certainly, he does not acknowledge a "right" to abortion, or to homosexual activity, or to any number of other newly fashioned "rights" that are the focus of rights in contemporary society. He would have argued that these "rights" are precisely against the natural law understood as the form of what human nature is in each person. Practicing these newly fashioned "rights" is the equivalent of the eye choosing not to see, not to be what it is. The eye, when open, must see the color before it. The will can choose to direct the mind to something else in order that it does not "see" everything it knows to be pertinent to a consideration. It is in this sense that I argue that what Maritain maintains about natural law remains more important than what he says about rights, because his effort to save rights, defensible as it is in itself, does not sufficiently prepare us for how rights have actually come to be used against his reasoned understanding of natural law.[18]

Maritain's use of the word "value," a word often related to "rights," serves further to illustrate this problem. By redefining the word "value," it can also be made to have a legitimate meaning. Maritain so redefines it. However, the word itself, as it is used in modern social philosophy, is most often a subjective word, one that specifically means that there is no possibility of arguing about or concluding to the truth of ultimate moral and philosophical issues. This inability to agree on meanings of terms and ideas is a factual situation that Maritain admits to be mostly the case in his explanation of the Democratic Charter.[19] We can thus argue about facts but not about values, which, in the tradition of Max Weber, are a matter of opinion or subjective choice. There is no way, it is said, to examine their truth either practically or speculatively.

"For a philosophy which recognizes Fact alone, the notion of Value—I mean Value objectively true in itself—is not conceivable," Maritain writes in *Man and the State*. "How, then, can one claim rights if one does not believe in values? If the affirmation of the intrinsic value and dignity of man is nonsense, the affirmation of the natural rights of man is nonsense also."[20] Maritain argues, rightly, that the only way that the word "value" is properly used is if it is an expression of something "objectively true in itself." But the word "value" almost never refers to that objective, ontological basis, but to a skepticism about its very possibility. It means a choice or feeling that cannot be grounded in any such objective reality. Thus, to say that "rights" are based in "values," or that what we need is a return to "values" to protect our "rights," will mean, in most modern discussions, that neither the one nor the other, neither rights nor values, is objectively grounded.

Thus, reading Maritain on rights and values requires a constant internal correction to recognize that what he means by these terms is something very different from what is generally meant by them in the culture. Whether Maritain's tactic to retain the use of the words, while reformulating their meaning, is the best one seems less viable in the years since his death in 1973. Both rights and values are generally understood in a subjective manner that allows no objective component that would examine the meaning or content of the values or rights proposed by comparing them with natural law, the content of which is not solely formulated by the subjective will. The reading of Maritain on natural law, rights, and values is an exercise on the condition of modern social philosophy.

To the careful reader, Maritain is in fact a good guide to the proper way of thinking through *what man is*. If we stick carefully to his articulated analysis, we can even express this guidance in terms of rights and values. Maritain is quite aware that rights without duties and values without objective grounding result in the sort of public philosophy that we do have in which values and rights have no real foundation other than individual or political will. What is right becomes practically identified with positive law. Democracy also comes to be defined in this light. Hence, by using the language of rights and values in the modern sense, over against the sense in which they exist in Maritain, we can, without changing the language, come to embody actions, institutions, and ways of life quite contradictory to natural law as Maritain explains it.

Until later in his life, Maritain seems to have expected that the philosophical and religious climate would preserve or change in the direction of classical philosophy and Christian revelation. With the publication of *The Peasant of the Garonne* (1966), he does come to suspect that the modern world is not morally and intellectually going in the direction that he had hoped.[21] Maritain is amazingly consistent in his intellectual life. "The principles of his philosophy remain always the same," Waldemar Gurian wrote of him in 1943; "their understanding and application are perfected more and more."[22] In the case of the natural law, Maritain sees it as a common ground between all philosophers, but he also knows that it needs development and perfection from experience and revelation. No doubt, the last thing he might have expected was to have to worry about changes in Christian thinkers and clerics sufficiently radical to embrace principles of modernity that he rejects in his philosophic studies.

Maritain's understanding of natural rights is in fact radically different from the way rights have come to be used even in some Catholic circles. His optimistic treatment of rights is even said to have been a contributory cause to this confusion.[23] Civilization did not follow the lines of revelation that supported classic reason but rather a line that separated itself from both the philosophic and revelational traditions. Maritain does not fail to notice this confusion. In 1967, Maritain responds to an accusation that his early book *Integral Humanism*, in which he first hammers out his ideas in social philosophy, is rejected in his later book, which he published as an old man. Maritain's reaction is most interesting and amusing in this regard:

> There are certain people in Italy who pretend that I have denied *Integral Humanism*! That is a stupidity and a calumny. I maintain more than ever all the positions of *Integral Humanism*. It is about the actual crisis being undergone by intelligence and faith with which I concerned myself in *The Peasant*. (That crisis is much more grave than many of our clerics wish to see). In many letters from unknown correspondents that I have received, I have found this phrase: "We do not know any longer that which is necessary to believe." How can someone give testimony to the Gospel if one does not know any longer whether that which it says is true?"[24]

Maritain knows there is serious confusion, but does not admit his principles as such are its cause.

The question of natural law and natural rights leads us directly, in the following chapter, to the consideration that Maritain examines in much of his political philosophy, namely, democracy with its philosophical and revelational foundations. Maritain wants to show the relation of natural law and natural rights to a proper understanding of democracy. The same problems that are found in natural-rights' thought reappear in different form in the analysis of democracy, in examining what, in fact, is the best regime and how this regime is to be understood.

NOTES

1. Jacques Maritain, "*Sur la Philosophie des Droits de l'Homme,*" *OCM*, vol. 8, 1088. This particular essay is listed as "*Réponse de Jacques Maritain à l'enquête de l'UNESCO,*" and is addressed from Rome in June of 1947, when Maritain was French Ambassador to the Holy See.

2. Jacques Maritain, *Man and the State* (Chicago: University of Chicago Press, 1951), 87.

3. Jacques Maritain, *The Rights of Man and the Natural Law* (San Francisco: Ignatius Press, 1986), 141.

4. Maritain, *Man and the State*, 88.

5. Jacques Maritain, "*Du Régime Temporel et de la Liberté,*" (1933), *OCM*, vol. 5, 334.

6. See John Finnis, *Natural Law and Natural Right* (New York: Oxford, 1980); Robert George, *Natural Law Theories: Contemporary Essays* (New York: Oxford, 1992); Russell Hittinger, *A Critique of New Natural Law Theory* (Notre Dame: University of Notre Dame Press, 1987); Henry Veatch, *Human Right: Fact or Fancy?* (Baton Rouge: Louisiana State University Press, 1985); Mary Ann Glendon, *Rights Talk: The Impoverishment of Political Discourse* (New York: The Free Press, 1991); James V. Schall, "The Natural Law Bibliography," *The American Journal of Jurisprudence* 40 (1995): 157–98; "On Being Dissatisfied with Compromises: Natural Law and Human Rights," *Loyola Law Review* (New Orleans) 38 n. 2, (1992): 299–309.

7. Thus, see, Jacques Maritain, *The Rights of Man and Natural Law*, 152–89.

8. See James V. Schall, "Human Rights as an Ideological Project," *The American Journal of Jurisprudence* 32 (1987): 47–61.

9. Maritain, *The Rights of Man and the Natural Law*, 140. It is not without a smile that when we read this almost identical passage in *Man and the State*, Mari-

tain adds the name of some philosopher who might actually speak this nonsense: "Since I have not time here to discuss nonsense, (we can always find very intelligent philosophers, not to quote Mr. Bertrand Russell, to defend it . . .)," 85.

10. Maritain, *The Rights of Man and the Natural Law*, 141.

11. Ibid., 141.

12. Maritain, *Man and the State*, 84, 89.

13. Ibid., 77.

14. Ibid., 89.

15. Ibid., 90.

16. Ibid., 91.

17. Ibid., 90.

18. David Walsh argues that Maritain is important in the effort to keep liberalism from simply embracing a complete relativism. The Christian insight into the transcendent origin of human dignity is reflected in liberalism's own effort to protect the dignity of human freedom. See *The Growth of the Liberal Soul* (Columbia: University of Missouri Press, 1997), 272–74.

19. Maritain, *Man and the State*, 108–46.

20. Ibid., 97.

21. Jacques Maritain, *The Peasant of the Garonne: An Old Layman Questions Himself about the Present Time*, trans. Michael Cuddihy and Elizabeth Hughes (New York: Holt, Rinehart, and Winston, 1968).

22. Waldemar Gurian, "On Maritain's Political Philosophy," *The Maritain Volume of the Thomist* (New York: Sheed & Ward, 1943), 20.

23. See Hamish Fraser, *Jacques Maritain and Saul David Alinsky: Fathers of the "Christian" Revolution* (Saltcoats, Scotland: Supplement to *Approaches* 71, n. d.).

24. Jacques Maritain, "*Le 'Paysan de la Garonne,' nous ecrit*," *OCM*, vol. 12, 1263.

6

DEMOCRACY: ANTHROPOCENTRIC
AND CHRISTIAN?

Let us now transpose *into the natural order* that phantom of evangelical egalitarianism: in place of an affirmation of the equal dependency of all people before the same Master, before a transcendent God, who is sovereignly free, we would have instead a vindication of equal independence for all formulated in the name of a god immanent in Nature. (This new god) displays sublime contempt for the rational and natural ordinations and hierarchies. They are all leveled equally before an idol of Justice, which is the soul of democratic egalitarianism.

—Jacques Maritain, *"Une Philosophie de l'Histoire Moderne"*[1]

It is high time for Christians to bring themselves back to to truth, reintegrating in the fullness of their original source those hopes for justice and those nostalgias for communion on which the world's sorrow feeds and which are themselves misdirected, thus awakening a cultural and temporal force of Christian inspiration able to act on history and to be a support of man.

—Jacques Maritain, *Integral Humanism*[2]

I.

The intention of this chapter is straightforward. Maritain understands that two theories of democracy are prevalent in the West. Each is grounded in a different theory about man. He recalls that one theory comes out of the classical and revelational tradition. It is based on natural law and natural rights; it is inspired by Gospel teachings about love of neighbor and the dignity of the person. He had hoped that this

99

view of man would come to prevail when the world saw, after World War II, the erroneous and dangerous intellectual premises of Nazi Germany and Marxism. In his examinations of the topic, Maritain considers his initial task to be twofold: (1) to teach primarily Christians about the relative autonomy of the political and economic orders and (2) to teach all men, whatever their religion or philosophy, the meaning of a limited state composed of human beings with a meaning and purpose beyond politics.

But Maritain also knows of a second concept of man that understands him to be a being who is "self-sufficient," centered on himself, a being not bound by any thing but that which he wills for himself, a being who has no normative relation to nature or nature's God. In the beginning, Maritain did not think that this latter view, with origins in Hobbes, Rousseau, and Nietzsche, could come to predominate over the classic understanding, but in his later years he begins to suspect that it might well do so. In any case, he devotes much of his intellectual life to understanding this "anthropocentric" philosophy as it develops in intellectual history. Maritain's own theory about democracy, as it develops, is one that seeks to give more independence to political life but, at the same time, more force to spiritual life. This spiritual life should influence the public order indirectly. It should foster an understanding of man that properly balances his contemplative and political life in the light of a full understanding of the various orders of reality in which he lives.

Maritain knows the world is likely to be messy, but he also maintains that the political world is worthy and of a high order of good. He wants to see just what this world should look like at its best. He thinks he is being practical and realistic in his proposals and does not intend to underestimate their difficulties. "Some seem to think that to put our hands to the real," he vividly writes in *Integral Humanism*, "to this concrete universe of human things and human relations where sin exists and circulates, is in itself to contract sin, as if sin were contracted from without, not from within. They claim therefore to forbid consciences to use all the means not evil in themselves to which men have given an impure context."[3] Initially, as we have seen, this blunt warning about failing to do what is possible because of fear of moral contamination seems Machiavellian. We cannot forget, however, that Maritain is aware that what man is up against, even in his very own project, must never be underestimated, never be met only with human means. Many people simply have not understood, he observes, "that the evils from which human beings suffer today are incurable if divine things are not brought into the depths of the human itself, of the secular, of the profane."[4] Describing how this bringing in is accomplished is one of his main purposes. But if divine things are not also attended to, as a result of an excluding political or philosophical principle, Maritain would expect to appear in the actual public order, not the rule of reason, but the rule of unreason, the rule based on a denial of *what man is.*

Maritain lived in an age when it was easier than in ours—and this is not a compliment to our age's concept of its own tolerance—to speak accurately of Christianity as a fundamental element in the definition, formation, and success of democracy. Democracy, however, that most complex of simple ideas, more and more is considered by many thinkers to have exclusively secular, even anti-Christian and skeptical foundations. Maritain realizes that a humanly self-enclosed concept of democracy, one that admits no opening to anything but itself, might come about as the operative political formation in history. But the degree and extent to which it did rapidly come about would probably have surprised him. Maritain himself frequently cites, with approval, a remark of his teacher, Henri Bergson, that democracy lives on implicit Christian inspiration. This recurrent theme recalls that, in Maritain's view, a relationship exists between democracy and Christianity, to the mutual benefit—indeed, to the mutual need of both in modern times. Yet and this was what is central to his thought and makes him unique in political philosophy, democracy is, for Maritain, something of reason, something of sound human inclination, not excluding the human inclination to the divine.

Let me, in the beginning, cite just one of Maritain's Bergsonian passages, from *Christianity and Democracy*:

> As Bergson has shown, . . . it is the urge of a love infinitely stronger than the philanthropy commended by the philosophers which caused human devotion to surmount the closed borders of the natural social groups—family group and national group—and extend it to the entire human race, because this love is the life in us of the very love which has created being and because it truly makes of each human being our neighbor. . . . That is the deepest principle of the democratic ideal,

which is the secular name for the ideal of Christendom. This is why Bergson writes, "democracy is evangelical in essence and . . . its motive power is love."[5]

What is affirmed here is not that democracy, as known by the philosophers, cannot in principle understand that it ought to include all men within its scope and interest, but that, without the inspiration of the Christian teaching about the love of neighbor as oneself and the love of God for each created person, thereby giving to each a unique dignity, this philosophic understanding did not in fact occur and, once discovered, would not continue in a manner that respects the essentials of human dignity. The implication is not necessarily that democracy, without a Christianity true to itself, is not possible. Rather, the implication is that it is not likely. This latter position is what, in Maritain's view, classical and modern political experience, as well as Christian theology, teaches us. In other words, something more than a political theory is needed even to have a political theory that justifies democracy.

II.

This is how Maritain describes, in words that need little changing even today, the two kinds of understanding of humanism, of what man is about, ways of understanding that lead to very different kinds of democracies. "The first kind of humanism recognizes that God is the center of man," Maritain writes in *True Humanism*,

> it implies the Christian conception of man, sinner and redeemed, and the Christian conception of grace and freedom. . . . The second kind of humanism believes that man himself is the center of man, and therefore of all things. It implies a naturalistic conception of man and of freedom. If this conception is false, one understands that anthropocentric humanism merits the name of inhuman humanism and that its dialectic must be regarded as the *tragedy of humanism*.[6]

Democracy based on one or the other conception of man will clearly produce different forms of regime. Yet democracy also means that within differing understandings of regime and man, citizens still can live by right in the same body politic.

Maritain recognizes, then, that democracy would have to be pluralist, in the sense of recognizing the differing concepts of what human life is about. As we saw in a previous chapter, he does not think that religious or philosophic differences, even of the deepest sort presented here, necessarily forbid living in the same body politic, provided it is clear what principles are at stake for all involved. Maritain distinguishes between "dogmatic intolerance, which holds the liberty to err to be a good in itself, and civil tolerance, which imposes on the State respect for consciences."[7] Understanding the difference between these two conceptions of tolerance is fundamental to understanding any regime in the light of Maritain's argument about the temporal order. Respect for the conscience as such does not imply that no truth exists, nor that it is not worthwhile to seek it by its own proper means. Dogmatic intolerance from whatever source—religious, political, or philosophical—would either deny in principle that truth exists, or affirm that only the truth officially recognized by the polity could be expressed either in public or private.

Maritain is quite aware of the rationalist dialectic that leads to a democracy based on skepticism, but at the same time, he wants to keep a place for refocusing attention on reason. He too wants to be "man-centered," as it were. At the same time, he rejects the view that man, because there is nothing else or because nothing else could be known, is the cause of all things, including himself. There are things about modernity that Maritain wants to incorporate within his system, chief among these are probably the notion of "rights," the institutions of popular rule, and the means for adequate economic goods, but in a way that does not lead to an "inhuman humanism." For all his realism and awareness of the dimensions of evil, Maritain is surprisingly optimistic about the chances of his new temporal project.

Indeed, an abiding criticism of Maritain is precisely his overestimation of the possibilities inherent in the natural order with its own forces and in a given time. It might even be wondered whether some of the movements he criticizes in *The Peasant of the Garonne* did not find their initial inspiration in Maritain's own attention to the secular order. But Maritain himself has a clear idea of the dangers of minimizing the secular order, to which he attempts to respond. The secular order, as he sees it, itself bears marks of evangelical inspiration not because the state is structured according to something found in the Gospel, but because those who live in and act in the state are in their own souls formed and guided by principles of reason that are themselves inspired by the Gospel, which is now unconsciously understood to be part of or essential to human nature with no further distinctions.

III

I titled this chapter, "Democracy: Anthropocentric and Christian?" At first, since Maritain considers "anthropocentric humanism" to be a false humanism, an "inhuman humanism," and hence the democracy based on it to be dangerous both to man and to Christianity, it seems as if the title should be "Anthropocentric *or* Christian?" The question mark in either title is important because it directs us to the heart of Maritain's whole democratic project, to what he is seeking to establish in his political philosophy. When Maritain proposes a relationship between Christianity and democracy, he does not intend to refashion a medieval Christendom in some modern garb. Maritain appreciates the medieval experience and learns from it; he agrees with many of its essentials. "The Middle Ages were just the opposite of a reflex age: a sort of fear or metaphysical modesty, and also a predominant concern to see things and to contemplate being, and to take the measure of the world, kept the gaze of medieval man turned away from himself. This characteristic we shall find everywhere."[8] It is the later turn of man "toward himself" that caused Maritain's concern with modern humanism and democracy. Democracy is about man, but not man turned in on himself, man thinking that there is only himself. This dichotomy between different views about democracy leads to Maritain's effort to distinguish between these two understandings of democracy.

Maritain also recognizes that in the realm of culture and politics, many varieties of forms and experiments are possible.[9] It is also possible to live a holy life in a disordered regime, in a disordered democracy. "One can be a Christian and achieve one's salvation while militating in favor of any political regime whatever, always on the condition that it does not trespass the natural law and the law of God," he reminds us in *Christianity and Democracy*.[10] But what Maritain concerns himself with is the place of the temporal order itself and its political structures, in the light of this realization that man is someone, who, in his personhood reaches beyond the political order itself. "The essential characteristics of the democratic philosophy of man and society, . . ." he writes in *Christianity and Democracy*, are the inalienable rights of the person, equality, political rights of the people whose consent is implied by any political regime and whose rulers rule as vicars of the people, absolute primacy of the relations of justice and law as the base of society, and an ideal not of war, prestige, and power, but of the amelioration and emancipation of human life—the ideal of fraternity.[11]

Maritain explains that working out the structures of a just society and participating in its operation are good and legitimate endeavors. It is worthwhile doing these political and social things, their very doing makes it more possible for the other important things in man also to take place. Politics is a nobility, but a limited nobility simply because the same men who are political are also more than political, even in being political.

Maritain is sometimes credited with taking a "new" position on the classic Aristotelian and Catholic teaching that several differing forms of regime—monarchy, aristocracy, polity—were legitimate. His position is said to deny the validity of any political form but the democratic (polity) one. However, on closer examination, as we have already seen in practice, he uses the word "democracy" as the equivalent of any good regime, no matter how it is configured in terms of office and administration. The British or Belgian monarchies can, in his sense, still be good regimes and can be called "democracies" in this technical sense of the word. For him, democracy is not one regime among the other regimes. It is not a bad regime, as it was in classical thought, wherein it was the best of the worst regimes. The three bad regimes—tyranny, oligarchy, and democracy—were bad because they were ordered to a particular good, the good of the ruling principle, and not to the common good.

"The word democracy, as used by modern peoples," Maritain writes in *Christianity and Democracy,*

has a wider meaning than in the classical treatment on the science of government. It designates first and foremost a general philosophy of human and political life and a state of mind. This philosophy and this state of mind do not exclude a priori any of the "regimes" or "forms of government" which were recognized as legitimate by classical tradition, that is, recognized as compatible with human dignity. Thus a monarchic regime can be democratic if it is consistent with this state of mind and the principles of this philosophy. However, from the moment that historical circumstances lend themselves, the dynamism of democratic thought leads, as though to its most natural form of realization, to the system of government of the same name, which consists, in the words of Abraham Lincoln, in "government of the people, by the people, for the people.[12]

How radically new Maritain is in this position about the natural form of democracy can be disputed; Aquinas had already taken much the same position. Maritain would certainly have agreed that, as Aristotle defined it, democracy was a bad form of rule when it means that the people only looked to their own will as its end. This latter understanding of the democratic form is, in fact, similar to the anthropocentric democracy that Maritain rejects. Essentially, he is asking: What would the essential elements be in any good state? He recognizes that a wide variety of good states would not only be possible but advisable. He understands the difference between the French and American forms of democracy; he neither identifies one with the other nor denies the name of democracy to either. He realizes that any form in practice can become distorted or corrupted.

Even though in *Man and the State* Maritain considers the question of world political order (chapter 11), he is careful to conceive it in terms of subsidiarity, of leaving authority at the lowest level possible, and in terms of a wide variety of differing nation-states. He assumes at the time he wrote that China and India would eventually come to belong to the community of nation-states in a form recognizable as democratic. The variety of states is itself a good. Maritain obviously shows a caution about the feasibility and the speed with which his proposal might come about. "I must confess that in my capacity as an Aristotelian I am not much of an idealist," he writes in his discussion of world government.

> If the idea of a world political society were only a beautiful idea, I would not care much for it. I hold it to be a great idea, but also a sound and right idea. Yet the greater the idea is with respect to the weakness and entanglements of the human condition, the more cautious one must be in handling it. And the more attentive one must be in *not* demanding its immediate realization.[13]

Having mentioned his own caution, Maritain then adds, quite amusingly, the following sentence in parentheses in the printed text, as a kind of insight into the character of his American audience. This is "a warning which, if I might be allowed to say, sounds especially distasteful to a generous country where good ideas are looked upon as something to be immediately applied and seem worthy of interest only to that extent."[14] Maritain's view of the possibility of the success of his own proposals is itself subject to his vigilant estimate of human nature, even redeemed human nature. The danger of a world tyranny cannot be ruled out of any discussion of a world order.

His Machiavellian discussion (chapter 1), that had initially appeared in *Integral Humanism*, prepares Maritain to acknowledge that sometimes, perhaps often, in actual circumstances, the only thing Christians could do would be to cling privately to the faith against an all-powerful state.[15] However, even here, Maritain insists that the extreme result of political hostility, that is, martyrdom, which numerically has almost occurred more in the twentieth century than in all the other centuries combined, would be authentic and praiseworthy only with some basic attention to acting forcefully in the political order. "Who knows if, from a long habit of being victims," Maritain writes in *Integral Humanism*,

> Christians do not count unconsciously on this as a solution? Martyr-dom is a solution, but a hyperbolic solution (and, for all those who prepare by their omissions and their torpor the martyrdom of *others*, a lazy solution). A St. Thomas More would, moreover, have held it presumptuous to brave the glory of being decapitated for God before having exhausted the solutions proportionate to nature. It will be nec-essary indeed that one day these should be found.[16]

This passage, I believe, contains, indirectly at least, the full force of Mari-tain's proposals for the validity of human activity in the world.

Notice how in this passage, Sir Thomas More (1478–1534) is praised. More is not praised specifically for his martyrdom, for giving us such a courageous example of how to die for the faith. Martyrdom is always a crucial instance of the failure of the state and spirit to meet, of a conflict about the highest human principles. Maritain maintains, in principle, that "solutions proportionate to nature" can be found. He is optimistic that they can be found "one day." To find these "solutions proportionate to nature" is what Maritain is about in his reflections in political philosophy. He holds that there is no reason why Sir Thomas More's arguments before more reasonable men cannot work. In effect, he praises More for his willingness and ability to persuade, to use, not to disdain, the human things, in this case, the things of the law.

IV.

Let us now look more carefully at Maritain's political and temporal order. To do this, it is important to remember that Maritain argues from a middle point against two opposing sides. First, he argues against a Christian tradition that insists on a public, political recognition of Christianity as natural and necessary both for the church and for the civil society. On the other side, he is arguing against those currents in modern thought, against anthropocentric—man-centered—theories, that would exclude any legitimate presence of religious inspiration and organization in the body politic. Maritain's position appears initially to be a downgrading of the spiritual loftiness of the temporal order. But he considers his purpose rather to present, perhaps for the first time in political philosophy, an account of the temporal order that is adequate to its own natural purpose. Maritain thinks that his position results in what is best both for church and for polity, as well as for the spiritual and temporal good of all citizens, whatever their religion or philosophic position.

A distinction exists in Maritain's analysis. One aspect is how a culture or polity actually proceeds and forms itself for action in the world; the other aspect includes the ideas or spiritual forces that inspire these same actions or institutions. He begins his approach to the proper aligning of the temporal order by examining why there is, in modern atheism, a particular "resentment" of Christianity and indeed of Platonism, ostensibly because they neglect this world. Maritain is careful to distinguish Church, Christianity, and the Christian world, though these distinctions are not always recognized in public debate.[17] Both Platonism and Christianity represent ideals to which practitioners of these lofty ideals seem unfaithful.[18] This resentment against the failures of those who claim to believe or follow a religion or philosophy ignores the fact that nothing in this world can be perfect. It also rejects any notion of grace, that is, that human ability to accomplish the true human good may not be totally a matter of human genius or effort. Maritain simply wants to indicate the fact of this evidently spiritual origin of modern atheism, something he examines carefully in different ways throughout his career.[19]

Maritain's response to this situation constitutes his new political thinking about the relative autonomy of the temporal order. To arrive at this position, he needs to discuss the various kinds of causality and the fact that something can be an end in one order and a means in another. Maritain wants to establish that there is a human purpose in the world that requires human action. But he does not want to call this activity the most important thing that human beings have to do in their lives. Neither does he want so to emphasize the most important things that the temporal endeavors are, as a result, reduced to relative insignificance. Ultimately, he takes the position that evangelical inspiration has provided a solution to this problem to which our attention is called by atheist or communist resentment.

Maritain does not think that the medieval solution is capable of being revived, nor does he think that it should be, except insofar as it has principles that can be applied in a different manner. Rather, he wants to propose a new way to relate the temporal and the eternal, by doing justice to both. Moreover, he realizes that his solution, if it ever comes about, would itself be temporal and subject to change to some other political or cultural configuration seeking to incarnate the same higher principles into worldly reality in a different fashion. Maritain's first task is to establish that what he is engaged in proposing is itself a Christian task, even though the political common good and its organization of regime to achieve it are not specifically Christian, except in the sense that its full realization may have been the result of revelation and not philosophy alone.

"There was for the Christian world a temporal task . . . because a civilization, as civilization, is directly ordered to an end specifically *temporal*," Maritain writes,

> a Christian *earthly* task. . . . The temporal task of the Christian world is to work on earth for a socio-temporal realization of the Gospel truths. For if the Gospel is concerned first of all with the things of eternal life and infinitely transcends any and all sociology and philosophy, nevertheless it gives us sovereign rules for the conduct of our lives, and traces for us a very precise ethical code to which any Christian civilization, so far as it is worthy of the name, should try to con-

form socio-temporal reality, with respect to varying historical conditions.[20]

Thus, the accusation is that the dire condition of the world causes the resentment that inspires the movements of modern ideology to try to substitute some better vision of life. To respond to this accusation, Maritain initially seeks to establish as clearly as possible that there is also an earthly task contained within Christian thought itself. Moreover, within the Gospel, there are guidelines for the proper conduct of life. Hence, political or cultural laws and customs ought to reflect this deeper inspiration arising from the inner thoughts of a good people.

One might ask, as it seems necessary to ask of more recent democratic theories and practices, whether ethical codes that are specifically against this "precise ethical code" make it necessary either to withdraw from political life or to seek to exclude these actions. Maritain's whole theory of natural law is designed to provide a way to deal with such questions, but these too presuppose a condition of common reason. This civil enforcement or promotion of practices against the natural law, of course, brings us back to the problem of anthropocentric and Christian conceptions of man and democracy, about whether Maritain's democratic project has any chance of succeeding. With startling frankness, Maritain rejects any notion of establishing some sort of religious or philosophic minimum that would provide a kind of least common denominator for agreement.

"Throughout the whole of the modern period, we have witnessed a very significant attempt of philosophy to fulfill the same cultural function as faith did in the Middle Ages," he writes;

> the philosophers haunted by the memory of medieval unity, whether it be Descartes, Leibniz, Hegel, or Auguste Comte, have called on reason to furnish temporal civilization with the supratemporal principle of perfect unity which it no longer found in faith. Their failure has been resounding. The lesson of this experience seems to me to be clear: nothing is more vain than to seek to unite men by a philosophic minimum.[21]

Maritain thinks that the alternative is a kind of practical solution supplemented by a civic, not dogmatic, tolerance that respects the personal dignity of others and is supported by a wide ranging good will, prudence, and civic friendship. Again, this position is not designed to lessen the importance that Maritain gives to philosophy as such. He knows that philosophy, reduced to a common denominator for political purposes, would not be consistent or deep enough to convince everyone. He prefers to leave a realm of freedom open in which philosophers could meet with one another with the full force of their arguments, convictions, and, no doubt, prejudices.

V.

One of the subheadings in the fifth chapter of *Integral Humanism* is, "The Autonomy of the Temporal."[22] Again, this heading is striking because we know that Maritain does not consider the temporal order to be completely "autonomous" but believes that it is itself created and created with some given order. This order is open to understanding by the human mind. Ultimately, the world exists for achieving human purposes, which are also given by nature. However, the context of this discussion on the autonomy of the temporal is not with anthropocentric humanists who deny any relation of man to a transcendent order. It is with Christians who seem to neglect the worldly order and hence give cause of scandal, resentment, and disorder in the world. In this context, Maritain begins by citing authority, namely that of Pope Leo XIII, who, following the Aristotelian tradition, argued that "the authority of the State is supreme in its own order."[23] Maritain's political philosophy thus must explain what it might mean for the authority of the state to be "supreme" but only "in its own order."

In part, the distinction in Matthew (22:22) of the things that are Caesar's and the things that are God's had the effect historically, in Maritain's view, of freeing Christians from the pagan state. In principle, this passage forms the basis for considering any state that claims itself to have complete religious competence. In this sense, the "secular" state can be seen to have arisen under Christian inspiration by freeing the state to be itself. This is what Maritain wants to establish. The "distinction [between God and Caesar] . . . has been unfolding throughout our history in the midst of accidents of all kinds . . . [it] frees religion from all temporal enslavements by stripping the State of all sacred pretensions, by giving the State secular standing."[24] Seen from this angle, the state is freed from the burden of religious questions, not by denying their importance but by affirming that they do not fall within its own competence. This is what Maritain means by the phrase that the state has a "secular standing."

Maritain is quite aware, however, that, in fact, in the modern era, the state would come to claim, largely because of the anthropological theories that Maritain examines, more for itself than is due to it. "All along the course of this evolution [of modern political thought], even and especially during the liberal and individualist democratic period, something has constantly increased and magnified its claims: the State, the sovereign machine in which political power takes flesh, and which imprints its anonymous countenance on the social community and on the obeying multitude."[25] Thus, Maritain in a sense has to develop a position that recognizes the dangers of the modern state, the dangers of a confessional state, and the dangers of a state built on a philosophy that does not recognize anything higher than man.

The basis of Maritain's understanding of the relative autonomy of the temporal or political order, something that is worth legitimate effort in itself, is clearly derived from Aristotle and St. Thomas. He vigorously denies that he thinks that politics is merely a matter of "individual morality."

> I do say, and Aristotle said it long ago, that political science constitutes a special branch of moral science—not that which concerns the individual, nor that which concerns the domestic society—but precisely that which concerns specifically the good of men assembled in political society, in other words, the good of the social whole: this good is an essentially human good, and this is measured above all by reference to the ends of the human being, and concerns the morals or manners of man, insofar as [he is a] free being having to use his freedom for his true ends.[26]

The operative phrase for Maritain is this: "the good of men assembled in political society." What Maritain proposes is to elaborate the terms of this real political good, relatively autonomous for its own purpose, but within a context that would limit it to its own sphere.

First, Maritain wants to establish that the political order does not act merely at the nod of the spiritual order, as its arm or instrument. He does not intend to deny that the political order is itself limited because human persons have a higher purpose than politics.

> The temporal order would be subordinate to the spiritual, no longer, of course, as an instrumental agent, as was so often the case in the Middle Ages, but as a *less elevated principal agent*; and above all, the earthly common good would no longer be taken as a mere means in relation to eternal life, but as what it essentially is in this regard, namely, as an *intermediary or infravalent end*. A real and effective subordination—that is, in the contrast with modern Gallican and "liberal" conceptions; but a subordination which no longer takes a purely ministerial form. . . . This means a body politic in which the secular and temporal have their full role and dignity as end and as principal agent, though not as ultimate end nor as the most elevated principal agent. This is the only sense in which the Christian can take the words "secular body politic."[27]

This passage is of great importance because it establishes for Maritain the notion that there is something to do in the world that can be seen as its own good, something worthwhile working for simply because it is a legitimate common good in some legitimate order.

VI.

In *The Peasant of the Garonne*, Maritain shows how he understands the dignity of the temporal order as something rightfully and honorably worth working for without, at the same time, divinizing it. Again in this latter work, Maritain clearly is critical of much that passed in ecclesiastical circles in the 1960s. But he retains the idea from his earlier discussions that the temporal order, while worthy in itself, is still not an absolute good that is completely independent of the spiritual ends and destiny of man. In this light, the question might be posed: What are we human beings doing in the world, anyhow, if our destiny is, and we hope it will be, in the transcendent order? Maritain, in other words, wrestles with the problem of whether the world and its activities have any inner worldly purpose that itself ought to be fulfilled. We have already seen that Maritain set out on his analytical enterprise here because Christians were accused, especially by Marx, of not giving enough attention to the world. The world was said not to be in the shape that it should be to meet human problems. This presumed failure is what gave rise to various accusations that classical Christian theology is, in part at least, the cause of the problems of the world by deflecting attention to the supernatural.

"I spoke just now of the natural end of the world. I would like to clarify this briefly," Maritain explains in *The Peasant of the Garonne*. "The absolute final end, the supreme end of the world is supramundane, it belongs to the supernatural order. But the world has also a natural end (*relatively* final, or final in a given order)."[28] No doubt, we do not at first appreciate the depth and breadth of what is behind Maritain's concern about "the natural end of the world." He does not deny that there is a supernatural end of man, that is, to be redeemed, to achieve the Beatific Vision as a proper end for each human being within that society known since St. Augustine as "the City of God." The supernatural end, its reality and importance, is what primarily prevents most people from making the state or some other worldly movement or order from becoming for them the highest end of man as such. Man is not the highest being; hence, politics is not the highest science. But it is a worthy science because it is a proper function of man's nature. This proper function is what Maritain is trying to establish in his own political thinking.

Yet Maritain's answer to the question of the natural end of man in the world is not simply an account of a valid end for human activity, even if it is not itself the highest end. Maritain recognizes that man's contemplative soul and his contemplative activities are also proper to him. Both the political and contemplative sides of the whole human experience have their proper exposition and goal. Maritain divides his response to the question about man's natural end into three parts. In his first element, he meets head on the question about human autonomy, that temptation that haunts the modern world. "In the first aspect, the natural end of the history of the world is the mastery of nature by man, and the conquest of human autonomy."[29] Maritain's response has taken its cue from Genesis, wherein man is commanded to "Be fruitful and multiply, and fill the earth and subdue it." Notice here that Maritain takes his philosophical position from a revelational source. That is to say, what is proposed in Genesis corresponds with and confirms a line of thought already present in Aristotle, in philosophy, about the purpose of man. Maritain is thus concerned to establish that there is a genuine goal that man can and should attain. And this valid but subordinate goal is one that will not be attained without his effort, without his mind and hand. The freedom of man has this goal as its worldly object.

> This goal is the conquest which man must achieve of his own auton-omy; as an earthly being who harbors within himself an immortal spirit he has a natural tendency to liberate himself progressively from the control exercised over him by the physical world. At the same time it is required of him to set the human person and the different human groups (races, classes, nations) free from servitude or subjection to other men, and from that violence by which one man imposes his power in another by treating him as a mere instrument.[30]

Maritain maintains that there is something to be done that imposes a duty on man for his own good.

The second worldly task is spiritual, that is, knowledge itself. "A second aspect of the natural end of the world is the development of the multiple immanent (self-perfecting) or spiritual activities of the human being, especially the development of knowledge in all its different de-grees."[31] Maritain would include here both art and ethics as things that need to be spelled out and developed.

The third aspect of the earthly end of man is "the manifestation of all the potentialities of human nature."[32] The fact that man is incarnate and not a "pure spirit" means, for Maritain, that all those things that are finite and changeable still have the potency to be fashioned into some higher beauty or goodness. Maritain maintains that the world awaits the imposition of the mark of man on it as its proper end. And the proper end of man is not merely this achievement, though that is a proper end, but the higher end to which all this earthly activity is ordered as a means.

Maritain will at least wonder how the potentialities for evil will affect this mission in the world. He will follow St. Thomas's principle that certain evils make other virtues possible; in particular, mercy cannot exist without prior fault. Thus, Maritain does not eschew in this discus-sion, lofty as it is, man's potential to evil. He proposes the conquest of evil, in the only way evil can be conquered, through forgiveness and the identification with what is lacking in something good (chapter 9).

VII.

Democracy thus will be for Maritain that aspect of the worldly mission that treats the proper understanding of the political and economic order. He does not intend to be utopian. He knows that a good order of economic or political things need not occur and may be prevented by accident or evil. What he concerns himself with is the accusation that Christianity is not able to act for justice and to support man. His response to this accusation is to rethink the various orientations that are given to man in their order of importance and in their interrelatedness.

Maritain would have no trouble in imagining a world full of two or three hundred or more differing polities, each unique or different and yet each still fulfilling the essential definitions of "democracy" in his positive sense of term. He would also expect that in actual fact, many regimes with a democratic constitutional form would in fact be disordered in the sense of not achieving this or that aspect of democratic life. Further, he could anticipate that some, perhaps many, regimes might well be "democratic" in the anthropocentric sense of excluding any form of natural law or revelation within their orbit. Obviously, what will actually happen in history, he could not and, in a sense, did not predict. As a philosopher what he could do is propose the essential principles and structures. "The democratic philosophy of man and society has faith in the resources and vocation of human nature," he writes challengingly. "In the greatest adventure of our life and our history it is placing its stakes on justice and generosity."[33] What Maritain seeks to set free is that combined philosophical and Christian effort to accomplish the purpose of man within history, not as the most important thing that man has to do, but rather as a significant thing precisely because it is reflective of what is the highest thing.

> The democratic society thrives on the unceasing work of invention, criticism and demands of individual conscience—it thrives on it and would die of it if it were not also living on the unceasing gift of self which must correspond to this unceasing work of criticism and demand; running counter to the natural bent of man's imagination, it denies to the rulers the right to consider themselves and be considered a superior race, and wills nevertheless that their authority be respected on a judicial basis. It does not admit that the State is a transcendent

power incorporating within itself all authority and imposed from above upon human life; it demands that autonomous organs, in possession of authority commensurate with their functions, emanate spontaneously from the civil community.[34]

Maritain's democracy is not centrist or monolithic, but composed of legitimate parts. Its people are not "sovereign" in the sense of being themselves subject to no higher law, but they do need freely to consent to be governed legally and constitutionally.

Maritain, in conclusion, gives a legitimacy to the temporal order; he gives it a worthwhile purpose within a theory of order that understands the place of politics as something that is highest in a certain order. Maritain is quite clear that the citizens who make up the democracy must themselves first be open to and motivated by the higher contemplative and revelational things. A democracy based only on the human will, itself subject to only itself, constitutes the gravest threat to democracy Maritain's democracy is, in the end, both man-centered because it seeks a legitimate place for the political and Christian because to be itself, its citizens themselves need some sense of things that are addressed to man's highest end, without which politics tend to substitute for the highest things.

Maritain thinks that the experience of the twentieth century shows that any democracy, based on anthropocentric principles that deny any higher principles to man, is contradictory to the true nature of democracy. What he does not foresee is that, having eliminated the principal ideologies of the early twentieth century, the earlier forms of anthropocentric humanism would become predominant in the culture. In this sense, the value of Maritain's nonsovereign democratic theory serves mainly as a contrast, as a critique, of the type of democracy that no longer admits any limits on the human will except power. Anthropocentric humanism based on a theory of relativist skepticism is not the only or best justification for democracy. In the forum of intellectual freedom, Maritain still makes his case for the complete humanism that makes democracy address itself to its own proper political end, the temporal common good.

NOTES

1. Jacques Maritain, "*Une Philosophie d'Histoire Moderne*," *OCM*, vol. 2., 1169.

2. Jacques Maritain, *Integral Humanism: Temporal and Spiritual Problems of a New Christendom*, trans. Joseph W. Evans (Notre Dame: The University of Notre Dame Press, 1973), 6.

3. Maritain, *Integral Humanism*, 249.

4. Ibid., 250.

5. Jacques Maritain, *Christianity and Democracy*, trans. Doris C. Anson (San Francisco: Ignatius Press, 1986), 53–54. (The citation from Bergson is from *The Two Sources of Morality and Religion*, 243.)

6. Maritain, *Christianity and Democracy*, 28.

7. Ibid., 172.

8. Ibid., 10.

9. Ibid., 138.

10. Ibid., 28.

11. Ibid., 57.

12. Maritain, *Christianity and Democracy*, 25. Maritain specifically noted that the word "people," recalling the earlier chapter on political definitions, is not some kind of abstract absolute. "I do not share the romantic optimism which ascribes to the people a judgment which is always just and instincts which are always upright." Ibid., 66. A government following Lincoln's definition must still be a government of reason, law, and truth, in Maritain's view. See John Hittinger, "Jacques Maritain and Yves Simon's Use of Thomas Aquinas in their Defense of Liberal Democracy," in *Thomas Aquinas and His Legacy*, ed. David W. Gallagher (Washington, D. C.: The Catholic University of America Press, 1994), 149–72.

13. Jacques Maritain, *Man and the State* (Chicago: University of Chicago Press, 1951), 200–201.

14. Ibid., 201.

15. Ibid., 159, 226–27.

16. Ibid., 286.

17. See Jacques Maritain, "Church and State," *Man and the State*, 147–87.

18. Maritain, *Integral Humanism*, 41.

19. See Jacques Maritain, *The Social and Political Philosophy of Jacques Maritain*, ed. Joseph W. Evans and Leo R. Ward (Notre Dame: University of Notre Dame Press, 1976), "The Meaning of Contemporary Atheism," 171–86; "The Roots of Soviet Atheism," 252–53.

20. Maritain, *Integral Humanism*, 42.

21. Ibid., 173–74.

22. Ibid., 176.

23. Ibid.

24. Maritain, *Christianity and Democracy*, 28.

25. Maritain, *Integral Humanism*, 160.

26. Ibid., 216.

27. Ibid., 177.

28. Jacques Maritain, *The Peasant of the Garonne: An Old Layman Questions Himself about the Present Time*, trans. Michael Cuddihy and Elizabeth Hughes (New York: Holt, Rinehart, and Winston, 1968), 40.

29. Ibid.

30. Ibid., 40–41.

31. Ibid., 41.

32. Ibid.

33. Maritain, *Christianity and Democracy*, 56.

34. Ibid., 58.

7

THE AUTHORITY OF FREEDOM AND THE FREEDOM OF AUTHORITY

> I mean by "authority" the right to direct and to command, to be listened to or obeyed by others. And I mean by "power" the *force,* which one can use, and with the aid of which one can oblige others to listen or to obey.
>
> —Jacques Maritain, "Democracy and Authority"[1]

> It is not true that the autonomy of an intelligent creature consists in not receiving any rule or objective measure from a being other than itself. It consists in conforming to such rules and measures voluntarily because they are known to be just and true, and because of a love for truth and justice. . . . [Man] becomes free, by warring upon himself and thanks to many sorrows; by the struggle of the spirit and virtue; by exercising his freedom he wins his freedom. So that at long last a freedom better than he expected is *given* to him. From the beginning to the end it is truth that liberates him.
>
> —Jacques Maritain, "The Conquest of Freedom"[2]

I.

Liberty and authority, reason and transcendence, nature and history can, with careful consideration, be seen to be properly related to each other. To be human means, all together, to be reasonable, to be free, to be creative, to be open to the transcendent, to be able to fashion the earth by forming ourselves. Maritain rejects a concept of liberty whose only purpose is its own exercise. Philosophy can understand the demands of and reasons for liberty and authority if man is to be as he is

121

found in nature, the rational animal. Freedom needs authority; authority needs freedom.

In approaching freedom and authority, Maritain presupposes an understanding of two points about genuine freedom: (1) that this process must begin within us—"in the hierarchy of values, it is the development of the life of the spirit, wisdom, and love which hold first place"[3]—and (2) that the conquest of freedom does not come quickly—"the freedom of expansion for the person . . . will need all human history to achieve the conquest of this freedom."[4] These cautionary observations are not intended to dampen enthusiasm for the task of ordering temporal society. However, they do remind us that external reforms in economics or politics, as well as claims to achieve freedom quickly, are often themselves the justification for tyrannies based on neither freedom nor authority.

As an "authority" on the subject of *authority,* Jacques Maritain's student and friend Yves Simon is perhaps better known than he. Maritain in fact wrote a perceptive review of Simon's famous work, *Nature and Function of Authority,* in *The Review of Politics* in 1941.[5] The striking intellectual project that Simon proposed was to inquire, whether, granted, contrary to fact, that all men were equally intelligent and virtuous, they would still need authority. Were liberty and authority, in other words, in fundamental opposition to each other, or did a healthy liberty require, as part of its own intellectual justification, the fact of authority? His conclusion is that authority is also needed in a society in which all are equally intelligent and virtuous. An argument, in fact two arguments, could be made to establish this need. Simon thought this natural need of authority arises in practical affairs, in the affairs of family and politics, when deciding either what specifically should be done by a group for its own proper good or who is to protect the particular good while fostering the common good.

Thus, authority is not simply, though it is that too, an instrument to remedy some disorder that ought not to exist in the first place, a position associated with St. Augustine.[6] Rather, authority is itself necessary and rational. It can be understood as such. To obey authority when it is legitimately established, both in argument and in practice, consequently, is neither irrational nor inhuman nor to be eventually eliminated in some more perfect status. By itself, authority is a considered act of freedom working for and establishing some true good. Thus, to obey authority can be, and can be known to be, a perfectly intelligent act. Obedience as such is in no way antiintellectual or a sign of human weakness or imperfection. The explanation of why authority could be considered reasonable constitutes the arguments for authority that Simon presents. These arguments are the ones that Maritain himself approved of and developed in his own right. The discussion about authority represents a fundamental aspect of his political philosophy.

To clarify the meaning and necessity of political authority, we need to spell out in particular why man, by nature, to use Aristotle's term, is a "political animal." We accept, perhaps, on the "authority" of Aristotle, that "man is a political animal." The arguments for authority draw out what this means in rational terms. We need not take the need for authority only "on authority." To say that man is a political animal is another way of saying that man needs authority to be himself, to be *what he is*. If man is "by nature" a political being, that is, if he needs a political organization for him in fact to bring into existence all or most of the potentialities he is provided in his given nature, then authority itself is natural, even though its particular form of exercise has to be deliberately set up by human beings organizing themselves formally in a polity. Treating this very point, Maritain writes:

> There is an order that it is the office of reason, as practical reason, to make: it is, to be exact, the order of human acts and operations. . . . To the natural law reason adds the determination of positive law; in this way are established organs of civil society which is indeed prescribed by nature and necessarily presupposes certain laws of nature but which is the work of reason and of virtue and has in Justice "the mystical basis of authority." The . . . whole order of human life is not ready-made in nature and in things; it is an Order of Freedom; it has not just to be discovered and accepted: it has also to be made.[7]

Many different ways can be conceived whereby a people can organize this authority and choose, in some prescribed manner, those who exercise it and how they are to exercise it. The form this configuration will take is largely a question of prudence and of political art under the control of prudence.[8] But that members of a polity must establish some form of rule, with the aid of their own reason and will—this necessity comes from their nature, from what they are. In the order of its coming about in history, a viable order of civil authority may be the last thing to be established even though it is first in the order of what man needs in nature to become fully *what he is*.

II.

The fact that man is a political animal, therefore, does not deny that there can be different kinds of regime, each of which has some designated source of political authority to make morally binding laws. How many and of what structure these regimes will be is itself a question of man's judgment of prudence and of his experience. Indeed, the variety of peoples and ways to achieve a worthy life suggests that, because of freedom, we should want and expect to see a wide assortment of legitimate and worthy political regimes or constitutions. We really do not want the French to be ruled like the Spaniards, nor the Japanese regime to look like that of the English. We are better off with variety. On the other hand, the fact that man needs actually to think out and set up an organized society as something that falls in his knowledge according to the logic of *what he is* means that the very political act of establishing a polity is itself known to him through his reason. The founding of a polity, to locate authority, is at some point a specific act of political reason.

Maritain explains this principle follows:

> If, in the cosmos, a nature, such as human nature, can be preserved and developed only in a state of culture, and if the state of culture necessarily entails the existence in the social group of a function of commandment and government directed to the common good, then this function is demanded by the Natural Law, and implies a *right* to command and govern.[9]

That no form or very imperfect forms of authority existed in earlier stages of human history is no argument against this position. Man's own intelligence and historical experience are themselves instruments that enable him to be what he ought to be in his flourishing or fullness.

Maritain is careful to point out that with regard to forms of rule as such, this decision is properly a responsibility of political philosophy, not revelation: "The Christian religion is annexed to no temporal regime; it is compatible with all forms of legitimate government; it is not its business to determine which type of civil rule men must adopt *hic et nunc*."[10] What legitimate political rule is not compatible with is a regime that denies human dignity or man's relation to God, though life with God can take place even under the worst regimes.

Maritain observes that presidents or prime ministers in diverse modern states are really "elected monarchs" whose function is to exercise or administer the authority of the people established in the state. The state itself is the highest agency of the body politic in which this authority is set down and articulated as to its limits, purpose, and mode of procedure.[11] In this sense, the organs of rule, of polity, are products of freedom and intelligence proposing and, if necessary, imposing order on human actions and passions in the name of a just common good. Ultimately, this order of public life is not possible without an authority that is also legitimate and intelligible. Maritian emphasizes the uniqueness of every practical judgment in the exercise of authority:

> The essential function of authority is a necessary one. The necessity is grounded in the fact that the prudential judgment is of an essentially different nature from scientific judgment, that the truth of prudence consists in the relation of conformity of the judgment with the requirements of right appetite of the end to be pursued, and that consequently the prudential judgment can never be demonstrated or intellectually intersubjectivized.[12]

Scientific judgments that claim to explain *what is* can be confirmed by repeating the demonstration or the experiment. In matters of action and decision, we put things into effect. What we put into effect need not be, or need not be this way or that. These things stemming from our causality are unique to the time and circumstances in which they occur. To those who lack wisdom, some things will never be clear.

By prudential decisions not being "intersubjectivized," Maritain means that the same evidence, with no interference of bad will or lack of capacity, still will not always or necessarily yield, to differing actors deliberating about them, the same clear choice in practical matters about what or how something is to be done. Thus, there will never come a time in practical matters when authority is not needed either to decide among differing good choices or to determine the identifying relationship of parts of the polity to the whole. This fact of differing opinions about real alternatives is, in itself, a good, not an evil. In practical matters, the more we know, the more we will need authority.

Authority and the obedience due to it by virtue of its own justification, then, will not somehow disappear in a world of perfect knowledge. Even less will it disappear in the actual, imperfect world we know. Obeying legitimate authority means to incorporate the norm or law presented by authority so that this norm or rule becomes the criterion of one's own action. We thus act according to the rule because what is proposed by authority is seen to be basically reasonable. Either we see that what is to be done makes sense, or we see that the authority appointed to decide on differing alternatives itself acts reasonably. Obedience, contrary to the way it is often depicted, is, when commanded by legitimate rule, in no wise an irrational act, except when authority is usurped or is clearly irrational. In fact, in practical matters, in spite of what we might initially suspect and on the assumption that people choose to remain in their polity, the more perfect the knowledge, the more the need of authority. Authority and obedience will be necessary because knowledge will offer more and more good alternatives from which to choose.

Generally speaking, a healthy and intelligent society will be filled with a wide and bewildering number of good alternatives of things that it may choose to do, but from which it must select a particular course. If no alternative is chosen, nothing can happen to achieve the purpose at issue in the polity. Hence, not to choose is itself a choice and often a sign of societal paralysis. Stagnation ensues when authority is not permitted or does not choose to act on its own best prudential judgment even when that judgment might validly be otherwise seen by others equally intelligent. When one alternative is chosen, others are rejected, even though they may also, for one reason or another, be good alternatives.

What the state is, in Maritain's understanding, is the recognized location of that human will or those human wills that are, by democratic process, appointed to make the laws or rules to be followed by other reasonable beings formally assembled together to achieve a polity's good. This good includes the flourishing of the various private and individual goods for the sake of which a polity is also composed. The constitutional or positive or civil law is the intelligible statement of this choice, of what in particular is to be done. What makes this chosen decision a law rather than just another opinion about what is to be done is that the recognized authority, by a proper procedure, understood it, willed it, communicated it, and seriously intended it to be carried out for a good purpose. The sanction imposed for breaking a law usually indicates the seriousness with which the lawmakers intended the law to be taken. Subsequently, the observance of the law is backed by official law enforcement agencies designed to see that the law is in effect even when free citizens do not choose to observe it.

This emphasis on will and reason in state and law is why Maritain distinguishes authority from power or coercion, which latter we too often confuse with the understanding or reason implicit in the law itself. He does not, be it noted, say that coercion, in theory or in use, is in itself always unreasonable or wrong. Maritain is neither a pacifist nor an anarchist. Coercion's proportioned use is sound when potentially reasonable beings are not in fact acting reasonably. "Force is necessary in civil communities because of men who are violent and inclined to vices, but it has a pedagogic office and ought to lead in the direction of freedom. It is only a substitute for those creations of freedom that we call virtues."[13] The notion that force leads "in the direction of freedom" means that it prevents or punishes acts that ought not to exist. It does not substitute for virtue but it can prevent acts that lead away from it.

Notice that Maritain carefully indicates that freedom relates to the observance of a good law, not to its nonobservance. But for the most part, authority and the law stemming from it ought not to have to use coercion or force. Many citizens obey the law not after the manner of coercion, of being forced to observe it, but after the manner of persuasion and virtue. That is, they see that what authority commands has some justification to it that can be established in reason. At the same time, they understand the argument about the natural need for this authority to make decisions for a common good. The good man "fulfills the law not out of compulsion but out of love and his own free will."[14] The educative function of the law is designed to direct the reason of the lawgiver to the reason of the citizen so that, as much as possible, the law will be observed through persuasion and reason, not through coercion. A society in which laws are observed mostly because of the fear of punishment is already a dangerously disoriented society.

III.

It is the burden of Maritain's discussions of freedom and authority patiently to spell out their separate meanings and to relate them in a manner in which both can be seen for what they are in the argument that establishes their intellectual purpose and necessity. I have called this chapter "The Authority of Freedom" *and* "The Freedom of Authority" to emphasize the paradox contained in both phrases. I included authority and freedom in both phrases of the title to emphasize what exactly is at stake in this long and controverted discussion in political philosophy. The word "authority" comes from a Latin word meaning "to grow" or "to cause to grow." Thus, authority has the connotation of something already being *what it is;* yet, at the same time, it, as still the same thing, develops into what it ought to be in its fullness or maturity. That is a particular instance of the classical principles of act and potency. A seedling of an oak thus does not grow up to be a chicken. If it did, it would not do so by "authority" of its natural form. The acorn or seedling inclines to grow to be a full oak tree, never something else.

Thus, the "authority" of freedom refers to Maritain's understanding of free will as a faculty itself given in nature. How free will works, what it is in its inception and in its perfection as free will, is seen in self-reflection. Man has a free will; in experience he knows he constantly uses it. It is not Maritain's position that knowledge of free will is only the result of some philosophic argument. The validity of arguments purporting to deny this faculty can be examined, of course. But that we possess this power or capacity is so obvious and clear that its denial generally constitutes by itself a sign that it exists and leads to a contradiction. Nothing is clearer, on any serious reflective perception of ourselves, than that we have free will. This is a power, implicit in our given being. It is not determined except in its end. This end is that the will (or man with his will) can, must, and does choose as the end of all its choices the good in general.

All choices freely made, when examined, are of some good or apparent good that will be defended as such when questioned, even in the case when there is some disorder or evil connected with them. Good, as such, is seen to be the will's highest end. All alternatives to achieve it in practice are presented to us from the intellect. It presents them to us, as real goods, participated goods. But they are not the final or general good in the light of which we choose all else. Since, however, in this life we are always confronted with finite or limited goods, we are never determined to do one or the other alternative, though we may freely do either. But each good we find is choiceworthy as a good even though it may not exhaust the full content of the good. Through our wills, we are free to specify what we intend to do. And even then, having specified what we might do, we are still free to act or not.

No amount of coercion or fear or desire will change the fact that we have free will. Such constraints may influence the act itself, reduce its voluntariness. But they will merely make it less free in particular circumstances. It is even possible that acts that appear to be free are not free because of these particular circumstances. This fact of free choice, moreover, does not yet bring up the question of how we use this choice. That we are morally good or bad is explained in retrospect by looking back at what we chose to do with our free will. Our character is the result of our choices. Our explanation of our goodness or badness is not sufficiently analyzed by the fact of the power of free will itself. It is only explained by our reflective reason seeking to state what it is we are and what we do with the faculties that we are given. The object of the will is always some good, so that every choice of the will, even a bad one, is done under the appearance of good and in fact need not have been chosen or acted on.

The freedom that Maritain is concerned with in political philosophy is not the metaphysical question of whether we have free will and how we explain it if we do. He thinks this latter explanation to be important, which is why we must study the speculative sciences to study politics. But to return to that notion of "autonomy" and its origins, he also maintains that a misplaced understanding of the place of free will lies at the basis of much modern intellectual disorder. "A prime error which seems to be the root error of many of our contemporaries," Maritain writes,

> lies in the confusion of the two kinds of Freedom that we have distin-
> guished: freedom of choice and freedom of autonomy. This error
> makes the higher form of freedom consist in freedom of choice; as if
> the reason for choosing were not to escape having to choose again!
> Free choice becomes an end in itself, and man, condemned to recur-
> rent acts of choice without ever being able to bind himself, is launched

into a dialectic of freedom which destroys freedom. In order always to be ready to make any fresh choice that the circumstances of the moment may suggest, he refuses to declare for an end which, once chosen, would limit the field of possible choices in the future. In order to enjoy as supreme good the pure exercise of his freedom he refuses to determine it by reference to a rational ground.[15]

This passage is remarkable in its analytic power and in its description of what comes about if freedom of choice is confused with freedom of autonomy, as Maritain understands it. The "freedom" not to be bound to anything, including one's own choices and the reasons for them, is implicitly to deprive the will of its very purpose.

Free will is indeed a power of the soul, given as a constituent element of any existing human nature. But its exercise is not for itself, for its own exercise. The will is actually to settle on some good, and on good itself, if that ever appears before it. Maritain's description of the will is illuminating:

The notion of Freedom is very much wider than the notion of Free Will. Free Will is indeed the source and spring of the world of Freedom: it is a datum of metaphysics; we inherit it with our rational nature; we do not have to achieve it: it appears within us as our initial form of Freedom. But this metaphysical root must grow and develop in the psychological and moral order. We are called upon to become in action what we are already in the metaphysical order: a Person. It is our duty by our own effort to make ourselves *persons* having dominion over our own acts and bring to ourselves a rounded and a whole existence. There we have another kind of Freedom, a freedom to gain for which we must pay a great price: Freedom of fulfillment. What shall we call it? We may say it is the Freedom of autonomy.[16]

Thus, when Maritain uses the term "freedom of autonomy" to refer to his understanding of the purpose for which free will exists in the first place, he means the freedom that comes when, through discipline, asceticism, habit, and purpose, a person can rule his acts to choose what in fact is good. The expression "we are to become what we are" implicitly refers to this relation between freedom of choice and freedom of autonomy when we rule ourselves for known and noble purposes given with our nature.

IV.

This discussion leads naturally to the question of how many beings, each of whom possess free will, act together? Sometimes, no doubt, human beings with free wills have to be "coerced" to do what is right or needed. This coercion, as we mentioned, may even be, indeed should be, "reasonable," in the sense that it substitutes for the right reason that is lacking in someone in such a manner that he harms himself or others. Thus, this coercion or force is a substitute, through another reasoned will in authority, for the will doing what it should do. The will itself is a human faculty of vast proportions and independence, but one whose object is the good, a good it is presented by the intellect, the object of which is to know what is true. Since the good of the intellect is what is true, the will's proper object is this true good presented to it for action by the intellect.

When I speak of the "authority" of freedom, I use the word authority paradoxically. What I mean is that freedom or liberty is such a central and vital matter to human life—indeed, it is the location of the person's independence and capacity to transcend itself—that it "calls for" its proper presence in every area of life. If we say that someone is an "authority" on baseball, we mean that he knows the history, rules, and lore of the game. The "authority" of freedom would mean that whatever is authentically a part of the human condition clearly ought to be related to or grounded in the given freedom that distinguishes the rational creature in all of his actions. The authority of freedom includes its capacity to choose what is true.

"In the order of the spiritual life, we may at once observe that all the sages, stoics, epicureans, and neoplatonists, yogi, rabbis, and sufi, Spinozists, and Nietzscheans," Maritain writes in a memorable passage,

> have always wished, whatever the name they use, to achieve the one thing: Freedom. All have maintained that its achievement requires a certain measure of asceticism (interpreted in one or another of many different ways) and that it implies a state of perfection beyond ordinary human reach. To propose to man a merely human end, said Aristotle, is to misunderstand his nature.[17]

Clearly, Maritain does not want to misunderstand human nature or its freedom. He understands that freedom implies a certain discipline. Freedom is not its own purpose but leads to a chosen good that is not totally of man's own making.

By the freedom of authority, in contrast, I mean the philosophical argument for the necessity of authority that Maritain proposed, about why we need authority in social and political matters. In this sense, the freedom "of" or "given by" authority implies that man's freedom goes into the very construction of the polity in which authority is exercised. Once a proper authority is established, the people under its rule become free to do those things for which human beings are constituted, including the highest things, a freedom they would not otherwise easily have without political authority. By political and social freedom, then, Maritain means the discovery and execution of a proper understanding of a political rule based on the natural ends and purposes of human beings.

In speaking of freedom, as we have seen, Maritain distinguishes freedom of choice and freedom of autonomy. He argues that the modern world is built on the proposition that the only freedom is freedom of choice, whereas the true meaning of freedom of choice can only be decided when we know what man is and what he does with his free will in using it. Maritian recognizes that the "freedom of autonomy" has two diametrically opposed meanings. He understands and uses both meanings, something that can be confusing because the notion of "autonomy" has come to mean precisely what Maritain foresaw and rejected when the term became associated with "free will" and not with what Maritain called "freedom of autonomy." Maritain sees early in his intellectual career that the concept of autonomy could signify complete independence from any law or standard other than itself. He writes to propose a more accurate understanding of both freedom and autonomy.

Maritain understands the background of the modern understanding of autonomy. "The false political emancipation (the false city of human rights) has as its principle the 'anthropocentric' conception that Rousseau and Kant had of the autonomy of the person," Maritain writes.

> According to them, man is free *only if he obeys himself alone,* and man is constituted by right of nature in such a state of freedom. . . . We have here the divinization of the individual, the logical consequences of which are, in the practical and social order: (1) a practical atheism in society. . . . (2) the theoretical and practical disappearance of the idea of common good; (3) the theoretical and practical disappearance of the idea of the responsible leader, and of the idea of authority falsely considered to be incompatible with freedom.[18]

Maritain immediately relates this practical atheism and autonomy of the isolated individual to the "social divinization of the State and of the anonymous mass incarnate in a Master who is no longer a normal ruler but a sort of inhuman monster whose omnipotence is based on myths and lies; and at the same time bourgeois liberalism makes way for revolutionary totalitarianism."[19] In the 1930s, Maritain connected the absolute autonomy of the individual with the rise of the State and of totalitarianism. Even with the demise of the three totalitarian regimes, his thought remains pertinent. Maritain writes his political philosophy to propose his particular alternative to the divinization of the individual and eventually the state that he saw as a result of trends in modern political philosophy. The fact that the particular totalitarian trends he immediately dealt with have disappeared does not mean that the Christian-oriented solutions he proposed and expected to have serious consideration in a new social order replaced them. In fact, the "autonomous man" rather than the "freedom of autonomy" is closer to what has occurred.

The structure of Maritain's argument about freedom begins with the fact that one species of physical being in nature is—evidently from this nature itself, for it has no other source—endowed with intelligence and will. Maritain speaks of this presence of free will in human nature as a metaphysical fact. He means that man did not create himself to possess these powers of will and intellect. He also means that the use of these powers, including their use to know what they are, is something given to someone who wants to use them. But what is chosen need not be. It could have been otherwise. Ethics and metaphysics are thus related, but they do not have the same objects. "The universe of Freedom presupposed the universe of Nature and constitutes nonetheless an order apart, irreducible to Nature, with a dynamic that leads from an initial term of freedom (which we call the Free Will) to a final term which may be called Freedom of Attainment or of Autonomy."[20]

Free will is something given. It is essential to *what man is*. Free will is what Maritain calls the natural basis of freedom of autonomy. Nature and freedom can be in opposition. Man exists. He exists with given powers of intellect, will, and senses. These powers operate in a certain way. The speculative intellect, reflecting on itself, understands the given nature of these realities. That is, it understands what these realities are. That there is a free will is not a question of ethics. Rather, ethics deals with what in fact one chooses and what ultimately one chooses for.

Maritain, moreover, will point out that the sphere of moral decision, what we do with our free will, constitutes a special sphere of reality unique to itself. It is precisely because particular decisions and choices need not exist or exist in this way rather than that way, that makes this sphere of freedom unique. It is the sphere that most immediately affects us because it is one for which we are directly responsible.

V.

In all his philosophical discourse, Maritain is noteworthy for keeping open, in precise terms, a place for freedom of transcendence, a place for revelation, or divine authority, within the human order. This consideration of transcendence, he argues, has a legitimate and intelligible place in human affairs, one that fosters, not negates, freedom. "The true city of human rights recognizes as God only one God: God Himself and no created thing," he writes in a passage that indicates why the state can never be divinized or absolutized.

> And this city understands that human society, despite the diverse religious families living within it, implies a religious principle and presupposes that God is accessible to our reason and is the last end of our existence. The city is founded upon the authentic notion of the common good; . . . it implies the effective respect for their rights and has, as its essential element, their access to the maximum development and freedom compatible with given historical conditions. And finally this city implies an authentic notion of authority.[21]

Maritain is careful to warn about setting up some pseudodivine power in the place of God—"God Himself and no created thing." The city has access to the notion of God not from itself but from the people who compose the society. In their own inner life by which they transcend the city, such notions arise among citizens.

Maritain is concerned to reconcile the freedom of God, who can in His wisdom create or not create, with the freedom of the rational being whose freedom consists of knowing and choosing what is already good, a good caused not by man's own making it so. The good to be chosen is the locus of what can in fact make man happy not by virtue of what he wants but by virtue of *what he is*. History, ultimately, is the place where these two freedoms meet. "We can form some idea of the drama of history, or rather the drama of the sacred element in history," Maritain writes.

> Despite all the mass of sensible material that conditions it in the order of nature, history is fashioned above all things by crossing and commingling, by chase and conflict, of Uncreated Freedom and created Freedom. . . . And divine Freedom is all the more wonderful and glorious for the liberty it gives to created freedom to undo its work; for only the Divine Freedom can out of a wealth of destruction draw forth a superabundance of Being.[22]

The root of Maritain's confidence in man's purpose in the world is no doubt located in a passage such as this, wherein the destructive effects of free will are both acknowledged and set in a higher, transcendent context. Students of Maritain are thus conscious that his intellectual system consistently provides for a place wherein we can consider not only philosophical and political liberty and authority, but also divine freedom and divine authority in their interrelationships.

But Maritain's general discussion of church and state or metaphysics and politics is designed not to "impose" by civil power either the discussion itself or any set of conclusions. He seeks to allow a place, because of the very nature of human freedom and the legitimacy of authority, for the highest things to exist within the human order. Maritain proposes three fundamental principles, in the light of which he relates human freedom and divine authority, wherein human freedom is enhanced by divine authority and divine authority is directed to the purpose of human freedom. These principles are, briefly: (1) the primacy of the spiritual, (2) the principle of freedom of the church to be itself, and (3) the principle of necessary cooperation between the church, the body politic, and the state.[23] What is remarkable about these principles in their interrelation with one another is their ability to protect and foster the relevant meanings of human freedom and authority into a coherent whole that recognizes the nature and limits of each.

The "primacy of the spiritual" is one of the earliest principles that Maritain develops in the political order after his experience with the *Action Française* in 1926 and 1927.[24] It comes primarily out of the Christian distinction between the things that are God's and the things that are

Caesar's. "The direct ordination of the human person to God transcends every created common good of the political society and the intrinsic common good of the universe," Maritain explains.

> Here is the rock of the dignity of the human person as well as of the unshakable requirement of the Christian message. Thus the indirect subordination of the body politic—not as a mere means, but as an end worthy in itself yet of lesser dignity—to the supratemporal values to which human life is appendant, refers first and foremost, as matter of fact, to the supernatural end to which the human person is directly ordained. To sum up all this in one single expression, . . . the law we are faced with here is the law of the *primacy of the spiritual*.[25]

This statement of principle of each person's openness to the transcendent is the "rock" of human dignity, as Maritain puts it.

The second principle follows: if authority is "the right to be listened to," then those to whom something is addressed are free only if they can listen to this authority in its own content. The church or the churches may look like and be defined as other voluntary associations; however, they "must enjoy that *right to freedom* which is but one, not only with the right to free association naturally belonging to the human person, but with the right freely to believe the truth recognized by one's conscience, that is, with the most basic and inalienable of all human rights."[26] Thus, Maritain does not present the case for the church in terms of authority but in terms of basic freedoms.

The second general principle is thus "the freedom of the Church to teach and preach and worship, the freedom of the Gospel, the freedom of the word of God."[27] Without this independent freedom on the part of the church, the primacy of the spiritual could not properly be communicated to those who are free to hear it. Maritain grants the church the freedom to be what it is. Its purpose is to free people so that they can hear the truth that they do not know.

The third principle of cooperation of church and body politic flows from these two principles: (1) that grace is built on nature and (2) that the limitation of political authority to temporal goods freed it from areas over which it was not competent. The church has her own organization and purpose. It deals within its own realm with its own autonomy and authority. "There is no distinction without an order of values," Maritain explains.

If the things that are God's are distinct from the things that are Caesar's, that means that they are better. . . . I do not say that the body
politic is by nature irreligious or indifferent to religion, . . . I say that
by nature the body politic, which belongs strictly speaking to the natural order, is only concerned with the temporal life of men and their
temporal common good.[28]

The freedom of the church, thus, is the other side of the discussion of
the authority that constitutes the state within the body politic, with a
legitimate but limited political purpose. Maritain's philosophy is designed to protect the state by defining what it is and to save liberty
by allowing even the transcendent order to address itself to the human
person.

In all of this discussion, Maritain's general principle remains, in a
phrase that has subsequently become almost universal within this discussion of politics and religion: "To hate evil is Christian: but to hate the
person of the wrongdoer will never be Christian."[29] This principle thus
acknowledges that evil can and does have terrible effects in the human
order, enough to suggest that something more than human power is
needed to confront it.

Thus what goes on in history is not a blind evolution, though there
is some of that on some levels. It is rather a drama—"chase and conflict"—that manifests the freedom of will and the actual choices that the
will makes for or against the norms or laws of human action. Maritain, in
recognizing the place of the spiritual power, does not lessen or denigrate
political power. He intends to be loyal to a fact of experience and to an
illumination of philosophy that does in fact come through the historic
experience of revelation. What makes Maritain both unique and relevant is the clarity with which he presents this approach within political
philosophy. Maritain's statement of what he is doing in his openness to
revelation is worth citing. It shows how he protects the philosophical
and hence the political order in their own relative autonomy. At the
same time, he does not deny the human intellect's openness to higher
authority if it is in fact encountered through unanswered philosophic or
political questions: "I note in passing that the light of Christian philosophy is not, like that of theology," Maritain writes, "the light of Faith
illuminating Reason in order to enable it to acquire some understanding
of revealed mysteries, but the light of reason comforted by Faith in order
to do better its own work of intellectual investigation."[30]

Maritain presents a forceful intellectual argument within the realms of political philosophy, itself open to the actual goods that exist within human experience, which includes religious experience. "The Catholic Church is sometimes reproached with being an 'authoritarian church,' " Maritain writes in *Man and the State*,

> as if the authority—that is the right to be listened to—that she exercises on her faithful in seeing to the preservation of revealed truth and Christian morality were to result in fostering authoritarian trends in the sphere of civil life and activities. May I be allowed to say that those who make such reproaches lack both in theological and historical insight.
>
> They lack historical insight, because they do not grasp the significance of the diversity of historical climates which in past times made the authority of the Church over the State—and now makes the mutual freedom of the State and the Church—mutual requisites of the common good of civilization.
>
> They lack theological insight, for they do not see that the authority of the Church in her own spiritual sphere is nothing else than her bondage to God and to her mission.[31]

If the essence of authority is the right to be listened to—with the corresponding duty to listen—then its purpose is to assure that what is taught or laid down from the beginning is to be continually present within civil and voluntary bodies in which this authority exists. Authority in religious matters is designed to keep what is revealed, as such, within the world. The freedom of the church is, in the civil order, rooted in the duty that people have to know the highest things addressed to themselves. Without this authority, in the religious realm, it is impossible to be free to know and observe the order of reality contained in revelation. "The true deification of man consists in opening himself to the gift which the Absolute makes of itself, and the descent of the divine plenitude into the intelligent creature."[32]

Maritain's discussions of freedom and authority, then, show how much is at stake in properly understanding how each is related to the other. Maritain understands the dangers of identifying political and religious freedom with the simple exercise of free will and not with the purpose for which free will exists. But we start with free will as a metaphysical fact, a given. Authority need not have a bad name. Indeed, authority in its proper meaning is an instrument of freedom, while freedom is the faculty by which we can choose what is right and what is true. That there is no freedom without truth and no truth without freedom seems obvious to Maritain. But what also seems clear to him is that authority is also a servant of both freedom and truth. Yet, to recall the English title of Raïssa Maritain's book, *We Have Been Friends Together,* or even the French title, *Les Grandes Amitiés,* the purpose and context of truth, freedom, and authority is friendship, the topic to which we shall next turn, a topic of great beauty that appears with such frequency in Maritain that it serves to enhance the spirit of all his social thought.

NOTES

1. Jacques Maritain, "Democracy and Authority," *Scholasticism and Politics,* trans. ed. by Mortimer J. Adler (Garden City, N. Y.: Doubleday, Image, 1960), 93–94.

2. Jacques Maritain, "The Conquest of Freedom," in *The Education of Man: The Educational Philosophy of Jacques Maritain,* ed. Donald and Idella Gallagher (Garden City, N. Y.: Doubleday, 1962), 138.

3. Ibid., 59.

4. Ibid., 51.

5. Jacques Maritain, "On Authority," *The Review of Politics* 3 (April 1941), 250–54. This review is found in *OCM,* vol. 7, 1288–1303. See also Yves Simon, *A General Theory of Authority* (Notre Dame: University of Notre Dame Press, 1980); "General Theory of Government," in Yves Simon, *Philosophy of Democratic Government* (Chicago: University of Chicago Press, 1951), 1–71.

6. See Herbert Deane, *The Political and Social Ideas of St. Augustine* (New York: Columbia University Press, 1956).

7. Jacques Maritain, *Freedom in the Modern World,* trans. Richard O'Sullivan (New York: Charles Scribner's Sons, 1936), 79–80.

8. For a related discussion of prudence, see Joseph Pieper, *The Four Cardinal Virtues* (Notre Dame: University of Notre Dame Press, 1975), 3–42.

9. Maritain, *Man and the State.,* 126.

10. Maritain, *Twilight of Civilization,* trans. Lionel Landry (New York: Sheed & Ward, 1943), 60.

11. See again, Maritain, *Man and the State,* 9–19.

12. Jacques Maritain, "On Authority," *OCM,* vol. 7, 1292. (Both French and English texts appear in this place.)

13. Maritain, *Freedom in the Modern World,* 79.

14. Ibid.

15. Ibid., 31–32.

16. Ibid., 29–30.

17. Ibid., 31.

18. Maritain, "The Conquest of Freedom," 169–170.

19. Ibid., 170.

20. Maritain, *Freedom in the Modern World*, vii.

21. Maritain, "The Conquest of Freedom," 171.

22. Maritain, *Freedom in the Modern World, 28.*

23. Maritain, *Man and the State,* 248–53.

24. See Jacques Maritain, *Primauté du Spirituel,* in *OCM,* vol. 3, 785–988.

25. Maritain, *Man and the State,* 149–50.

26. Ibid., 150.

27. Ibid., 151–52.

28. Ibid., 153.

29. Maritain, *Twilight of Civilization,* 41.

30. Jacques Maritain, *On the Grace and Humanity of Jesus,* trans. Joseph W. Evans (New York: Herder & Herder, 1969), 11.

31. Maritain, *Man and the State.,* 184.

32. Maritain, "The Conquest of Freedom," 177.

8

THE FRIENDSHIP THAT LEADS TO LAW AND JUSTICE

If the person has the opportunity of being treated as a person in social life, and if the unpleasant works which this life imposes can be made easy and happy and even exalting, it is first of all due to the development of law and to institutions of law. But it is also and indispensably due to the development of civic friendship, with the confidence and mutual devotion it implies on the part of those who carry it out. For the true city of human rights, fraternity is not a privilege of nature which flows from the natural goodness of man and which the State need only proclaim. It is the end of a slow and difficult conquest which demands virtue and sacrifice and a perpetual victory of man over himself. In this sense, we can say that the heroic ideal towards which true political emancipation tends is the inauguration of the fraternal city.

—Jacques Maritain, "The Conquest of Freedom"[1]

In . . . friendship the friend, in giving what he has, also gives . . . in a certain manner . . . that which he is, his proper person or subjectivity itself. . . . He gives himself . . . in a hidden way or indirectly, by another thing, . . . by the means and by the intermediary of gifts that hide under these signs the gift of himself and parcel it out. . . . These gifts permit him to reserve his proper self . . . insofar as he has not given absolutely all that he has.

—Jacques Maritain, *"Amour et Amitié"*[2]

I.

At first, we might expect the title of this chapter to be phrased the other way around, namely, that law and justice are what lead to

141

friendship. There is truth to this converse statement; Maritain acknowledges that "law and the instruments of law" can provide a space for relative human happiness and comfort. And yet we have in Maritain an abiding suspicion that something else is required within the natural order even for it to be precisely natural, almost as if that something permits justice and law to be themselves and have their proper effects. Following the discussion on freedom, we suspect we are most free when we are most bound to our friends by something more than justice. Maritain does not first propose to build a worthy human city by natural means, only then to confront the things of the higher orders. It might be nice if it were this way, but human experience does not encourage us to believe that the natural order can do its best work in isolation.

Maritain comes by this suspicion naturally, no doubt. Rationalism, the idea that human reason is open only to itself, stands in contrast to the Thomist idea that reason is open to *whatever is*. "The essence of rationalism consists in making the human reason and its ideological content the measure of what is: truly, it is the extreme of madness, for the human reason has no content but what it has received from external objects."[3] Finite spiritual beings, in fact, find their completion in being open to what is not themselves, both in the order of knowledge and in the order of love. "For the very quality of spiritual beings is that they are not confined within their separate being and can increase intrinsically by the being of what is not themselves."[4] When an "object" to which human beings are open is another personal being, a being that can also know, will, and choose, this ensuing relationship is precisely in the realm of friendship. It represents something that, as Aristotle said, we could not be happy without, even if we possessed all else in the world.

The particular idea of "civic friendship" is found in Aristotle and St. Thomas within the more general discussion of friendship, generally translated as concord (1167a23–b16). It adds something to justice and makes justice work. Civic friendship is based on that agreement of civic life that citizens of one polity have in common. Justice by itself, though noble, is a cold and impersonal virtue. Aristotle and Thomas often indicate, if only by the fact that they devote more time to it, that friendship is more important than justice, without intending to deny the importance of justice. What we find in Maritain is that both justice and friendship are seen in their philosophic purity. Yet they are also seen in their relation to revelation, particularly to charity and to love, that seem somehow necessary for friendship to be itself.

II.

During World War II, a series of short essays that Maritain had written was published under the title, *De la justice politique*. I want to introduce Maritain's reflections of friendship through his discussions in these essays on justice. If justice is not enough to satisfy human living, it is still a beginning whose initial alternative is not friendship but injustice. Maritain begins this essay by observing that a minimum knowledge of history would convince us that "except in the case of certain holy kings, the leaders of peoples are never very much concerned with justice in politics."[5] Evidently, justice and political expediency have been mixed together and confused since the very beginning of human experience (chapter 1). People just do not expect politics to be fair or moral. Christian language speaks of this situation in terms of "The Fall" and of the fact that all men are sinners. The question to ask, however, is whether this conflict of justice and political immorality is normal, something required *"par la nature politique elle-même."*[6] The lesson seems clear: if justice and political expediency are confused, human life will not be able to provide a setting for human happiness. Especially in Christian centuries, Maritain thinks, we find at least an awareness that even if we do act unjustly, we should not do so. Certain rules of right and codes of honor, even when ignored, did serve to limit the evil of blatant injustice. Even the classical Chinese thought politics to be a branch of ethics.[7]

The difference in the 1940s, Maritain thinks, is that "politics believes that it is of its very essence (and thus an obligation) to ignore entirely morality and justice."[8] He points to the contemporary experience surrounding World War II to suggest the dire way in which this division between morality and politics works itself out. He contrasts this position with a remark of Catherine of Siena, who said that the power that preserves cities is rather *"la sainte justice."* He adds that, "The great despots who believe themselves today to be the masters of history are certain that justice in politics is the sure means to lose all; and what is worse is that without having their cynicism, many people, by a smallness of spirit, think lazily what the tyrants think violently."[9] What Maritain first wants to establish, then, is that politics does not have as its primary option the use of evil or injustice as a valid means of political action. Secondly, he wants to show that standards of justice, even when not practiced, are valuable instruments of justice because people still know that they act in a manner in which they should not. Finally, he knows that not only the brutal tyrants of his time, but ordinary politicians and people are willing, because of a kind of moral laziness, to accept as perfectly normal the separation of politics from morality in public life.

Maritain is convinced that it is worth thinking through ideas of justice and injustice precisely to prevent their being confused or identified. That is, the first step leading to things higher than justice is to have the distinction between justice and injustice clearly in mind. Friendship, love, benevolence, or charity, virtues that transcend justice and even can deal with the results of injustice in actual human lives, have to begin with the validity of the distinction between justice and injustice. "The first idea to purify here is that of justice itself. There is a true and a false justice. The tragedy of our epoch is that false justice has aided, by masking and disfiguring true justice, in the triumph of injustice erected into a principle. This [masked injustice] has aided in the diffusion of that universal skepticism in matters of political morality that is one of the plagues of our time."[10] Thus, Maritain implies that false justice can mask itself to look like true justice. If there is a universal skepticism in moral matters, it is related to this confusion caused by the inability of justice to make its presence felt in politics. People thus come to think that what politics is about is merely the replacement of one form of injustice with another.

Maritain distinguishes true and false injustice in a surprising way. He argues that the failure of the League of Nations to prevent World War II, for instance, was a failure in terms of a false idea of justice. With great perception, Maritain recognizes that modern ideology is itself conceived in terms not of injustice but of a purer and more dangerous form of justice. The extremes of injustice in contemporary politics, which he deplores, are the results not of injustice as such but of a false justice that holds itself free to use any means to achieve its purposes. As he writes in a short essay in *The Commonweal* in 1933: "All things begin by the spirit; temporal transformations have their origins in the supratemporal. . . . The first supporters of the October Revolution in Russia were intellectuals who, desiring a 'spiritual revolution,' mistook for the radicalism demanded by the spirit the radicalism of a visible and tangible upheaval masking the old evil of the modern mind."[11] What Maritain means by "false justice" is a kind of abstract formula or theory that is not modified by or related to the concrete reality and variety of existence or to natural law.

Maritain's understanding of justice is based on his idea of the uniqueness and irreplaceability of each human being. In Maritain's thought, it is precisely this aspect of justice that leads naturally to friendship and love.

> True justice, which is, as it were, the sap or strength of creation, is concrete and living; it takes into account the particular cases and circumstances. It treats men as persons holding all in the same essential dignity even with different qualities, not as interchangeable things. It establishes among persons (individual persons or "collective" persons) an equality of proportion. It admits and sanctions the variety of customs; it recognizes the diversity of historical conditions. It does not give to the child the same rights as to the adult, nor to the furious the same liberty and the same powers as to the healthy of spirit.[12]

This description of "true" justice recognizes that justice must include or account for the existential variety of existing human beings in their differing conditions. Contained within Maritain's description of true justice are interwoven Aristotle's general, commutative, and distributive justice. Likewise, equity or *epichia,* the virtue that repairs the failures of general and particular justice, is found because of the incapacity of general rules to reach the singular.

Justice is a moral virtue whereby we render to each his due, with all the ramifications of justice that are commonplace from the classical discussion of justice. The basic difficulty with justice is that it is indifferent to the uniqueness of the person to be dealt with in the exchange of justice. It looks to a relationship under which something is exchanged or due, not to the person who is the object of that relationship. It is clear that even in the classics, friendship is more important than justice, both for individual life and for the city. Moreover, both *eros* and *caritas* have a relation to justice and friendship. Maritain never denigrates the efforts to define and achieve justice, but he likewise never thinks justice is enough. Almost anywhere we go in Maritain, we run into the need to explain why the natural virtues by themselves do not work to reach easily and surely their own noble ends. What is said to be "natural" seems uncommonly difficult to attain by ordinary means.

Part of the reason why injustice seems to be the natural condition of men, then, is the failure of virtue to sustain itself. From the other side, however, from the side of revelation, the reason that justice seems inadequate is that the natural virtues themselves, even when they are achieved in some satisfactory sense, point towards realities that are not fully accounted for by the natural virtues. In his preface to *The Degrees of Knowledge,* Maritain writes to this effect:

> I am in fact convinced that when the philosopher takes as his subject matter the study of anything which bears on the existential conditions of man and his activity as a free personality, . . . he can only proceed scientifically as long as he respects the integrity of his subject and therefore, those realities of a supernatural order which are in fact implied in it. . . . No philosophical pretensions can abrogate the fact that man as we know him is not in a state of pure nature, but of nature at once fallen and redeemed. The first obligation for a philosopher is to recognize what is.[13]

For Maritain, then, it is simply unscientific not to recognize that the difficulty of historic mankind to reach its own natural virtues and just relationships is evidence that human nature is in a situation that does not yield its own full explanation of itself.

III.

Early in Raïssa Maritain's autobiography, *We Have Been Friends Together,* a book that is itself an account of friends—Ernest Psichiari, Charles Péguy, Léon Bloy, among many others—she devotes a few pages to "The Greatest of My Friends," of course, to her husband Jacques Maritain. What she says of their first meeting serves to set the tone for much of what Maritain would say on this most fundamental of human subjects:

> For the first time I had met someone who at the outset inspired me with absolute confidence; someone who from that moment I knew

would never disappoint me; someone with whom I could so readily come to an understanding of all things. Another Someone had preestablished between us, and in spite of such great differences of temperament and of origin, a sovereign harmony.[14]

The many levels of this remark of Raïssa Maritain—of fidelity, of providence, of growth in intelligence, and of the harmony that results from true friendships—are found everywhere in Jacques Maritain's reflections on friendship and its consequences.

Aside from the classical discussions of friendship in Plato, Aristotle, and Cicero, we can find among more recent authors several discussions of love and friendship that serve to relate the way classical and revelational thought on this topic is found in Maritain. The most insightful books on this topic are: C. S. Lewis, *The Four Loves;* Denis de Rougemont, *Love in the Western World;* and Josef Pieper, *About Love.*[15] Maritain himself seems to have come late to this topic. However, his discussion of "Marriage and Happiness," in *Reflections on America,* contains most of the basic points that we find in his treatments of these issues a few years later.[16]

The same general discussion about love and friendship that is found in his late *Approches sans entraves* appears in his *Notebooks.* Maritain, in these passages, is commenting on a footnote of his that appeared in Raïssa Maritain's own *Journal.* Maritain confesses that here he speaks primarily as an old man (the passage was published in 1965; Maritain was born in 1882). "I am merely proposing some refections drawn from the experience of an old man who has seen many things."[17] He further appeals to Aristotle who remarks that old men can have their own valid insights. Maritain is encouraged to expand on a remark he made in a footnote of Raïssa's *Journal,* but he decides to add his more extensive remarks as a chapter to his own *Notebooks* as well as a chapter in *Approaches sans entraves.*

The issue at hand is the nature and relation of love and friendship. No doubt this question is, at least in part, ethical and political as it is treated by the classical philosophical authors. But, following the principle that Maritain elucidates in *The Degrees of Knowledge,* a good deal of the discussion of love and friendship is also found to be incited and deepened by revelational sources. The philosopher cannot simply ignore this source as it sheds light on his own methods, purposes, and unresolved enigmas. Essentially, Maritain wants to relate justice, love, friendship, and charity in one coherent whole, which does not mean that one is absorbed into the other but that each has a proper place and limit.

Maritain's reflections begin with the following comment of Raïssa: "The essence of love is in the communication of oneself, with fullness of joy and delight in the possession of the beloved. The essence of friendship is in desire for the good of one's friend, strong enough to sacrifice oneself for him."[18] This is the statement that gives rise to Maritain's own quiet reflections over the years on the topic of love and friendship. In his original editing of his wife's *Journal,* after her death, Maritain adds the following footnote:

> Raïssa uses here the words *love* and *friendship* in their currently accepted senses, and one that corresponds to very obvious realities of experience. The love, which is *eros* in the realm of passion, is already, though on a lower level, *eros-agapé* in the truly human world: and it is also—I mean in an analogical and absolutely supereminent manner in which all that pertains to the passions is transcended—*eros-agapé,* "mad," boundless love, the love of total mutual self-giving in the spiritual order. (There is, no doubt, a distinction of meaning between *eros* and *agapé,* but the radical opposition people choose to make between them nowadays [Maritain was probably thinking of the Swedish theologian Anders Nygren's *Eros and Agapé*] has no foundation.)
>
> Friendship which is *agapé-philia,* the love of mutual goodwill, in our human world, (for the Greeks it deviated towards *eros-philia*), is also—I mean in an analogical and absolutely supereminent manner—*agapé-philia* in the spiritual order. It is important to understand that what, in opposition to *amour-concupiscentiae,* St. Thomas calls *amour-amicitiae,* comprises as subdivision both senses ("love" and "friendship") here mentioned.[19]

This was the basic passage on which Maritain was urged to elaborate.

Maritain's initial remarks show how he tries to distinguish and relate the various forms of love to one another. The key notion of *agapé* or its Latin equivalent, *caritas,* the love with which God has loved us, the sacrificial love, does not necessarily appear in opposition to *eros* or *amicitia (philia)* but subsumes them. The natural virtue or experience, as it were, leads to something beyond itself but not by excluding what it is. In all this discussion of friendship, Maritain keeps carefully in mind the legitimacy of the natural order, yet also its limitations even to achieve itself by its own powers.

Maritain's essential point is that the highest things do not take place in the order of justice. On the other hand, to speak of the friendship of "unjust people" is not possible except in the sense of some immediate pleasurable or utilitarian purpose that is not sufficient to meet the requirements of the highest form of friendship, that of good people exchanging what they know and have. Friendship and love have this in common: they cannot be commanded by law or cannot be due in justice. They belong rather to a realm of freedom and of delight that calls forth a response that is wholly unnecessary, that is wholly chosen. Maritain is careful to distinguish love and friendship, even though it is proper to talk of friendship as a love and to speak, in the case of marriage, of *eros* and *amicitia* belonging to the same relationship.

Indeed, following the Christian notion of marriage in the context of the classical discussions of friendship, it will be seen as the one relation that most aptly fills the requirements of true friendship. But for this same reason, other forms of genuine friendship do not have the same intensity of living together, self-giving, permanency in life, natural purpose, and delight that is characteristic of this relationship. Moreover, with the proper distinctions, it is this relationship that is seen by Maritain to best describe our relation to God in a love or friendship that was thought impossible in the natural order by Aristotle. The case becomes even more delicate to understand in the case of Maritain and his wife, to whom a mystical vocation seems to have been given. This vocation involves a certain rarely given or even rarely advisable giving up, at a certain point in their lives, of marital relations precisely so that the reality of a total mystical vocation to God can occur.[20]

The discussion of marriage in *Reflections on America,* gives Maritain's thought on this topic:

> Far from having as its essential aim to bring romantic love to perfect fulfillment, marriage has to perform in human hearts quite another work—an infinitely deeper and more mysterious, alchemical operation: I mean to say, it has to *transmute* romantic love, or what existed of it in the beginning, into real and indestructible human love, which does not elude sex, of course, but which grows more and more independent of sex, and even can be, in the highest forms, completely free

from sexual desire and intercourse, because it is essentially spiritual in nature—a complete and irrevocable gift of the one to the other, for the sake of the other.[21]

Maritain sees romantic love, however necessary and fascinating, as itself needing a further completion in a permanent friendship that looks to what he calls the "complete and irrevocable gift" of persons to each other.

Maritain, explaining Raïssa's remarks on love and friendship, maintains that "all disinterested love is gift of self."[22] This "gift of self," the capacity of the spiritual being as spiritual, is what distinguishes all Maritain's thought on this subject from an individualism in which we have a "right" to everything. Love is an act of the will and is always other-oriented. But this other-orientation does not mean that there is no order to love. Aristotle himself had said that we cannot expect to have many real friends. We have neither the time nor opportunity to do so in this life. Indeed, to seek to do so is to betray the possibility of any real friendship of any sort. This does not mean there can be no real and valuable friendships of pleasure or utility. Political friendship itself is of this sort. Maritain's chapter, "American Kindness and Sense of Fellowship" in *Reflections on America,* concerns precisely this matter. In what seems nowadays an unexpected compliment, Maritain writes of America in this regard: "America is the only country in the world where the vital importance of the sense of human fellowship is recognized in such a basic manner by the nation as a whole."[23] But the rarity of human friendship in the deepest sense means that the reality of friendship is something that is multiplied in a different manner. All good men and women should have a few, or in the case of marriage, one, good friendship, rather than everyone being common to everyone. The healthy society of a web of true friendships, each of which is unique and irrepealable according to its nature.

At first, Maritain's distinction between love and friendship will seem unexpected. The gift of the self can take place in different sorts of communication or situations. The ultimate act of friendship is the laying down of one's life for one's friend. Clearly, this is not something due in justice, even though there are cases wherein justice may demand our laying down our lives for another, for someone who is by no means our friend. Again it is to be remembered that for Maritain, love and friendship are reflections of God's love and friendship both within the inner life of God and of God's relation to human persons through the Incarnation. This sense that love and friendship are of God is ultimately why it is proper to speak of "giving one's life for one's friend" in a way that does not imply a sort of blind act of nothingness or despair.

The gift of self, Maritain observes, is manifested in two different manners. The first is the way of friendship. Here what is given is what one has, whether goods, services, knowledge, sympathy, or guidance. This benevolence or devotion to another also includes possibly one's life. But this gift is more indirect than in the case of love. The friend "no doubt gives himself, and really, but *covertly and indirectly, through something else,* in other words through the means and intermediary of the gifts which hide his gift of himself under signs and more or less parcels it out, and which permit him to more or less reserve his own self as long as he has not given absolutely all that he has."[24] If this explanation of friendship at first seems to lessen its importance, it is because Maritain recognizes that the communication or relationship between friends necessitates differing sorts of exchange.

IV.

In his study, *Love in the Western World,* Denis de Rougemont remarks that there is a certain tragic flaw in a concept of human love that seeks to make lovers such as Tristan and Isolde consume each other in erotic love to the exclusion of all else, even unto death. He suggests that the only proper place for erotic love is in fact in marriage.[25] Maritain seems to have referred to this position, indirectly at least, in *Reflections on America:*

> Love is not sex, and that kind of love on which marriage must be founded is not primarily sensual passion, *l'amour passion,* nor romantic love and that philtre by which Tristan and Isolde were divinely intoxicated—but a deeper and more lasting love, into which . . . romantic love must be transmuted, and in which sex and passion are but a prime incentive. This deeper and more lasting love takes root and develops at the properly human and spiritual level where the one accepts to be entrusted with the revelation of, and the care for, all that the other *is*

in his or her deepest human depths, and where the will is fully dedicated to the good and happiness of the one loved.[26]

Maritain's discussion of love thus begins with the idea that all love is self-disinterested, not in the sense that the self has nothing to do with it, but in the sense that the focus of the love is the other as other, as particular. In this sense there is a certain parallel between Maritain's discussion of true justice and true love, in that both must take into consideration the particular differences and distinctions that properly belong to the objects of justice or love. The difference is that the object of justice is a relationship of exchange, whereas the object of love is the other person as such and the gift intended is the mutual gift of the person.

Maritain's statement of the matter is worth considerable attention. What is engaged in love, Maritain begins, is "the spirit." That is, our capacity to comprehend and know ourselves, what we are, is what is directly involved in love.

> The person or subjectivity gives himself *directly, openly, or nakedly,* without hiding himself under the forms of any other gift less absolutely total, he gives himself wholly from the very first in giving or communicating to the beloved, in ecstasizing in him that which he *is.* It is the very person of the lover which is the Gift, simple, unique, and without any possible reserve, made to the beloved. This is why love, especially in the extreme sense in which we are taking it here, is gift-of-self *absolutely and preeminently.*[27]

Thus, Maritain considers that the difference between friendship and love is not that both are not gifts of the self or both in fact disinterested, but that love can be more open. *"The very person of the lover is the Gift."* Friendship is likewise concerned with the good of the friend but admits that the differing kinds of relationships—brotherly, sisterly, fatherly, motherly, and their analogies—will indicate the differing ways in which concern for the good of the friend will be manifest. Friendship will still remain a disinterested love for the good of the other.

"The difference between love and friendship is not necessarily a difference in the *intensity* or the greatness of disinterested love," Maritain continues. "The difference between love and friendship is a difference in the *intrinsic quality* of disinterested love or the *ontological level* at which it constitutes itself in the soul, in other words, in the power which it has of alienating the soul from itself."[28] This passage can be misunderstood. The expression "alienating the soul from itself" has many possible unacceptable overtones. The very ontology that Maritain follows suggests that the person is an absolute; it cannot in reality "be" someone else. If it gives itself, it also remains itself. Further, as Aristotle remarked, we do not want our friend to cease being himself, or to be someone else. If such were the case, friendship would be a sort of despair about the actual person loved. This same ontological permanence is true of ourselves also in any relationship, particularly the highest ones.

Friendship and love in their disinterested concern for the other, in their giving directly or indirectly to the other what we are, do not imply that either we or the friend ceases to be. The point Maritain is trying to make in using the expression of the soul "alienating itself" is, it seems, an effort to separate any sort of disinterested love from a reserve of selfishness in which the other is somehow an object of use or pleasure alone. What the notion of friendship adds to this love, which Maritain will call in a perhaps infelicitous phrase, though one he vigorously defends, *"amour fou"* or in the English translations "mad, boundless love," is the notion of mutuality. Love and friendship, to be complete, always imply precisely a mutual gift.

Maritain clarifies what he means by the "alienation" remark in referring indirectly to the point de Rougemont made above about the relation of *eros* and marriage.

This love in which the very person of each gives itself to the other in all truth and reality is, in the order of the ontological perfections of nature, the summit of love between Man and Woman. Then the lover truly gives himself to his beloved, and she truly gives herself to him, *as to his or her Whole,* in other words, ecstasizes in her or in him, making himself or herself—although remaining ontologically a person—a part which no longer exists except through and in this Whole which is his or her Whole. This extreme love is *amour fou* (mad, boundless love); and such a name properly befits it, because it accomplishes (in the special order or, if you will, in the magic and spiritual "superexistence" of love) precisely that which is itself impossible and insane in the order of mere existence or simply of being, in which each person continues to be a whole and cannot become a mere part of another whole. This is the proper paradox of love: it requires on the one hand the ontologically indestructible duality of persons, and on the other hand it demands, and *in its own way,* accomplishes the unbroken unity, the actually consummated unity of these two persons.[29]

This passage recalls Maritain's distinction between the individual and the person wherein the person, as such, is a whole and transcends in this ontological capacity and permanency the whole of the relational social order because it is directed to the knowledge and boundless love of other "wholes," including God.

Can the love of another finite person interfere with our love for God, or is it precisely a way to God, a reflection on the finite side of God's love? Maritain is remarkably perceptive on this question. First of all, he does not think that if the possibility of love and friendship exists in the first place, as seems to be the case in human experience, it can be explained in terms of itself. It seems to exist at the peak of human order, that to which all other relationships are somehow ordained, at least symbolically, without ceasing to be themselves. Maritain has taken the first step in explaining what is at issue when he describes love and friendship themselves as they are in their purity. Clearly, they are the most important things in human life, not merely in making its reality an exchange of wholes that are selves giving disinterestedly to one another what is to their good, but in providing a way for the highest things to be freely exchanged. Moreover, it seems clear that man does not himself "create" or "invent" what love and friendship are about. Rather, he discovers them and finds not only that this is what he wants, but that most of his disorders can be reduced to loving wrongly or to betraying his friends.

In the natural order, Maritain sees that, at its best, "mad, boundless love" is "an ontological perfection of nature." And, he reminds us, that as such "it is available to the best and to the worst." But, if it is available morally "to the worst," does not this somehow corrupt the very idea of love and friendship? Human history has recognized that in love and friendship there are both "splendor" and "ambiguity." Why is this? It is because the proper object of love or friendship is "a created object." This means that "he who loves with a mad, boundless love gives himself totally; the *object* of his love is a limited, fragile, and mortal creature." The logic of the analysis requires us to acknowledge that such is the status of any human person who is loved. As such, this is the way it must be. Men are not gods. But, in revelational teaching at least, they are given God's love as also theirs.

Maritain adds a patient observation about the fallen human condition:

> It would be to ignore the grandeurs of our nature to believe that this creature loved with mad, boundless love *necessarily* becomes an idol for the lover, and it is *necessarily* loved by him more than God. But it would be to ignore the miseries of our nature to believe that she *cannot* be loved more than God by him who loves her with mad, boundless love, and *cannot* become an idol for him. Human mad, boundless love can radiate within a life morally upright and submissive to the order of charity. It can likewise radiate (and not only outside marriage, but in the state of marriage also) within a life of sin.[30]

Maritain is thus quite aware that the highest things are also potentially the most dangerous things. The crucial issue about love and friendship is, thus, not the emotion itself, the feeling of being outside of oneself and devoted totally to another, but rather the worthiness and legitimacy of the object of our love itself and the grounds on which we are to pursue it, be that love or friendship.

V.

Maritain's reflection of the love of God is of great beauty. Maritain addresses his own revelational solution to the classical problem, already appearing in Aristotle, of whether we can be friends with God. The ancients thought divine friendship to be impossible. In suggesting that human beings can have a boundless love for God that is disinterested and involves a gift of the self, Maritain does not intend to imply any sort of pantheism or absorption of the creature into God. The Whole that is God and the whole that is the unique person remain. What he maintains is that love and friendship exist in the center of the Trinitarian existence of God. This is why in some finite sense they can exist in the human level, since human beings are created in God's precise image. The essence of friendship in a mutual giving and receiving, however, does remain and defines the central relationship.

"In God *friendship* and *love* are only two aspects of one and the same infinitely perfect disinterested love, which is the transcendent God Himself—two aspects which we distinguish according to our human mode of conceiving and by analogy with that which appears in human disinterested love, all of whose qualities and perfections are supereminently contained in their uncreated Exemplar," Maritain thus explains the reasons why the examination of human love pertains to the understanding of divine love, its origin.[31] That which is united in its origin may be separated in the natural order wherein the highest forms of love and affection can and sometimes are joined together in a single love. "In the creature (and to consider things in their natural order) *friendship* and *love* between two human beings are two different kinds of disinterested love (and, in *love*—because on this wholly human plane where the differences of the sexes enter into play, the flesh is also interested—the love of covetousness is joined to disinterested love)."[32]

Maritain explains that in her passage on love and friendship, what Raïssa primarily had in mind was not human love "but the love of God for man (uncreated Love) and of the love of man for God (love of charity)."[33] Thus when it comes to charity, to the grace by which we can love God and one another in God, "friendship and love (mad, boundless love) are clearly not two distinct species, they are two different degrees (not necessarily in intensity, but as to the power of alienating the soul from itself)—and, at least in a certain sense—inseparable—of one and the same disinterested love."[34] Maritain is at pains to emphasize that this love for God is first a love of God and not the self. "It is not for itself, it is *for* God first loved that the soul wishes God to itself."[35]

God has no need of anything but Himself. To those creatures capable of knowing and loving God through His own grace, what is given to them is, after the manner of His grace, not just themselves in creation, but Himself as their end. If we are commanded to love God, it is not because God is lacking something, particularly our own love. This would make God dependent on creatures and in principle reduce love to need. The whole point of Maritain's discussion is that love and friendships are not, properly speaking, "needs" but "gifts." Here Maritain cites the famous sentence from Aquinas—*"Deus suam gloriam non quaerit propter se, sed propter nos"* (II-II, 132. 1, ad 1), that is, God does not seek His glory for Himself but for us.[36] Maritain concludes with a further reflection of Raïssa, who remarks that even uncreated Love "remains love and consequently is not satisfied unless another expansion responds to its expansion and makes union possible."[37]

Maritain is aware of the profundity that exists in any consideration of the relationship between friendship and justice. Both are considered in their natural terms, and both are seen in relation to each other. Moreover, there are things about both justice and friendship that seem insolvable on a philosophical level. Maritain's reflections on those passages in his wife's *Journal* are his way to complete his discussion of justice, friendship, and love as these realities reach into and beyond themselves. If friendship leads to justice, to the constant habit of returning what is due, it also leads to the disinterested gift of oneself in a mutual exchange of life, fidelity, and wisdom. A city is not complete if it is only just. It is not complete if it is not composed of a myriad of active friendships and loves that have their vigor and reality beyond the city.

Maritain realizes that a society of human beings would have to include an ability to forgive, to account for the failures of justice and love.

> For the gospel law of mutual forgiveness expresses, I believe, a fundamental requirement which is valid not only in the supernatural order, but in the terrestrial and temporal order as well, and for basically natural societies like domestic society and even political society. Each one, in other words, may then become really dedicated to the good and salvation of the other.[38]

No order of justice or friendship can be complete without some fundamental way to live with human failures to be just or loving. The friendship that leads to justice is first based on fidelity, a mutual gift, but includes the capacity to forgive. For Maritain, the tractates on justice and the tractates on friendship are interwoven with each other and with, in addition, the tractates on love, charity, and forgiveness. To repeat in conclusion what was cited in the beginning from *The Conquest of Freedom:* "The heroic ideal towards which true political emancipation tends is the inauguration of the fraternal city."

NOTES

1. Jacques Maritain, "The Conquest of Freedom," *The Education of Man: The Educational Philosophy of Jacques Maritain,* ed. Donald and Idella Gallagher (Garden City: N. Y.: Doubleday, 1962), 172–73.

2. Jacques Maritain, *"Amour et Amitié," Approches sans entraves, OCM,* vol. 13, 703.

3. Jacques Maritain, *The Three Reformers: Luther—Descartes—Rousseau* (New York: Charles Scribner's Sons, 1970), 85.

4. Ibid., 47.

5. Jacques Maritain, *De la justice politique, OCM,* vol. 7, 321.

6. "By the nature of politics itself." Ibid.

7. Ibid., 322–23.

8. Ibid., 322.

9. Ibid., 323.

10. Ibid., 323–24.

11. Jacques Maritain, "A Note on the Bourgeois World," *The Commonweal,* 18 (2 June 1933): 120.

12. Ibid., 324.

13. Jacques Maritain, *The Degrees of Knowledge,* trans. from the 2d rev. French ed. by Bernard Wall and Margot Adamson (New York: Charles Scribner's Sons, 1938), xii. The University of Notre Dame Press has issued its translation of this volume from the new French *Opera Omnia.*

14. Raïssa Maritain, *We Have Been Friends Together,* trans. Julie Kernan (New York: Longmans, Green and Co., 1943), 41–42.

15. C. S. Lewis, *The Four Loves* (New York: Harcourt, 1971); Denis de Rougemont, *Love in the Western World,* trans. Montgomery Belgion (New York: Schocken, 1967); Josef Pieper, *About Love,* trans. Richard and Clara Winston (Chicago: Franciscan Herald, 1974). See also Gilbert C. Mailaender, *Friendship: A Study in Theological Ethics* (Notre Dame: University of Notre Dame Press, 1981); Martin C. D'Arcy, *The Mind of Heart and Love* (New York: Holt, 1947). See also James V. Schall, "Aristotle on Friendship," *The Classical Bulletin 65,* nos. 3 and 4 (1989), 83–88; "Unknown to the Ancients: God and Friendship," *What Is God Like?* (Collegeville, Minn.: Michael Glazier/Liturgical Press, 1992), 140–70.

16. See Maritain, *"Amour et Amitié," OCM,* vol. 13, 701–64. Maritain, *Reflections on America* (New York: Charles Scribner's Sons, 1958), 137–46.

17. Jacques Maritain, *Notebooks,* trans. Joseph W. Evans (Albany, N.Y.: Magi Books, 1984), 219.

18. Raïssa Maritain, *Journal,* ed. Jacques Maritain (Albany, N. Y.: Magi Books, 1974), Entry for Easter Sunday, 20 April 1924, 162.

19. Jacques Maritain, n. 2, ibid.

20. Maritain's analysis of the theological and philosophical reasons for this way of life is best explained in his own words in his *Notebooks,* ibid., 248–51.

21. Maritain, *Reflections on America,* 140.

22. Maritain, *Notebooks,* 221.

23. Maritain, *Reflections on America*, 72.

24. Ibid., 221.

25. de Rougemont, *op. cit.*, 299–323.

26. Maritain, *Reflections on America*, 143.

27. Maritain, *Notebooks*, 221.

28. Ibid., 222.

29. Ibid., 223–24. "It is through renouncement of such self-realization that real loves lead man and woman to a superior form of freedom and happiness, which is purified, and spiritual in nature, and in which the personality of each one is enlarged and uplifted, each one being henceforth primarily centered *in the other,* or having his or her dearest self *in the other.*" Maritain, *Reflections on America*, 144.

30. Maritain, *Notebooks*, 224. The word "mad" as a translation of the French *"fou"* may not be altogether the best word. The idea has a long tradition going back to the Greek idea where it means being out of oneself, or completely absorbed, not in the sense of insane but in the sense of delight and joy.

31. Ibid., 222.

32. Ibid.

33. Ibid., 226.

34. Ibid.

35. Ibid.

36. Ibid., 227.

37. Ibid.

38. Jacques Maritain, *Reflections on America*, 141.

9

MARITAIN ON THE ENIGMA AND INTELLIGIBILITY OF EVIL

We know that concerning the metaphysics of evil, St. Thomas represented and deepened the great Augustinian themes: evil is neither an essence, nor a nature, nor a form, nor a being; evil is an absence of being; it is not a simple absence or negation, but a *privation*: the privation of a good that ought to exist in a thing.

—Jacques Maritain, *De Bergson à Thomas D'Aquin*[1]

The sin of the angel does not presuppose either ignorance or error in the functioning of the intellect as such. His sin thereby reveals to us the frightening and, as it were, infinite power proper to free will. That will can choose evil in full light, by a purely voluntary act, and without the intellect's being victim of any previous error. . . . The sin of the angel, consequently, has as its matter or object something (for example, the love of his own natural perfection) which is in itself morally good and worthy of the angelic nature; and his sin consists in doing beyond due measure something which is in itself good.

—Jacques Maritain, *The Sin of the Angel*[2]

I.

Without denying its good, the monstrous moral evils experienced in the twentieth century—the two great wars, the many "minor" wars, the totalitarian regimes, death camps, persecutions, the rise of a culture of death—leave little choice but to acknowledge their dire presence and to attempt some account of their cause. The question here is not to give another account of the particulars of these events

161

but to reflect on the deeper question of what evil means and how it is caused.

The transition from a chapter on love and friendship to a chapter on evil might, at first, seem unexpected, if not downright odd. However, a certain logic stands behind such a treatment. From Plato and Aristotle, we have learned that the highest theme of political philosophy is not justice but contemplation, love, and friendship. To discuss friendship itself, we must discuss how it relates to justice and duty. The loss of friendship is often more serious than the violation of justice. If there is no greater love than to lay down one's life for one's friend, so there is no greater violation than to betray one's friend. What links friendship and love with evil is that each is rooted in the same faculty or power of will.

This power of the free will fascinated Maritain. Just as there can be no friendship, even friendship with God, without freedom, so there can be no evil, particularly moral evil, without freedom. What is wrongly chosen needs to be located in a responsible agent to identify how and where the evil in question came about, how and where we can assign praise or blame. Love, to be love, has to be someone's love. Evil, to be evil, has to be someone's evil. If love is coerced or imposed on someone, it is not love; evil that is forced is not moral evil. Moreover, free will is not its own object. The will must always be directed to something other than itself, to some good that it knows to be good. Choice itself is not an object of free will. Its object is always something definite besides the will itself.

In his famous lecture, *St. Thomas and the Problem of Evil,* Maritain discusses the difference between a purely philosophical understanding of evil, something that he found in the German philosopher Leibniz (1646–1716), and a philosophical understanding of evil that is pursued in the light of revelation, an understanding that takes up where the pure philosophic analysis leaves off. St. Thomas had argued that the world, itself not necessary or self-caused, is created in the particular form in which it appears as a product of the divine art in which all the parts are themselves; that is, each is a genuinely distinct being. As such, in being itself, each being is related to the whole. The whole is an order. This artistic creation that came to exist in fact imitated, in a finite way, the divine being or goodness. The world and all in it, though finite, are, as such, good. The problem of evil is to be worked out against the background of a God and a world that are good.

This artistic result, the world or cosmos, means that all the ways whereby God might be imitated are present in creation. The whole creation, with all its parts, is necessary to reflect, but not equal, the divine grandeur. Within this creation is the possibility, indeed the centrality, of particular beings who possess intellect and freedom. These rational beings exist as wholes or persons, for their own sakes. By their nature, angelic or human, these free beings have a possible natural end, a happiness that is due to them by virtue of what they are. But this natural end is not immediately the divine goodness or any direct personal relation with it, however the divine goodness exists in itself. Human and angelic beings, in other words, are not gods, but they exist and are worthy of existence.

Aquinas holds, however, that even though such a natural creation as described might have been possible, it did *not* happen in the order of history in which we exist. Rather, what happened was that, from the very beginning, God intended that the free and rational creatures be offered, not simply imposed upon or given, an end or happiness higher than that which is due to them by virtue of what they are in themselves. This offer puts every rational creature in a different position from that in which he would have been had this offer not been given to him. The completion of every rational being, human or angelic, now requires that being to choose or reject its elevated end. In other words, no actually existing rational creature can ever find a happiness that will satisfy him unless it is the divine being itself for which each rational being is in fact specifically created. The real drama in the universe has to do with how each rational and free being thinks and chooses about this proffered end or destiny as manifested in each particular choice of his life. Maritain's reflections about angels and men consider how this free choice comes about and what its characteristics and consequences are. For Maritain, freedom always has consequences, good or bad, following the exercise of free will.

However, many free creatures, because they can fail, will fail; that is, they will choose some end other than what has been offered to them as the completion of their being. No finite creature as such can, by virtue of its own powers alone, be guaranteed the gift of eternal life. All it can be guaranteed is the power and practice of its freedom to choose or reject such a gift within the confines of its own free life. Jacques Maritain spends considerable scholarly effort to establish the intellectual creature's freedom and in what it consists because he sees here the foundation of its dignity and the worthiness of its life, including its life with God. Thomas Aquinas understood this relationship to God to be a "friendship." The other side of this same freedom, which cannot not exist if rational creatures are to exist at all, is that the same creature by the same powers can choose to reject what does not originate in itself. It has the power to reject what is not caused to exist by virtue of its own choices. Implicitly, the creature, in all its actions, can choose for itself absolute autonomy.

The perfection of the universe, consequently, requires that there be within it creatures that can in principle fail. The very good of some natural creatures, moreover, cannot exist without the destruction of others. The lion exists by the destruction of the hart, even though the existence of both the lion and the hart is an ordered good.[3] In logic, the only way for God to have chosen in such a way that there was no possible evil, no animals eating other animals, would have been for Him not to have created anything at all. This latter possibility—that, in the name of the good, it is best that there be nothing but God—turns out, on reflection, to be a different good by contrast to the universe that is in fact created wherein beings other than God also exist and act. God does not become more or less good if there is or is not a creation of what is not Himself. Thus, following St. Augustine, if God is going to have certain goods, the good in particular of free beings, as well as the good of nonrational beings, He must *permit*—a carefully chosen word—evil in some circumstances, but only if from this "permitted" evil He can bring forth a greater good.[4] This "greater good" is the key overarching principle in thinking about why evil might be found amidst otherwise good but finite beings, including human, free beings.

II.

Maritain next considers evil in Leibniz's philosophical theodicy and contrasts it with St. Thomas's analysis. Maritain's presentation is of interest here because, as it turns out, it is on the issue of friendship and its implications that the whole matter of the existence of evil hinges. Evil, that is, is not overcome by evil but by suffering evil without doing it, a position that already has intimations in the trial of Socrates. Yet a philosopher can read all of Aquinas's arguments to conclude that evil exists in the world because it is necessary for the good of the whole, not merely permitted. What follows from this? "A philosopher like Leibniz," Maritain observes, "adopts the truths contained in the text from St. Thomas I have just read, in a merely philosophical sense; and as a satisfactory answer given by pure philosophy, this philosopher, then, will tell us it is a good thing for a mother to bewail the death of her child, because the machine of the world required it in order to be more perfect."[5]

Maritain indicates what is at stake here, that is, the natural worth yet simultaneous insufficiency of pure philosophy to reach to the essence of the problem. "Explain this Leibnizian position to the mother in question, tell her this thing was necessary in order that every degree of being should be filled, and she will answer that she cares not a whit for the machine of the world—let them give her back her child!"[6] To this motherly protest, Maritain simply agrees that she, not the philosopher, is right, even though what the philosopher says, in one sense, is true. The philosophic answer, as it stands, is not adequate, even though the principle at stake, that all the grades of being ought to be manifest and operative in the world in relation to one another, is valid. Does this philosophic conclusion mean that there is no answer to the mother's grief?

To the mother's agony, Maritain simply remarks that "such questions are not resolved by the machine of the world but in the darkness of faith, and by the cross of Jesus."[7] And while this is a revelational answer, Maritain understands that this revelational answer incites further philosophic deepening about the nature of evil itself. The mother's child, be it noted, could have died because of either an ontological evil (a tree fell on it) or a moral evil (someone shot it). Evil requires a proper response to it consistent with the sort of free beings that we actually are. The mother must know that ultimately her child reached the end for which he was created. Evil requires, in other words, a free response or rejection consonant with the freedom that caused it in the first place.

Maritain argues that friendship and evil are related. Both are concerned with a freedom that is "fallibly" free; that is, a freedom that may, but need not, choose the real good that is offered to it.

The creature's liability to sin is thus the price paid for the outpouring of creative Goodness, which in order to *give itself personally* to the extent that it transforms into itself something other than itself, must be *freely loved with friendship's love and communion,* and which to be freely loved with friendship's love and communion must create *free* creatures, and which in order to create them free must create them *fallibly* free. Without fallible freedom there can be no created freedom; without created freedom there can be no love in mutual friendship between God and creature; without love in mutual friendship between God and creature, there can be no supernatural transformation of the creature into God, no entering of the creature into the joy of his Lord. Sin—evil—is the price of glory.[8]

What this remarkable passage suggests from a political point of view, of course, is that there is no "external" cure to the problem of evil; its possibility will always recur in every regime because its possibility will occur in every personal free will, wherever found.

Thus, the acceptance or rejection of what is good always lies within the being that is free. It cannot be eradicated until the being has chosen its final good, a finality generally associated with death. In human life, evil can happen wherever freedom is present. Nothing can change that situation. But the reason why evil is possible in the world, looking at it from the divine viewpoint, is not that it be chosen for some necessary order, but that something greater is possible, namely friendship with other personal realities, including God, without which freedom, there can be no love or friendship. To have the latter possibility, the possibility of evil is necessary. When evil happens, we are to respond to it, not with evil, but with good.

III.

The student of political philosophy often lacks a clear and straight-forward discussion of evil as this often perplexing topic has been considered in Western philosophic tradition. Maritain himself recalls that the famous French socialist and sociologist, Georges Sorel, held that the "crucial work of the philosophers, in the new age into which we are entering, would consist in recasting and penetrating more deeply into the problem of evil."[9] Maritain adds that if we are going to understand the reality of the twentieth (or any other) century we cannot avoid "a theory of evil." All students need some reflection on what evil might be, how it comes about, what its consequences are.

At some point, politics presupposes metaphysics, the study of the reality of *what is,* and will not be able to explain itself to itself without it. The existence and mystery of evil is broader than a political consideration. But politics as we know it cannot be properly understood without some effort to come to intellectual terms with evil. The serious consideration of evil as an intellectual and moral problem is something incumbent on every human being, but something particularly important to students seeking to know the dimensions of what they must deal with, including the problem of evil as it exists in themselves. While no one, therefore, can pretend easily or definitively to "solve" the problem of evil in a chapter or essay, or even within a lifetime, still the main elements in the consideration of what evil is or is not and what causes it are strikingly pertinent to political philosophy.

Certain positions in the revelational tradition have become key elements in understanding what we mean by evil. In themselves, they cause us to think. One does not have to be a "believer" to understand the significance of these considerations. No one has to be a Jew or Christian to understand the pertinence of the account of "The Fall" in the Book of Genesis, wherein, in a world created specifically "good," disorder and evil come through the workings of the free will in angelic and rational beings, also themselves good. Nor does one have to be a philosopher of the caliber of Thomas Aquinas to recognize, as he did, that the major argument against the existence of God is the perplexity caused by the "reality" of evil. And when we ask, "What sort of a 'reality' is evil, anyhow?" we reckon with the heritage of Plato, Augustine, and Aquinas that evil is not, as such, a "being," a "thing," but rather a lack of something that ought to be in a good being but is not. All discussion of evil takes place against the background of a good God "allowing," not causing, evil things to happen to rational beings with free will.

Maritain's central discussion of evil is lucid and penetrating. Few in the twentieth century can match the clarity and directness of his reflections on this enigmatic topic. Maritain acknowledges that he is, in this question, a student of Thomas Aquinas:

> But now, let us consider the world of freedom, the world of free acts.
> In that case, what is the cause of [the] evil of action? What, in the

order of metaphysical connections, is it that causes free action to be bad, or, if I may be allowed to express it this way, bitten by nothingness? This is a particularly difficult problem. I believe St. Thomas is the only thinker who has considered it in all its difficulty, and I think the solution he proposes is one of the most original of his philosophical discoveries.[10]

Evil is an abiding and serious problem for every person and in every philosophical, theological, or political system. It is not simply relative to a culture. Maritain sees that a complete philosophy gives considerable attention to the matter of evil.

IV.

Maritain divides his consideration of evil into two related issues. The first wants to know whether there is any meaning to the existence of evil in the world. The second reflection wants to know what causes evil when free will is engaged.[11] The first question is discussed under the heading of "ontological" evil; the second is usually called "moral" evil. Both indicate something is lacking. Maritain does not think that a world in which there is only "ontological" evil could exist. Ontological evil—pain, suffering, and loss—exists as background for the kind of finite, free beings we are. In other words, if we understand why human beings as persons exist, we will understand why a world in which they can exist has come to be. Maritain is not asking here a question about evolution or temporal sequence, but about the purpose of things in their very being.

As noted in the first passage at the head of this chapter, Maritain associates himself with St. Augustine in a famous consideration about evil that goes back in part to Plato. Thus, evil is not a thing, either physical or spiritual, that exists by itself, with its own relative autonomy. Pure evil is not something we will ever have to worry about walking into in the streets at night, though we might have to worry about falling into manholes or being accosted by robbers. Nor is there a god of Good and a god of Evil standing in opposition to each other as two warring beings. This theory is traditionally called Manicheanism wherein the god of Good creates spirit and the god of Evil creates matter. This Manicheanism has in fact taken many forms in the history of philosophy. At bottom, as Augustine tells us in his *Confessions,* it is an attempt to free ourselves from responsibility for our own evil choices by holding, contrary to fact, that matter, not a choice of the will, is the locus of evil. No physical or spiritual thing, as a being, is evil. How then do we deal with what is called evil?

The first thing to clarify is what we do and do not mean when we say that evil "exists." Strictly speaking, only things, which are good, exist. But evil is not an "illusion." We cannot simply deny its existence and make it go away.[12] Maritain makes two points. When something that ought to be present is lacking, real consequences follow that would not have happened were the absent good present. Secondly, the power of evil is and can only be effective through the remaining good that bears what is lacking. The coward who runs away from battle may still do some other good because he continues to exist. Maritain's explication of these points is worth considerable reflection:

> Evil does exist in things; it is terribly present in them. Evil is real, it actually exists like a wound or mutilation of the being; evil is there in all reality whenever a thing—which, insofar as it is, and has being, is good—is deprived of some being or some good it should have. Thus, evil exists *in good,* that is, the bearer of evil is good, insofar as it is being. And evil works *through good,* since evil, being in itself a privation or non-being, has no causality of its own. Evil is therefore efficacious not by itself but through the good it wounds and preys upon as a parasite, efficacious through a good that is wanting or deflected, and whose action is to that extent vitiated. What is thus the power of evil? It is the very power of the good that evil wounds and preys upon.[13]

Thus, evil as such cannot totally prevent good from appearing in its very midst. An evil action can in a new way occasion a new development of good. This presence of evil as a parasite on the good explains why it is never right to despair because of the existence of evil, no matter how awful. This lack of existence called evil always depends on what is good, a good whose activity continues in spite of that which is lacking in it.

If we compare ontological evil and moral evil, it is moral evil that is by far the more serious problem. Moral evil "affects man's will and his liberty, making him evil himself and offending to the Principle of his being."[14] Moral evil can have direct effects when it is chosen. The initial temptation is to say that it should be counteracted in kind, that is, evil with evil. But if evil lies in a free will, it is only the same free will that can ultimately counteract it. But what about one's reaction to being the object of someone else's evil action, the problem of rights and duties? Maritain is not opposed, as we have seen, to resisting attacks of evil men by appropriate means. Good and innocent persons do suffer because of the evil activities of others. Thus, we can contrast the evil that exists in the will of the evildoer with the attitude of the person who suffers from this same action. Hence the classical questions that arise already in Plato: Is it better to do evil or to suffer it? And how do I repair my evil deeds? Maritain answers as Socrates did; namely, (1) it is better to suffer evil than to do it, and (2) "it is better to be punished than to be guilty."[15] We have touched on this latter point earlier, but here suffice it to suggest why, contrary to what we might at first expect, punishment is, in Maritain's view, better than guilt. To be guilty of an action means that the action is in fact caused by us. We have done wrong to someone else. Our being is now formed by our choice.

Punishment, especially punishment undergone willingly, on the other hand, is a sign to ourselves and to others that we, who caused the disorder, we who sinned and thus were guilty in the first place, now recognize, with our own intelligence, that what we did, that is, the fact that we did not put into our actions the order or rule that should govern them, hurt others, and distorted our own souls. The acceptance of punishment is, in this sense, neither morbid nor irrational, but the open acknowledgement that we irresponsibly broke the rule of reason. By acknowledging our guilt and accepting punishment, we restore the order of reason that ought to exist in our actions and through which we are properly related to others. However, even with sorrow or punishment, the suffering that we caused others continues to be present in the world. The murdered son's mother continues to grieve. Thus, we can respond to evil by suffering it and not doing it. But we can also respond to it by ourselves, as objects of someone else's evil act, doing a further evil. Therefore, we perpetuate it, even after the original cause may have suffered punishment.

These latter remarks help to illuminate Maritain's philosophy of actual history that sees historical reality to be composed of a long series of intertwined good and evil acts, each producing its own results. "The whole spectacle of things," he writes, "is that of a procession of things good, of a procession of goods, wounded by nonbeing and producing by their activity an indefinite—increasing accumulation of being and of good, in which that same activity also carries the indefinitely-growing wound—as long as the world exists—of non-being and of evil."[16] Such a penetrating passage explains why Maritain is basically hopeful about the good but also realistic about the on-going results of evil even within otherwise good and noble things.[17]

V.

The possibility of evil in the form that we know it is permitted because, without this permission, what God had in mind in creating beings other than Himself in the first place could not be possible. God, as it were, was in a dilemma: either (1) no world, hence no evil; or (2) a natural world with ontological evil and a natural but less fitting end; or (3) a supernatural world that could be rejected by the free creature but whose initial offer is the highest possible good that could come to any being less than God. Again, the link between evil and love or friendship is at the point of freedom. In examining creation itself and the beings in it, we see that matter is not evil. All beings as such, in time, are good. Each of these things, including human persons, is in some sense finite, not infinite. It could not be otherwise, lest God be creating Himself over and over again, a contradiction.

What concerns Maritain here is to establish that evil, in itself, is a kind of nothingness, of nonbeing. God creates only reality, being, and being is good. No thing is evil. And as we indicated in the second citation at the head of this chapter, Maritain does not think that either ignorance or error, as such, are the immediate causes of evil. The immediate cause is that we choose without, at the same instant, taking into consideration all that ought to be looked at in producing our actions. Anything less than God can and often will fall into error or be ignorant. This is simply what it means to be a limited being. But since man as a work of divine art is part of the world that is good, the existence and faculties of man that make him to be what he is, including his will, cannot as such be anything other than good. Yet the faculty or power of will, of freedom, can be looked upon not just as a power, in which case it is good, but as a power designed to do something. In this latter sense, Maritain thinks, in a highly perceptive remark, that the "universe of freedom" presupposes "the world of nature, but is quite distinct from it."[18] In what does this distinction consist?

Following St. Thomas, Maritain writes, "the free act is not a part of *this world,* but of an original universe of its own, the universe of freedom."[19] As a created being, man is involved in the interrelation of things. Trees can fall on him through the normal workings of wind and snow. But man is also not merely another part of the world, but a person, a whole, with a spiritual soul and powers that stand outside of time.[20] In the case of ontological evil, say, the wind blowing the tree over on us, we understand that the wind is merely doing what wind does. But in the world of persons with an acting freedom that does not exist directly in time, something more ominous results. "The sin of man is the sin of a person, the disaster of a universe and a wounding of God (not as far as God's being is concerned but as concerns His love.)"[21] Notice what is said here. Consistent with his whole approach to evil and love, Maritain explains that, since the purpose of creation is to make possible an offer of friendship between man and God, God can paradoxically be "wounded," not in any physical sense, but in the way we wound those who are our friends by not being honorable or truthful in our relationships to them. In this sense, God can be said to be vulnerable.

In this arena of timelessness in which freedom exists and in this rational awareness of the mystery of suffering found in wholes who are persons, suffering caused by both moral and ontological evil, Maritain finds the most profound reason why revelation is offered to human beings in the particular way it is, through suffering. To the objection that God cannot exist because of evil, Maritain responds that God too suffers from our evils. Understanding the order of nature as a work of art or a complete order with all the grades of being is not sufficient to explain the permission of the actual sufferings that arise from evil actions in this world. "God, in actual fact," Maritain writes, "would not have made nature if he had not destined it to grace."[22] Ultimately, this destiny to grace means that the mystery of suffering and evil is to be resolved at the level of the purpose of the highest cause of evil and suffering, which lies in free will. Thus, if there is a purpose for a free will that cannot as such negate the will's possibility of choosing evil, then it seems that the possibility of freely choosing the highest good is what makes it possible to permit any evil to exist in order to achieve the purpose of creation in the first place. The consequences of evil both in suffering and death are in fact the context and purpose of the Redemption.

Maritain puts the issue in this way:

> The person asks,—from a desire which is "conditional" and "ineffi-cacious," but real and natural—to see the first cause of its essence, it asks to be *free without being able to sin,* it asks that it should not suffer, should not die. In the state of pure nature, these aspirations of the person would have remained forever unsatisfied; grace causes us to reach up toward a final state where these aspirations will be super-abundantly satisfied by a gift which surpasses all nature, being a formal participation in the Deity.[23]

Thus, it is not a question of justice or necessity that such an elevated purpose be given to the rational, free being. Rather it is "fitting" be-cause it corresponds with the conditions in which man finds himself in his own natural powers, that is, incapable of really knowing the life of the highest things.

Thus, "the motive of the Incarnation is Redemption; it is to redeem sinful man. . . . Freedom that can err was created for the love of charity between God and creature."[24] The reason for this redemptive purpose is because it is the only response to evil that allows for a free creature to be open to God—"a free creature, naturally impeccable, would be a squared circle."[25] Maritain's thinking here is very tight. He does not say that God is pure will and could have made a free creature who, by its own powers, could not err or sin. "These necessities themselves depend on His very essence as His intelligence sees it, seeing at the same time all those ways in which that very essence can be participated in."[26] Essen-tially, Maritain holds that evil is possible because without its possibility, the purpose of the actual universe as intended by God could not be possible. That is, unless friendship of the free creature with God could be freely and mutually chosen, even though this possibility requires grace, there would have been no universe.

In the universe that is created, where the free creature can possibly reject the destiny offered to it by God, evil and suffering result from actions of the free creature. The Redemption, the Cross, is God's way of responding to chosen evil and innocent suffering, a response that necessarily leaves the creature free but gives it an example of what the consequences are of choosing evil. The consequences of a free creature's rejecting this graced offer are also in the order of freedom and timelessness, in a world in which the creature remains stable in its choice of itself. This condition is generally known as Hell, itself the result not directly of God's punishment but of the creature's choice of itself and what this choice involves, the choice to make itself the center of reality.

VI.

Granted this ontological and theological aspect of the consideration of evil, Maritain's second task is "the cause of evil." This cause is free will. Maritain shows how the will operates when it chooses what we designate as evil in its action. He wants to establish that, while acknowledging that the will as a faculty is good, nevertheless, under the power of the person using it, it places by its own causality some action in the world that lacks something that ought to be there. The cause of the lack is not nature, hence not a being, but freedom, hence something of the spiritual order of the person.

> Evil of action or of operation always derives from a certain presupposed defect in the being or the active powers of the agent, . . . in this case, in the will. But this time the defect itself, that failure in the being which is the root of evil of action, must be a *voluntary and free* defect since it is the evil of a free action or a free choice which results from it.[27]

Thus, Maritain wants to examine this defect that takes place prior to choice that makes it possible to put an evil action into the world. Here Maritain's discussion of the rule of reason in natural law links up with his discussion of evil in action (chapter 5). The existence of the rule or the law, itself good and prior to action, makes the action chosen in spite of reason or law to be culpable.

The cause of moral evil is the will, or better, the person using his will. The person does this by putting into existence, as it were, something that is lacking. Moral evil remains the lack of something that ought to be there but is not because its presence or use is knowingly avoided by the will. Maritain stresses the power of the will not to be coerced. It can choose what it wants, even the principle or object of its own operation, which is given to it by the mind or intellect. In itself, this lack or defect as such is not an evil but merely the condition of freedom.[28] Perhaps the point becomes clearer by recalling Aristotle's famous double syllogism that he uses to explain moral fault. Aristotle proposes that in an evil or good act, the mind has available to it many propositions that are true.

To give a brief example, we know the following things: This is ice cream. Ice cream is good. This ice cream belongs to someone else. I like ice cream. When, considering this situation, I decide either to eat or not to eat the ice cream. I can justify or explain my action. We always act for a reason. We have a norm or rule of action in one of the true propositions. If I decide not to eat the ice cream, I do so because I did not pay for it or because it is not mine. My rule of action is what is just. If I decide to eat it, I do so because it is good, and I am hungry or desirous of something sweet. I thus choose the argument that allows me to eat it. I ignore the argument that would forbid me to eat it even though I understand it. (I protest against people eating my ice cream.) Since all of these arguments are available to me in my mind, what I do is to use my will to focus on the major premise that will allow me to eat or incite me to reject eating the ice cream. My vice or virtue results from the unavoidable situation of my knowing many things about the ice cream and my relation to others.

Maritain puts this argument in this way:

> Evil lies in acting without reference to the rule; and in this concrete whole, acting without consideration of the rule, there are two moments to be distinguished, not with regard to time but according to ontological order: *first movement, not considering the rule,* which is a negation, an absence, the lack of a good which is not yet due; and *second movement, acting with that negation,* which, from the sole fact that one acts with it, becomes a privation, an absence of a due good in the action.[29]

When we wish to do something, our mind gives us all sorts of intelligible alternatives, each of which is true in its own way. The fact that I can look over all these various alternatives to see what they are is not a sin or a disorder but the very nature of the relation of will to intellect. To know evil is not to do it. But if I choose not to understand the relationship of all these possible things to each other, if I neglect one of the norms or standards by which I properly judge something—say, if I look at the ice cream only as something tasty but not as something belonging to someone else—then I have introduced "a certain nothingness" into the beginning of my act.[30] Since I "want" to reach a certain conclusion no matter what, I simply do not look at the proper rule by which I decide whether the whole action is right but only at the one that gives me what I want.

Thus, in thinking about how evil is chosen, there is a free choice not to look at the whole rule or whole reality. "This moment of non-consideration of the rule is so to speak the spiritual element of sin."[31] Maritain speaks of evil as putting "nothingness" into our choices.[32] Evil in this sense is a profound aspect of the meditation on nothingness, of why is there something rather than nothing, a meditation that stands at the root of any philosophy of being, of *what is*. The creature is the first cause of evil or the nothingness or lack of being that it always implies. The nothingness that surrounds evil actions, therefore, has a cause, namely, the free will not putting into action what ought to be there and is expected to be there. What is not there is a privation of a good and hence the remaining good limps along without what it ought to have.

The evil that is done can itself cause two sorts of reaction in those whom it affects. They can imitate the action and increase the evil, or they can suffer it and reject it as a principle of action for themselves. Moral evil is thus the privation of a good, a norm, that ought to be in human-willed action but is not there. It is not there because, by the power of his will, the person freely directs his attention to a principle or proposition that allows him to affirm that what he does is good or reasonable. A person always, to himself, defends his evil acts as reasonable under some heading. But in doing this, he leaves out of his consideration those rules or propositions that would have shown him what the wholeness of his action was. The recipient of the evil action rightly expects it to contain a consideration of the rule or reason whereby it is put in proper order. The fact that this evil action is possible to the human being is but the other side of the fact that he can likewise respond positively to the good that exists in reality. Whether and what we choose to love or hate, to accept or reject, is where the drama of life in free beings is located.

In conclusion, Maritain is careful to indicate why the world is not a kind of deterministic working out of a divine plan, a kind of necessitarian predestination.

> The divine scheme is not a scenario written at a previous time, which is later to be performed by creatures. The divine scheme is simultaneous, just as eternity itself, with every moment of time. And thus the will and the permission of God eternally determine this eternal plan with regard to the presence or absence, at each moment of time, of a moment of non-consideration of the rule in human free will, which in this way does or does not by its own deficient first initiative, fail divine action.[33]

We can speak of "bringing good out of evil" but only if we mean bringing further good out of the good in which evil necessarily exists. The drama of evil is, thus, a very active enterprise. Each act of good or evil provides us with the next act of how we will respond to such an act. What is often forgotten is that we, as free beings, need not respond to good by good. Nor do we need to respond to an evil act by evil. Since we are free, we can choose evil or good. What we cannot do is make good to be evil or to evil be good. This is why the moral content of our actions indicates that with which we choose to fill ourselves, good or evil, and so present ourselves to others in the world.

Maritain's reflections on evil thus can be seen as an essential background for the perplexing task of accounting for evil in the political and historical orders. Maritain's essential reminder is that God "did not invent evil; it is we who invented it. We are its first cause. It is our creation."[34] To the question, "well, then, why would a good God allow man his evil?", Maritain answers first, because He has no other alternative if man is to exist and to be free, which is what he is, and secondly, that evil is permitted because man is offered something that must be chosen freely, or else it cannot exist, namely, God's friendship.

Maritain is right in thinking that the great problem in the political philosophy of our time is the abiding, if not increasing, presence of evil as a factor in human living. Maritain thinks, as a philosopher, that, thought through properly, something incumbent on every student and responsible person, the dimensions of evil and its subordination to good in fact will make an essential contribution to just regimes. Once we understand that we can do evil presupposing neither ignorance or error, we can begin to see the extent of the conflict in human living between a world open only to man's own definition of himself and one open to a right order that in fact corresponds to *what man is* and to what he is invited to become.

NOTES

1. Jacques Maritain, "Saint Thomas D'Aquin et le Problème du Mal," *De Bergson à Thomas D'Aquin, OCM,* vol. 8, 127.

2. Jacques Maritain, *The Sin of the Angel: An Essay on a Reinterpretation of Some Thomistic Positions,* trans. William Rossner, S. J. (Westminster, Md.: The Newman Press, 1959), 9.

3. Susan Orr, in reading this text, at least notes the question of whether the suffering of animals is absolutely natural in every conceivable order. C. S. Lewis had also remarked on this issue in his discussion of "Animal Pain," in *The Problem of Pain* (New York: Macmillan, 1962), 129–43.

4. Jacques Maritain, *St. Thomas and the Problem of Evil* (The Aquinas Lecture; Milwaukee: Marquette University Press, 1942), 7. (This lecture was subsequently published in three French journals or books: "Saint Thomas D'Aquin et le Problème du Mal," *La vie intellectuelle* 13 (July 1945): 30–49; chapter VII of *De Bergson à Thomas D'Aquin,* and in *Le Mal Parmi Nous* (Paris: Plon, 1948), 279–306.)

5. Maritain, *St. Thomas and the Problem of Evil,* 8.

6. Ibid.

7. Ibid.

8. Ibid., 18–19.

9. Ibid., 39.

10. Ibid.

11. Ibid., 1.

12. Ibid., 1–2.

13. Ibid., 2.

14. Ibid., 3.

15. Ibid., 4.

16. Ibid., 3.

17. See also Maritain's discussion of evil in his *Existence and the Existent,* trans. Lewis Galantiere and Gerald B. Phelan (Garden City, N. Y.: Doubleday, Image, 1975), 120–28.

18. Maritain, *St. Thomas and the Problem of Evil,* 10.

19. Ibid.

20. Ibid., 11.

21. Ibid., 12.

22. Ibid., 17–18.

23. Ibid., 12–13. "Since the evil of the free act is our creation, it is in letting our monsters proliferate to the very end, and allowing the infinite resources of our power of nihilating to develop all forms of degradation and corruption of being, that divine liberty manifests the sublimity of its omnipotence by drawing *from that itself* the higher good which God designed, not for Himself but for us. . . . A more than human grandeur is dissembled in our creeping destinies. A sense is given to our wretched condition; and this is probably what matters most to us. It remains a wretched condition—but the existent who vegetates in it is cut out to become God by participation." Maritain, *Existence and the Existent,* 127–28.

24. *St. Thomas and the Problem of Evil,* 13–14. See also Jacques Maritain, "The Human Person and Society," *Scholasticism and Politics* (Garden City, N. Y.: Doubleday, Image, 1960), 61–90.

25. *St. Thomas and the Problem of Evil,* 15.

26. Ibid., 16–17.

27. Ibid., 23.

28. Ibid., 25–56.

29. Ibid., 31.

30. Ibid.

31. Ibid., 32.

32. Ibid., 34.

33. Ibid., 38–39.

34. Maritain, *Existence and the Existent,* 120.

10

MARITAIN ON "THE MYSTERY OF ISRAEL"

[Israel] is not only a people, but a people endowed with a mission which pertained to the very order of the redemption of mankind. And Israel's mission continues in a certain manner—no longer as an "ecclesial mission"—after its lapse, because it cannot help being the chosen people, for the gifts of God are without repentance, and the Jews are still beloved because of their fathers. So we might say that whereas the Church is assigned the task of the supernatural and supratemporal saving of the world, to Israel is assigned, in the order of temporal history and its own finalities, the work of the *earthly leavening* of the world. Israel is here . . . to irritate the world, to prod it, to move it. It teaches the world to be dissatisfied and restless so long as it has not God, as long as it has not justice on earth. Its indestructible hope stimulates the life forces of history.

—Jacques Maritain, *On the Philosophy of History*[1]

I am not a charismatic author. I can justly say that which the poor eyes of a philosopher believe to perceive in the entanglements of history. It seems to me that to be authentic, the friendship in question (between Jews and Christians) presupposes on both sides a purification of thought. It is necessary that Christians truly understand that God has not reproved, but always continued to love the children of Israel, and that it is His love which has permitted this long passion. It is also necessary that Jews truly understand that it is not the will to power, but the charity of Christ, that animates the effort of the Church towards men. It also seems to me that if this friendship is affirmed, it will be the foretaste of great things, and eventually of a common action to bear help to the world that is in danger, but in all corners of which there are souls who die of thirst.

—Jacques Maritain, *De l'Église du Christ*[2]

181

I.

That some link might exist between the chapter on evil and the chapter occasioned in part by the treatment of Jews in the twentieth century seems obvious enough. Not even an ardent cultural relativist or an adamant opponent of universal natural law will admit that this massacre of the Jews in Germany was anything but evil on a massive scale. The very fact that Raïssa Maritain was born of Jewish parents in Russia makes it inevitable that she and her husband are brought directly into the tragedies of the twentieth century once the war came to France in the 1930s and 1940s. Her Jewish heritage explains the origins of the Maritain's long-term residence in the United States. Raïssa Maritain had written of her Jewish background and its relation to Christianity and to philosophy.[3] The place of Israel in history and the roots of anti-Semitism were long concerns of Jacques Maritain.[4]

To recall his discussion of Machiavellianism (chapter 1), Maritain argued that evil, even in vast proportions, can triumph for a time but that it cannot last, a position that seems born out in the cases both in Nazi and communist experience. In the midst of World War II, Maritain writes,

> Never before in the history of the world have the Jews been so universally persecuted; and never before has this persecution fallen, as it does today, on Jew and Christian alike. It is a sign of the profound disturbance of our civilization. But let us have no fear. For a time, the unjust, triumphant, can do what they please. They know themselves that their time is short. That is why they show such monstrous haste.[5]

In the previous chapter, we saw that evil is "permitted" only that some greater good might appear. Maritain understands that such great human aberrations need acute intellectual reflection. As a philosopher, a Christian, a Frenchman, and a human being, Maritain devotes much of his intellectual energy to understand, in the light of his general considerations on being, good, and evil, what these historical events concerning the Jews of his time mean.

In *We Have Been Friends Together,* Raïssa Maritain speaks in particular of the French novelist Léon Bloy, whom she and Jacques had just met. "We read this book (of Bloy) in the country during the month of August, 1905," she writes.

It revealed Saint Paul to us, and the extraordinary ninth, tenth, and eleventh chapters of the Epistle to the Romans, from which Léon Bloy took the inscription for his title-page and the support for his exegesis in *"Le Salut par les Juifs"* (Salvation through the Jews). . . . But the first line of that great lyrical and scriptural poem which is *Le Salut par les Juifs* has a still higher reference: *"Salus ex Judaeis est.* Salvation is of the Jews." Christ's words in the Gospel of Saint John, chap. 4:22.[6]

The careful effort to make sense of the political events of his time involves Maritain in considering the meaning and destiny of Israel and the Jews in the Diaspora. We must be aware that he writes as a Christian and as a philosopher as well as someone for whom the Old Testament is a revealed book.

Maritain seeks to give an accurate Christian and, to the extent possible, philosophic understanding concerning the destiny of Israel in the world. This is why Maritain's work includes not only a discussion of political philosophy about what sort of a "nation"or "people" Israel is, but also what is the meaning of the human history in which it appears, its vocation as it were. The fact that he must ask about Israel, which exists both as a faith and eventually as a political society, implies that, in this consideration, he must be aware of other peoples, the Gentiles, of other faiths and nations. No wonder then, that in order to be a complete philosopher, he writes a book precisely *On the Philosophy of History* as well as a book on St. Paul, the young Pharisee. Paul, in the Epistle to the Galatians, explains his original attitude: "You know I went to extremes in persecuting the Church of God and tried to destroy it . . ." (1:13). Only later, after his own conversion on the road to Damascus, did Paul come to analyze, in the classic text in the Epistle to the Romans, the relation of Israel to God, to the Church, and to the nations.

What Maritain does not think is that the events surrounding the "fate" of the Jews in the twentieth century can be adequately or even minimally explained by political philosophy alone or by any purely human reflection. Maritain understands, however, that a knowledge of political tyranny, for example, might be of help in analyzing the totalitarian treatment of the Jews. There is an intellectual history to political events that helps explain them. Maritain spends much time in studying Machiavelli, Luther, Descartes, Rousseau, Kant, Hegel, Marx, and

Nietzsche because he does think that intellectual history explains, to some extent, how things come about in the real order.

However, in this case, Maritain often returns to the term "mystery" to remind us that something beyond human and political considerations surrounds the place of Israel and the Jews in the world. He is aware that, independently of his own explication, there is a modern Jewish analysis of the meaning and nature of this "mystery." In fact, there may be several such attempts to analyze the meaning of Israel in the world, a Muslim one, or a purely philosophic one. The "mystery of Israel" is considered because it has again arisen in Maritain's time. He intends to be loyal to his sources and loyal to the facts.

II.

"The End of Machiavellianism" appeared in different books and journals. In this essay, Maritain considers the questions: does the end after all justify the means and is anything wrong in dealing with human beings solely for political reasons? In *The Range of Reason,* "The End of Machiavellianism" is preceded by an essay entitled, "The Christian Teaching on the Story of the Crucifixion."[7] This juxtaposition may be accidental, but it does bring us to the heart of our considerations about the "mystery of Israel." The death of Christ along with the death of Socrates provide the existential context for the classic question of the fate of the good man in any existing polity.[8] The question of who was legally, morally, and politically responsible for the death of Christ must be answered at many different levels. The effort to come to the clearest terms here takes on major importance because the involvement of a certain few Jewish leaders in Christ's death was sometimes used subsequently as an excuse to separate or persecute Jews.[9] Maritain's clarifications here are of considerable importance in his further considerations of the "mystery of Israel."

The origin of this analysis of the responsibility for Christ's death is a letter that Maritain wrote to Hayim Greenberg, the Editor of the *Jewish Frontier,* in August 1944. Greenberg had earlier (August 1939) published his own letter on this topic to a protestant minister, a letter that Greenberg had sent on to Maritain. Maritain compliments Greenberg for his understanding of Christian thinking on this subject. "For a Christian aware of the significance of his own creed," Maritain writes,

> Christ's condemnation and death are a divine mystery, the most awesome irruption of God's secret purposes into human history, a mystery which can be looked at only in the light of supernatural faith, and you are perfectly right in stating that "as long as your pupils will think of this problem in terms of a lynching party or of a judicial frame-up, they will remain on a low, non-metaphysical plane that has nothing to do with Christianity."[10]

Maritain is not denying that there may have been some legal or moral irregularity in Christ's trial. Rather, he is saying that the Christian understanding of what went on there has to do with redemption, "with God's secret purposes in human history."

Maritain next adds a point that follows from his earlier discussion of the freedom connected with evil in human affairs. Greenberg has used the expression "tragic guilt" of those connected with the death of Christ. (The same problem occurs when we use the word "fate" of the Jews.) Maritain worries that the word "tragic" gives the impression that this guilt has to do with "fate," which has something inevitable and deterministic about it. In both the Old and New Testaments, "guilt is not made inevitable by fate. It is involved in the unbreakable plan of eternal wisdom, yet human freedom stays real under the will of God, and does freely the good which God has eternally decided to predetermine, the evil which He has eternally decided to permit."[11] Maritain thus does not see the death of Christ as simply a Greek tragedy. There is real freedom and responsibility involved in the death of Christ, and therefore guilt. Otherwise, the death of Christ or the massacre of the Jews is merely a necessary event, the determined working out of natural forces in human form.

Who bears this guilt? Not very many people. Pilate, a few priests, to some degree the mob, perhaps some Roman soldiers by their cruelty. From the Christian view, on the basis of who Christ is in its understanding of the Incarnation, this death can rightly be called a "deicide," a murder of God, but Maritain points out that those few people who were in fact guilty of the unjust civil execution of what they took to be a man, Christ, did not think they were killing God or man-God. Maritain recalls that Peter in the Acts of the Apostles (3:17) specifically states that the Jewish rulers killed Christ "in ignorance" of who He is. What the Apostles and Paul accuse the Jewish leaders of is not "deicide" but of refusing to believe, in spite of evidence and testimony, who He is.[12]

While taking care to point out that "every Jew today is as innocent of the murder of Christ as every Catholic of today is of the murder of Jeanne d'Arc," still Maritain maintains that for the Christian understanding, this rejection of Christ as the promised Messiah had the necessary effect of banding together in a kind of *"corpus mysticum"* the majority of Jews who followed or accepted this rejection. This rejection is not, however, a rejection of Yahweh's original selection of His people but a rejection of a certain unanticipated way it is said to be carried out in history. Maritain's point, by analogy, seems to be this: if some group of, say, Englishmen called Pilgrims band together and abandon England to form their own compact about what they believe and in what land they will live, this very fact separates them from England and forms them into a new corporate body with a new history. Likewise, had the Jewish leaders chosen to believe that Christ was their Messiah, their subsequent history would necessarily have been quite different from what it was on the basis of the rejection of Christ. Maritain points out this matter objectively as something that follows logically from a proper understanding of what is at issue in human choices and their consequences. It is also the Christian understanding of these events. It is another instance of living with our choices.

In Catholic thought itself, no actual Jew, historic or present, is responsible for the legal killing of Christ, except for those few who played key roles in an actual historical event. Even these few did not know who in reality Christ was. Very few, if any, lawyers or philosophers, Jewish, Christian, or whatever, looking at this particular trial in retrospect, would maintain that Christ, whoever He be, was condemned justly. Maritain next proceeds to the more fundamental question about the existential cause of the execution of Christ. Beginning with the theological idea that Christ is sent to redeem us from our sins, it is clear that Christ's death, even though it involved Pilate, Annas, Caiphas, and perhaps a few others at a given historical moment, was caused by the sins, freely chosen evils, of all of us, for the forgiveness of which Christ was sent as a ransom.

Who killed Christ? The Jews? The Romans? I have killed Him, I am killing Him every day through my sins. There is no other Christian answer, since He died voluntarily for my sins, and to exhaust the justice of God upon Himself. Jews, Romans, executioners, all were but instruments, free and pitiable instruments, of His will to redeem and sacrifice. This is what Christian teachers ought to indicate to their pupils.[13]

None of this means that Christ killed Himself or was killed by the Heavenly Father. What it does indicate is the seriousness of evil caused by the free will of finite beings that carries itself out even to the extent of killing Christ, clearly an innocent man, but in Christian understanding, the Son of God.

On this basis, Maritain can talk more clearly of "that monstrosity, Christians who are anti-Semites." Granted that Christ died for everyone's sins, including those of Christians themselves, those who blame someone else for Christ's death, the Jews, say, are actually "seeking an alibi for their innermost sense of guilt." In not recognizing that Christ died primarily for one's own sins, that is to say, for everyone's, this very fact indicates a desire "not to be redeemed."[14] In other words, Maritain sees in anti-Semitism not only an evil against the Jews but an implicit rejection of the fundamental teaching of Christianity, by some Christians themselves.

The rejection of Christ by the Jews taken as a fact, however, does leave us with the thought-provoking question of their subsequent meaning in the world long after these events of the first century of our era. This is what Maritain means by "the mystery of Israel." Granted that God never goes back on His promises and granted that the Jews of history and of the present are not guilty by some sort of collective guilt (guilt must always be personal and chosen), where can we gain some understanding of this subsequent history that seems to identify them as a separate nation even in their diaspora in other nations? Their history has not only led, to name the most notorious, to the terrible events surrounding World War II, but also to the refounding, after two millennia, of Israel as a political state. Is the refounding and structure of this particular state a subject primarily and exclusively of political technique, with nothing to do with the Old or New Testament?

Maritain himself tells us that "never did I see so acutely the essentially anti-Christian madness of anti-Semitism as when preparing a book on St. Paul and gathering together his texts on the mystery of Israel. St. Paul teaches that 'the gifts and the call of God are without repentance,' so that the people of Israel continue 'ever beloved for the fathers' sake' " (Romans, 11:28, 19).[15] As a Christian and as a philosopher basing himself on empirical evidence, Maritain takes seriously the fact that something unusual and special surrounds Israel throughout history and that the events of our time, especially those involving the Jews, are not merely blind accidents that have no intrinsic meaning.

III.

With some humor, the novelist Walker Percy once asked, I think, in the *Second Coming,* "Why are there no Hittites in New York City?" The question implies that there must be something unusual about an ancient Middle Eastern tribe still being in existence, while other tribes have long since disappeared or been absorbed indistinguishably into other races and religions. We could try to answer this unexpected question in many ways. We could turn to sociology or anthropology to find some purely rational answer, but the persistence of the Jews throughout history seems to defy all scientific explications.[16] We could turn to the Old Testament itself, to the constant reflection that Jewish rabbis and thinkers have made of their lot over the centuries, of their expectation of a Messiah and what it might mean. We could also see it in the light of both these sources and of the New Testament, particularly St. Paul, himself a Jew, who more than any other early Christian thinker, sought to address this question. Thus, although Paul himself did not specifically wonder why there were no Hittites in New York City, he would have shown little surprise to find the many Jews there.

In the revision of his earlier 1937 essay, "The Mystery of Israel," Maritain confesses his embarrassment as a Frenchman at the anti-Semitism that manifested itself in France under the Vichy regime of World War II. He thinks it anti-French. A philosopher ought to grapple with such issues that cause great perplexity. Then, in a marvelous sentence, he adds, "We must never despair of intelligence and the healing power of its dispassionate attempt toward understanding."[17] Friendly or objective descriptions of the faults of any group, especially the Jews, ought not to be taken to mean that Maritain himself does not write with the "deepest esteem and love for the Jewish people."[18] Maritain, indeed, takes considerable pains to establish his motives as genuinely philosophic and rooted in his own effort to understand what his own faith had to say about the "mystery" of Israel.

This "mystery of Israel" is, initially, a Jewish mystery arising from within the history and sources of Jewish experience. However, this history is also an essential aspect of Christianity's understanding of itself and the world.

> If these pages are seen by Jewish readers, I hope they will agree that as a Christian I could only try from a Christian perspective to understand the history of their people. When this essay was published in France, there were some who . . . tried to see latent intentions of proselytism where only a desire for truth engaged my mind; others took as personal "reproaches" what was only a statement of the consequences of the drama of Calvary regarding the relation of Israel to the world. They were mistaken. I am perfectly aware that before agreeing with the statements proposed in my essay, it is necessary to admit, as a prerequisite, the whole Christian outlook; therefore it would be inconsistent to hope for any agreement from a reader who does not place himself in this perspective. I do not intend to try to convince such a reader, but, for the sake of mutual understanding, I think it would perhaps be interesting for him to know how a Christian philosopher considers the question.[19]

This sensitive passage of Maritain indicates the careful way that he approaches this topic. It reminds us that even if we do not "believe" this or that position arising from sources in philosophy or faith, it is illiberal to refuse to understand how such positions are argued or presented.

And lest someone might think it somehow anti-Semitic even to talk about such issues, Maritain adds: "The simple fact of feeling no sympathy for the Jews or being more sensitive to their faults than to their virtues is not anti-Semitism. Anti-Semitism is fear, scorn, and hate of the Jewish race or people, and desire to subject them to discriminative measures."[20] Simply to dislike or disagree with an individual Jew or with a widely known Jewish political position cannot be called anti-Semitism. To do so confuses the main issue with another kind of prejudice.

Following the discussion about political definitions (chapter 4), Maritain seeks to define the use of political words when applied to Israel and the Jews. In what sense can the Jews be called a "race"? "Actually the Jews are not a 'race' in the biological sense of the word."[21] The fact is that no pure "race" exists in any large-scale political grouping in the world today. Jews come from many different blood streams. The only way the word "race" can be used of the Jews is when the reference is to "a community of mental and moral patterns, of ancestral experience, of memories and desires, and where hereditary tendencies, the blood strain and somatic type play a more or less important part of the material foundation."[22] Clearly, this usage of the word "race" is too broad and must be distinguished from a deterministic use of the word that takes blood alone to define a people.

What about the word "nation," whose root means "to be born of"? Are the Jews a nation? The three or so million Jews in Israel by no means include the other Jews who are members of other political societies. If nation means "an historical group of men bound together by a unity of origin or birth . . . and jointly leading or aspiring to lead a political life," then all Jews do not constitute a nation.[23] Maritain points out elsewhere that the land of Palestine, the physical foundation of this nation, has a transcendent origin:

> By a strange paradox, we see today contested against the Israeli, by the states that are their neighbors, the only territory to which, considered under the entire spectacle of human history, it is absolutely, divinely certain that a people has incontestably a right. For the people of Israel is the only people in the world to whom a land, the land of Canaan, has been given by the one God. . . . And that which God has given once is given for always.[24]

Israel is chosen as the least among the nations. The idea of a chosen people or nation is something in political philosophy that finds a parallel in Plato's foundation myth in *The Republic,* about gold, silver, and bronze children in their diversity forming a single society.

The understanding of a people or nation divinely given a particular land depends, of course, on the validity of the revelation given to Israel in the first place, but its reality has always been a principal factor in culturally uniting Jews of all ages and nations. Of the State of Israel,

Maritain writes, "a small number of Jews (500,000 in 1940), gathered together in Palestine, constitute a nation, and Hebrew is their national language. They are a special and separate group bearing witness that the other Jews (there are about sixteen million in the world [1940]), are not a nation."[25] Maritain acknowledges the possibility of differing citizenship for Jews outside of Israel. He also affirms that, at the level of faith, these same Jews are related to the historic land and people of Israel.

Maritain, recall, distinguishes nation and state; a nation is a community and a state a society, the one more instinctive and rooted in history, the other in conscious reason. In this sense, Maritain (writing in 1940) thinks that the Jews in Palestine "are tending to become a state," something that later became a fact. Thus, using the word Israel in its broadest religious sense to include all Jews in the world whatever their citizenship, Maritain does not think that, of their own volition, they "tend to set up a temporal society." That is, all of spiritual Israel is not a single nation or a state, at least, he adds, "so long as it has not brought to completion its mysterious historic mission."[26] Maritain is conscious of the fact that, in trying to understand Israel, we will not reach any understanding of its historic record if we are not aware of the workings of this "mysterious historic mission."

Likewise, the Jews cannot be called a "people" if we mean a group gathered in the same place with an identical, unified population. We can, however, call the Jews "a people" if we mean by this term rather a community nourished "by the same spiritual and moral tradition and responding to the same vocation."[27] But in analyzing these terms, Maritain speaks as a philosopher in considering this particular people. With all these categories, however, something still stands out about the historic experience of Israel. "Israel is a mystery. Of the same order as the mystery of the world or the mystery of the Church. Like them, it lies at the heart of the Redemption. A philosophy of history, aware of theology, can attempt to reach some knowledge of this mystery, but the mystery will surpass that knowledge in all directions."[28] For Maritain, "mystery" is not opposed to knowledge. Rather, it is a source of a knowing that, of its very nature, incites further human knowing.

IV.

The "mystery" is, to recall, the fact of Israel's persistence in time, through the five thousand years of its history. This persistence would not be possible in the course of normal human events in time. Looking at this abidingness of Israel in time, we can mistakenly call it, perhaps, a "problem," as if it can, like certain other problems, be fully understood or resolved by human means. Indeed, as Maritain points out, the attempt to "solve" the Jewish "problem" can have many dangerous overtones. But it must also be seen as a reminder of the spiritual and supernatural elements that are in fact in this order of man's history. "St. Paul was right," Maritain wrote, "we shall have to call the *Jewish problem* a problem *without solution*—that is, until the great reintegration foreseen by the apostle. . . . To wish to find . . . a *solution* of the problem of Israel, is to attempt to stop the movement of history."[29] This is another way of saying that the purpose of Israel in human history is real enough, but it is not a "purpose" under the direct control of human political forces. To try to solve it by human or political means is, implicitly, a claim to divine power, one likely to have terrible consequences.

Thus, Israel is, Maritain repeats, a kind of *corpus mysticum* in time. It is bound together by God's promises that will not fail and by the subsequent choices of its leaders not to recognize the particular mission that Christ represents as the purpose of Israel in the world. From the Christian point of view, this rejection is not only a part of Christian history, but of Israel's history. "The Synagogue still moves forward in the universe of God's plans. It is itself only gropingly aware of this its path in history."[30] Why then, it might be asked, is Israel a continuing presence in the world? Maritain's answer at first seems surprising. He knows that God's purposes will be carried out even if the free will of this or that person rejects what ought to be done. The fact that the Messiah, in the Christian sense, is rejected is simply that, a fact. That there is a cohesive unity of those who live according to this rejection is likewise the consequence of a fact. "The drama of Israel is to struggle against the Prince of this world while yet loving the world and being attracted to the world; and while knowing better than anyone else the value of the world."[31] It is with Israel's relation to the world that Maritain will find the answer, insofar as we can understand it, of the mystery of Israel.

Israel has a twofold purpose in the history of the world. Its first, which it did fulfill, was to "give the saviour to the world." Having done this, it remains as a "witness" to its own history. It preserves its scripture and thus is "a living and indestructible depository of the promise of God."[32] But Maritain thinks that there are things that "indirectly" serve "the salvation of the world" that the abiding existence of Israel in the world fosters even after the destruction of the Temple and the longstanding Diaspora in which Jews in history have mostly lived. Maritain thinks that these indirect elements serve to shed much light on "enigmas" that seem otherwise unintelligible. "Whereas the Church is assigned the task of the supernatural and supratemporal saving of the world, to Israel is assigned, in the order of temporal history and its own finalities, the work of the *earthly leavening* of the world. Israel is here—Israel which is not of the world—at the deepest core of the world, to irritate it, to exasperate it, to *move* it."[33]

Why does Maritain see as something to be praised this inner-worldly function of Israel as causing unrest and unsettlement in the world? His answer goes to the core of political philosophy itself, to the question of whether a complete or reasonably happy political life is enough for man, or whether it is that political life to which he is really ordained. The unrest that Israel, in the world but not of it, causes is designed to prevent mankind from misplacing the real reason for the world's existence. Israel "teaches the world to be dissatisfied and restless so long as it has not God; it stimulates the movement of history." The Cross and sufferings of Christ are primarily for the redemption of each individual insofar as he commits evil and disorders his world so that he can, through grace and forgiveness, reach that end offered to each human being in his creation. Human suffering does have a meaning. "The passion of Israel is not, like that of the Church, a passion of co-redemption, completing what is lacking in the sufferings of the Saviour," Maritain writes. "This passion is not suffered for the eternal salvation of souls, but for the stimulation and emancipation of temporal life."[34] We should not pass over this sentence lightly. It implies that the natural ends rooted in creation, that is, that there be a decent civil order ordained to temporal happiness, are not unworthy ones even if they are not the highest ones for which each human being is given existence. In differing ways, both the natural and transcendent purposes of creation are rooted and protected in revelation.

The oft-heard notion that somehow concern for the next life means, as such, unconcern for this life is here, by implication, rejected. The temporal mission of Israel witnesses both to the validity of a land, a chosen people, and to the unrest that would result by wholly identifying the life of this land or of that polity with human purpose as such. "Let us consider once more this strange intercrossing symmetry which holds our attention," Maritain asks us by way of summary:

> As to Christians, the Church follows her divine vocation, and it is not Christianity, it is Christendom, the Christian world, which has failed (in the temporal order) without [*sic,* that is, by not] being willing to hear the voice of the Church who, while she directs men toward eternal life, also requires them to help the development of life on earth along the lines of the Gospel. For the Jews, it is Israel as a Church, it is Judaism which has failed (in the spiritual order); and it is Israel still as the chosen people . . . which pursues in history a supernatural (yet ambiguous) vocation.[35]

These are indeed concerns that "hold our attention" for it seems clear that a plan or order of history is broken so that certain things that ought to belong together do not. Yet their very breaking apart has not stopped the purpose that was originally intended to work itself out in a different way.

Maritain next endeavors to examine the reasons that are given for disliking or hating Jews. "Those who want to hate a people," he remarks, "never lack a pretext." But Maritain is trying to find out whether there is any reason for this hatred that might be related to the transcendent purpose of the continuance of Israel in the world. "Jews are on the average more intelligent and quicker than Gentiles. They profit thereby; they do not know how to make people forgive them their success." And certainly, many instances "when they gather in the high places of culture to worship the idols of the nations, Jews become corrupted." Again, Maritain insists that there is nothing anti-Semitic in acknowledging these tendencies. But the fact is that "Jews have more good qualities than defects." Maritain mentions many of these good qualities—a sincere kindness, capacity for friendship, and a devotion to ideas.[36] But in listing these natural reasons for liking or disliking Jews, Maritain sees that something else is at work, something not often mentioned or understood, still something that needs to be accounted for.

Maritain turns to the notion that the Jew is never really satisfied in the world and thus causes an unrest, the purpose of which not even he is clearly certain. "If the world hates the Jews, it is because the world is well aware that they will always be *supernaturally* strangers to it; it is because the world detests their passion for the absolute and the unbearable action with which this passion stimulates it. It is the vocation of Israel which the world execrates."[37] Maritain thinks that Jews and Christians alike may well come to be hated by the world insofar as the one senses that there is something incomplete about the worldly order, and the other frankly maintains that we are strangers in this world and made for something that is not political or of this world.[38]

Maritain mentions the two strategies that various Jews have tried to develop to prevent any hatred or persecution, that of being totally assimilated in one nation or another and that of Zionism that seeks to put all Jews in the same homeland.

> Assimilation is not the solution of Israel's problem, any more Yiddishism or Zionism; but assimilation, like autonomy and Zionism, is a partial accommodation, a compromise solution, good and desirable to the extent that it is possible. . . . Yet it [assimilation] carries with it a risk—as does also Zionism (as a state)—the risk of the Jews becoming settled, becoming *like others* (I mean spiritually). Never had there been Jews more assimilated than the German Jews.[39]

Maritain implies here that we cannot look at what happens to the Jews wholly from outside their own vocation and purpose in the world.

Maritain's discussion of the history of both Israel and Christianity, in the light of St. Paul's position that it was precisely the rejection of Christ that opened the way of salvation to other nations, leads him to conclude that in one sense the unified project of God's plan is in fact being carried out both by Jews and Christians within the nations of the world. The dynamism of the Jewish unsettlement with the world and the Church's teaching of everlasting life are both addressed to the nations who are so busy with their own affairs that they will not listen to an account of their proper purpose or the purpose of individual human beings. "The hatred of the Jews and the hatred of the Christians spring from the same source, from the same will of the world *which refuses to be wounded* either with the wounds of Adam, or with the wounds of the Messiah, or by the spear of Israel for its movement in time, or by the Cross of Jesus for eternal life."[40] What Maritain suggests here is that in their own ways the combined history of Israel and Christianity, when looked at as an on-going reality of world history, reveals a limiting of political purposes and an abiding confrontation with the world and how it relates to redemption.

What Maritain seeks finally to ask, in the light of these transcendent reflections on the mystery of Israel, is whether there is any sort of possible political order that can allow the Jews to be Jews and Christians to be Christians while at the same time encouraging their spiritual teachings to be freely lived and taught. Maritain thinks, indeed, that the very structure of the mystery of Israel, with its relation of Jew, Christian, and Gentile, and their respective vocations, makes it necessary that the history of the world is to be included in one history. He maintains that, however it is to be considered or to come about, the relation of Israel and the Church is a key element in understanding the content of history. "On the spiritual level, the drama of love between Israel and its God, which makes Gentile participation in the economy of salvation, and which is but one element in the universal history of salvation, will be resolved only in the reconciliation of the Synagogue and the Church."[41] Thus, when Maritain says that the Jewish problem is humanly "without solution" and the attempt to solve it by political means is implicitly an attempt to "stop the movement of history," he is saying that the purpose contained in history itself has to do with the carrying out in history of the redemptive purpose implicit in the relation of Israel, the Church, and the nations.

Maritain's analysis of the mystery of Israel in terms of his own Christian background and in terms of modern political philosophy is a remarkable instance of faith seeking understanding and of intelligence seeking to comprehend and to order the temporal dimensions of transcendent explanations of human history and meaning. Maritain recognizes that the long history of Israel is perplexing both in its length—"why are there no Hittites in New York?"—and in its effect on the other nations. This abiding presence in history indicates an intelligibility that is also something we cannot fully understand. But the fact that something is a mystery does not mean that we can learn nothing from it. We can and do learn much about the nature of political things and about the forces and ferments that are at work in the world at its deepest levels.

Maritain's political philosophy in this sense is an effort to recognize the rights and purposes of those who belong to religious traditions, to allow them their due and their freedom, while at the same time to provide a political order in which these pursued purposes take place "civilly." Maritain's solution is designed primarily to allow the highest things to have their freedom because he sees that the purpose of the world in history is worked out at this level. On the other hand, he understands that hatreds and terrible consequences result from free human beings seeking to resolve at an earthly level what can only be resolved in the personal freedom and grace that are given to each person.

We can conclude by recalling the two passages that stood at the beginning of this chapter: First, Israel teaches the world to be "restless so long as it has not God." The mystery of Israel leads to the question of God. A valid political order is one that does not prevent this effort from flourishing. Secondly, in all the corners of the world, we find people who have the "thirst" for God. The purpose of politics if fulfilled best when, in doing what politics does, it does not deny either the restlessness or the thirst.

NOTES

1. Jacques Maritain, *On the Philosophy of History,* ed. Joseph W. Evans (New York: Charles Scribner's Sons, 1957), 92.

2. Jacques Maritain, *De l'Église du Christ, OCM,* vol. 13, 298.

3. Raïssa Maritain, *Histoire d'Abraham ou les Premiers Âges de la Conscience Morale, OCM,* vol. 14. See also the account of her Russian Jewish background and of her family, in *We Have Been Friends Together: Memoirs,* trans. Julie Kernan (New York: Longmans, Green, and Co., 1943), 1–15, 121–40. See also James V. Schall, "Everything that Can Be Saved, Will Be Saved," in *What Is God Like?* (Collegeville, Minn.: Michael Glazier/The Liturgical Press, 1992), 43–63.

4. Many of Maritain's essays on Israel, including "The Mystery of Israel," are collected in *Le Mystère d'Israël,* 1965, *OCM,* vol. 12, 428–660. See also, among other places, his "Anti-Semitism as a Problem for the Jew," 1942, *OCM,* vol. 8, 734–54; *"Réponse à André Gide sur les Juifs," OCM,* vol. 6, 1159–61; "The Mystery of Israel," *The Living Thoughts of St. Paul,* texts selected with comments by Jacques Maritain, trans. Harry L. Binsse (New York: Longmans, Green, and Co., 1941), chap. 4; in *OCM,* vol. 7, 519–30; *"L'Inauguration du Monument aux Martyrs Juifs,"* Rome, 8 July 1947, *OCM,* vol. 9, 1075; *"À Propos de la Question Juive," OCM,* vol. 2, 1196–1203. See also James V. Schall, "The Mystery of 'The Mystery of Israel,' " *Jacques Maritain and the Jews,* ed. Robert

Royal (Notre Dame: University of Notre Dame Press in association with the American Maritain Association, 1994), 51–71.

5. Jacques Maritain, *The Twilight of Civilization,* trans. Lionel Landry (New York: Sheed & Ward, 1943), 47.

6. Raïssa Maritain, *We Have Been Friends Together,* 121.

7. Jacques Maritain, *The Range of Reason* (New York: Charles Scribner's Sons, 1952), 129–33. The French version, dated 1944, is found in *OCM,* vol. 12, 631–36.

8. See my consideration of this topic, "The Death of Christ and Political Theory," in *The Politics of Heaven and Hell: Christian Themes from Classical, Medieval, and Modern Political Philosophy* (Lanham, MD.: University Press of America, 1984), 21–38; "The Death of Christ and the Death of Socrates," *At the Limits of Political Philosophy* (Washington: The Catholic University of America Press, 1996), 123–44.

9. See Jacques Maritain, *"Les Juifs parmi les nations,"* *OCM,* vol. 12, 481–553; "Anti-Semitism as a Problem for the Jew," *OCM,* vol. 8, 734–54. The following short essays or lectures are important, all found in *OCM, Le Mystère d'Israël,* vol. 12: *"Lettre à la Conférence du Seelisberg"* (1947), 637–43; *"Une Remarque sur la Diaspora* (1961), 647–48; *"Une Remarque sur les Responsabilités du Monde Chrétien,"* 649–50; *"Post-Scriptum,"* (1964), 651–60.

10. Maritain, *The Range of Reason,* 129.

11. Ibid., 130.

12. Ibid.

13. Ibid., 132.

14. Ibid.

15. Ibid.

16. "The Jews are a stumbling block to theory. They cannot be subsumed under any social or political theory." Walker Percy, "Parting Reflections," *Crisis* 8 (September 1990), 18.

17. Jacques Maritain, "The Mystery of Israel," (1943) *The Social and Political Philosophy of Jacques Maritain,* ed. Joseph W. Evans and Leo R. Ward (Notre Dame: University of Notre Dame Press, 1955), 195.

18. Ibid., 196.

19. Ibid., 196.

20. Ibid., 197.

21. Ibid., 199–200.

22. Ibid. 200.

23. Ibid.

24. Jacques Maritain, *"Post-Scriptum,"* (1964), *Le Mystère d'Israël,"* *OCM,* vol. 12, 651.

25. Maritain, "Le Mystère d'Israel," 200.

26. Ibid.
27. Ibid., 201.
28. Ibid.
29. Ibid., 201.
30. Ibid., 203.
31. Ibid., 205.
32. Ibid.
33. Ibid.
34. Ibid.
35. Ibid., 206.
36. Ibid., 208.
37. Ibid.
38. Ibid., 208–09.
39. Ibid., 209.
40. Ibid.
41. Ibid., 211.

11

THE POSSIBILITY OF A WORLD COMMON GOOD

The aspiration to communion in liberty can be efficacious only if the idea of the common good exercises in our souls a primary reality. It asks that each of us think of the common good, and that is neither so easy nor so natural as it might seem. . . . In spite of the self-criticism so dear to Frenchmen, they have understood today . . . that they have sought to work together for the common good, not of a group, but of the nation. . . . I mean to say that an interior renewal of conscience is above all necessary. Every technique of international organization, however just or wise as one might suppose, is empty of its effect if at the same time people do not understand this very simple truth, that states do not exist for themselves, but for the civilized community of which they are members.

—Jacques Maritain, *"Bien Commun National et Bien Commun International"*[1]

The common good is something ethically good. Included in it, as an essential element, is the maximum possible development, here and now, of the persons making up the united multitude to the end of forming a people, organized not by force alone, but by justice. Historical conditions and the still inferior development of humanity make difficult the full achievement of the end of social life. But the end to which it tends is to procure the common good of the multitude in such a way that the concrete person gains the greatest possible measure, compatible with the good of the whole, of real independence from the servitude of nature.

—Jacques Maritain, *The Person and the Common Good*[2]

I.

Acknowledging the magnitude of evil possible in the world, especially that caused by politics, and, at the same time, avoiding quick utopian solutions, many philosophers, including Maritain, have wondered whether a world political order of some sane and practical sort could be a logical means to repair the disorders of the twentieth century. In fact, the politicians of this era have twice tried to establish a system of world order, first in the League of Nations in Geneva and then in the United Nations in New York. The failure of the first and the limited success of the second are subjects of endless studies. No one would maintain that the United Nations is anything but a pale imitation of, when it is not a parody of, an adequate world organization commensurate with the needs of mankind.

A major reason for the difficulties of the United Nations in particular was, no doubt, the presence of Marxist states as impossible elements within the structure of this international body. With the demise of most of the Marxist system, therefore, together with the de facto spread of an intricate world economy of great magnitude at the turn of the twenty-first century, a renewed consideration of what Maritain called "the problem of world government" seems in order.[3]

Maritain specifically calls the issue of world government a "problem," one to be considered in the light of his own considerations of the accurate political definitions of body politic, state, people, society, and government. The use of the word "problem" rather than "mystery," indicates that Maritain does not in principle consider that world government—though he will decide that "government" is not the best terminology for what he has in mind—is impossible. Nor does he think that the question of a feasible international order arises solely because of the dangers associated with nuclear arms—from fear, in other words. Philosophers, he quips, do "not have to be stimulated by the atomic bomb to think."[4] He does acknowledge, however, that this particular weapon does in fact help many to think about this issue.

The reason Maritain insists that the "problem" of world government did not arise simply because of the bomb is of some interest in a man who identifies himself simply as "a philosopher." For the logic, if not the details, of this problem of world order has been in the literature since Aristotle and St. Thomas. Indeed, Maritain admires the book of his friend, Robert Hutchins, *St. Thomas and the World Order.*[5] The world order, Maritain thinks, without being in the least unaware of the darker side of the human record, is an aspect of what the common good of mankind entails.

Moreover, Maritain maintains that the question of the international community arises within political philosophy itself and therefore is worthy of serious treatment. It involves a practical conclusion of the human mind about what life in the city ultimately involves. To the objection that such an international organization is simply "a fine and beautiful [idea], but utterly impossible of realization, and therefore dangerous," Maritain replies not by denying the dangers or the difficulties involved, but by affirming that "if the idea is grounded, as we believe, on true and sound political philosophy, it cannot be impossible in *itself*."⁶ This is a remarkable response, true to the character of a philosopher who maintains that thought does arise in and does subsequently direct itself back to reality. Maritain continues, showing great confidence in the practical intellect he has often described: "therefore it is up to human intelligence and energy to make it, in the long run, not impossible *with respect to* the enormous yet contingent obstacles and impediments that the sociological and historical conditions which lie heavy on mankind have piled up against it."⁷ Moral and political means that do not exist at one time can be discovered out of the prudent fertility of human intelligence at other times when conditions and experience are more favorable. In the sphere of practical intellect, such as the case here, the impossible can be sometimes made to be "not impossible," as Maritain puts it. The "impossibility" Maritain speaks of is analogous to the "impossibility" that men once held when they were told to anticipate four-wheeled vehicles that ran by themselves and not using horses.

Aristotle remarks that only a divine mind can put order into infinity. Often, looking at international relations, a viable world order is seen to be a task analogous to putting order into infinity. The international world could only be, it was thought by Aristotle at least, a chaos of sovereign states at war with one another. The world orders of Alexander the Great or the Romans were thought to exist only because of force. Without a divine mind in charge, then, it is best not to propose a world political order on the international scale. It could only end up in a greater tyranny than anything so far imagined. While not denying that certain forms of international order can be dangerous, Maritain essentially argues that a world political order is needed and possible. He had implicitly rejected, in his analysis of the idea of sovereignty, the notion that it is best to maintain a multiplicity of varied national states, all with their own autonomous internal order and their own complete control over foreign affairs. Because a world tyranny is likely in practice, a multi-plicity of separate states is considered the only way to guarantee that at least somewhere a good political regime may accidentally happen.[8] Maritain rejects both of these alternatives because of the confidence he has in the capacities of practical reason to establish a genuine political order that can obviate the danger of a world tyranny or the depressing fact that a good regime appears only rarely.

II.

The "practicalness" of Maritain's proposed world polity is rooted in his notion, from St. Thomas, of a "common good." This concept has a long history in metaphysics and theology, as well as in political philoso-phy. The common "good" is itself also a "good." It is not something opposed to other goods but a good "diffusive of itself," to use Aquinas's phrase. It is a good designed to allow and encourage all goods to be what they are, including the good of the human intellect reflecting on and establishing a fit polity. The polity, for Maritain, is both an end and a means. The polity, including the body politic and the state, is an end, a good, that needs to be put into existence in some concrete, practical fashion in order that all the varieties of human activities or perfections can exist and prosper. It provides an order or structure in which what could not otherwise be can exist. The common good itself, moreover, is ordered to the end of the persons who make up the polity. This end is not itself political, but it is a good. All goods are ordered to each other.

Following St. Thomas, Maritain speaks of an internal common good of the universe and an external or extrinsic one. This difference lies at the foundation of human dignity and explains the basis of all order in reason. The example generally given is that of an army, whose end is external to its internal organization by which it achieves its end. Its end is victory; its internal order is the relation of units to command. The external common good—God, that is—is that to which the whole of the internal order of the universe is ordained. The internal order is ulti-mately directed to the person, to the rational creature, who alone can potentially reach, after the manner of knowing and willing, the external common good. No state or society, be it noted, is a person. Thus, no state can reach the external common good because it is not a "being" with these personal powers. The state is subordinate to and stands in the service of the reality of the person who has freedom and intelligence and who is directly related to the external common good.

In *Man and the State,* Maritain affirms that the state is not and cannot be a person. The idea that the state is a person lies behind much of modern tyranny. The person becomes the state's servant.

> The modern States were Hegelian in practice long before Hegel and his theory. The modern State, heir to the kings of old, has conceived of itself as a person superior to the body politic, either dominating the body politic from above or absorbing the body politic into itself. Now, since the State in actual fact is not a person, but an impersonal mechanism of abstract law and concrete power, it is this impersonal mechanism which will become suprahuman, when that vicious idea comes to develop its whole potentialities; and as a result the natural order of things will be turned upside down: the State will no longer be at the service of men, men will be in the service of the peculiar ends of the State.[9]

Maritain's political philosophy, at every level, local, national, and international, points to the fact that any political common good is always itself related to the individual persons whose good it fosters and that it is their good or purpose, not its own, for which any organized civil society exists.

Human dignity is grounded in the direct relation of each person to the extrinsic common good of the universe. This is a good that is not to be achieved in a deterministic fashion by man but one that he can accept or reject. The political order at whatever level is a good, the purpose of which is to foster in their proper order the other goods, including the highest, that belong to human persons who alone are the proper bearers of substantial being endowed with will and intelligence.

> In comparing the intellectual substance and the universe, St. Thomas emphasizes that intellectual creatures, though they, like all creatures, are ordained to the perfection of the created whole, are willed and governed for their own sakes. Divine Providence takes care of each one of them for its own sake and not at all as a mere cog in the machinery of the world. Obviously, this does not prevent them from

being related first to God and then to the order and perfection of the created universe, of which they are the most noble constitutive parts.[10]

What is at stake here, of course, is whether any political order is itself completely autonomous or whether its purpose is subordinate and directed to a higher purpose.

In maintaining that intellectual creatures are willed for themselves and have an end that is the extrinsic end or good of the universe itself, which only they can attain directly, Maritain keeps alive the crucial question about the scope of even an international political order. He wants to know whether it can be limited and intellectually directed to its own purposes that are also proper ones, if understood correctly. This is why Maritain had said that the question of international order is properly one of political philosophy to understand and of political prudence to bring about. It is possible, not impossible, but it is not itself the highest purpose for which each member of any international order is created.

Maritain, in fact, gives a very good, concrete description of what he means by the "common good"—that is, the purpose of the people in the body politic and the instrument the state:

> The common good is not only the collection of public commodities and services which the organization of common life presupposes: a sound fiscal condition, a strong military force; the body of just laws, good customs, and wise institutions which provide the political society with its structure; the heritage of its great historical remembrances, its symbols and its glories, its living traditions and its cultural treasures. The common good also includes the sociological integration of all the civic conscience, political virtues and sense of law and freedom, of all the activity, material prosperity and spiritual riches, of unconsciously operating hereditary wisdom, of moral rectitude, justice, friendship, happiness, virtue and heroism in the individual lives of the members of the body politic. To the extent to which all these things are, in a certain measure, *communicable* and revert to each member, helping him to perfect his life and liberty as a person, they all constitute the good human life of the multitude.[11]

The common good described here, as it exists within the polity, is precisely a good and, at the same time, a good ordered to something higher, to the end of each person in his relation to the external common good of the universe itself.

III.

We can "think" about the proper ordering of the world in terms of the inner-worldly purpose for which the political animal exists. We can consider this problem particularly in our time, Maritain thinks, because growing economic interdependence, something good in itself as a means of creating and distributing wealth, seems to lead to political order. But "an essentially *economic* interdependence, without any corresponding fundamental recasting of *moral* and *political* structures of human existence, can but impose by material necessity a partial and fragmentary . . . political interdependence."[12] The reason for this difficulty, Maritain thinks, is the theory of the modern state that implies that each state is totally sovereign, totally autonomous, both with regard to any higher law and with regard to any internal restrictions. Internally, at least, many states in modern times could be said to be limited by the democratic process, provided this process is not itself based on philosophical relativism. On the international level, however, states are subject to no law but their own. To this situation Maritain wishes to propose an intellectual, practical alternative.

Maritain, consequently, restates his position, elaborated early in his discussion of political definitions, about the term "sovereignty." Properly understood, it means that authority rises over and above the political body. As such it is an improper political idea. Sovereignty literally means a divine power that no state possesses because it is limited by what man is and what the state is. The latter is not a person, but a relation of order between human persons. Maritain thinks that there are and ought to be differing political societies, each with a sphere of limited "autonomy," that is, each with the capacity to make its own laws subject always to natural law and right. There is only a relative amount of economic and political self-sufficiency in any actual state. He does not see this as at all bad. Maritain states his objection to the word "sovereignty" in the context of an international society in order to develop his own justification for the possibility of a reasoned world order.

> And we must realize that the State is not and has never been sovereign, because *sovereignty* means a *natural* right (which does not belong to the State but to the body politic as perfect society) to a supreme power and independence which are supreme *separately from* and *above* the whole that the sovereign rules (and of which neither the State nor the body politic is possessed). If the State were sovereign in the genuine sense of that word, it could never surrender its sovereignty, nor even have it restricted. Whereas the body politic, which is not sovereign, but has a right to full autonomy, can surrender this right if it recognizes that it is no longer a perfect society, and decides to enter a larger, truly perfect political society.[13]

What Maritain explains in his political philosophy is why it is prudentially advisable to have a world political order. But he denies it absolute sovereignty to decide all questions. He requires that even a world order is at the service of ends of man higher than any politics.

The problem we deal with is one of political prudence. It is the "oldest problem" of politics in new historical and material conditions, namely, "how to find government for a community that lacked it, even if each fraction of the community already lived under a government of its own."[14] With the Aristotelian notion of "self-sufficiency," Maritain examines "communities" under their own governments. The evidence implies that the only body that is any longer "self-sufficient" is the world community. But this same community lacks proper political structure. Natural law and the law of nations *(jus gentium)* do provide some informal or even customary structures to deal with certain problems of trade, war, or communication. He contends, however, that, as these issues become more complex and diverse, their proper solution or order demands legal and juridical structure, including a constitution, so that the common good as something actually existing can find some more defined and clear basis.[15] Though cautious about any utopianism, Maritain does not seem to be overly concerned that a world polity might become a world tyranny so that a multiplicity of states ought to be preserved. Admittedly, he was writing before any actual world body had time to manifest its limited character.

IV.

Maritain, at this point, wonders if his purpose as a philosopher has not been completed with the basic statement that a world order is beneficial. This situation arises because, whether a given world order is good or bad, will require evidence of how it operates. History indicates that the earlier solutions were temporary or incomplete. This task needs some further elaboration precisely in the light of his discussion of political definitions. Maritain worries that the problem of world society will be conceived exclusively in terms of state and government, in which case it will be very dangerous and unsatisfactory. He calls this theory he worries about a "merely governmental theory" of world order.[16] The position he prefers sees the problem under the heading of "the universal or integral consideration of the *body politic* or *political society*," what he calls "the *fully political* theory of world organization." The notion of "fully political" is opposed to the state-government mode of conceiving the organization of the world society. The highest goods are as such not purely "political." The connotation of "fully political" acknowledges that man's social and political nature itself is ordered to things that are not political. But these higher things will not be fully themselves or capable of fitting realization without a proper political order.

What is wrong with a "governmental" approach to a world order? Basically, Maritain sees it as a top-down approach, one that separates the state and government from the people from whom it in theory arises or for whose benefit it functions. "Let me emphasize once again that the basic political reality is not the State, but the body politic with its multifarious institutions, the multiple communities which it involves, and the moral community which grows out of it."[17] Not forgetting what he said about evil that can affect all human beings including rulers at every level and the spiritual and political means needed to counteract it, the State remains the top-most agency whose function is to look to the good of the body politic, not to its own good. Government usually means the actual officials with their politics who are legally in charge, but only because they fill positions defined ultimately from the body politic. The people, not the state or government, rationally consider how they best achieve their own good in the light of what they are as people. If the world is organized on the model of a state or government, Maritain holds, it would reenact the old idea of a universal empire on the basis not of a monarchy but of a perverted democracy.[18]

Maritain's concern about a theory of international order modeled on the notion of a state-government, and not on the notion of the people-body politic from which the state arises, shows that he understands the dangers of misconstruing what can happen when a society of any sort is built upon a purely governmental theory. This is why Maritain insists that initially this "problem" is considered to be precisely one of political philosophy, not of economics, law, or military security. And within political philosophy, he holds that the world "state" and "government" must not be considered separately from the notion of a world "body politic" and the true meaning of people.

> What I just called a *merely governmental* theory would consider the whole thing, Existence and Nature of World Government, as well as Passage from the present state of affairs to the World Government, in the perspective of the State and government, *separately* from that of the body politic. As a result, we would have to contemplate a process developed artificially, and against the grain of nature, resulting in a State without a body politic or a political society of its own, a world brain without a world body; and the World Government would be an absolute Super-state, or a superior State deprived of a body politic and merely *superimposed* on and interfering with the life of the particular States—even though it were born of popular election and representation.[19]

This passage in Maritain, I think, is important because it reveals that he is not a naive utopian or a "one-worlder" at any cost. He is a thinker who realizes the complexity of his own proposal. He can put his finger on what is likely to be the main problem of any world organization, that is, its theoretical and practical independence of the people it is supposed to rule. Any concrete effort to carry out Maritain's ideas would have constantly to account for this concern.

The contemporary world is obviously composed of a multitude of nations and communities that are, as such, not directly products of reason, but of blood, loyalty, birth, tradition, and many other valuable and worthy components. These elements are themselves goods. Looking at them in the light of both nature and reason, what is clear is that the good of all these realities needs also to be understood and placed in order, recognized and protected. While man is a political being, he still, as part of what it means to be political, must establish or construct the institutions that allow all goods to flourish. What Maritain does is to propose a "fully political theory of world organization" in order to obviate the potential danger of a world government tyrannically or absolutely ruling without adequate moral and popular basis. He holds optimistically that a proper popular structure of a world state would counteract the dangers of imposed tyranny.

In a brief historical reference, Maritain points out that from ancient times, the idea of a world order was often dreamed of. Both the Alexandrine and the Roman Empires were thought to be "world" empires in which there was to be a common people, brotherhood, law, and, usually, language. These efforts were not always bad. After time, they often developed into relatively tolerable systems. Many ways to bring about world order have been attempted in history, but few of them were rooted in the essential notion of political freedom. Both the League of Nations and the United Nations tried, with varying degrees of success, to ground themselves in political freedom. Maritain acknowledges this freedom today as necessary for any real hope of a true political solution to the problem of world order.

> Now, if a world political society is some day founded, it will be by means of freedom. *It is by means of freedom that the peoples of the earth will have been brought to a common will to live together.* This simple sentence makes us measure the magnitude of the moral revolution—the *real* revolution now proposed to the hopes and virtues of mankind. . . . *Living together* does not mean occupying the same place in space. It does not mean either being subjected to the same physical or external conditions or pressures or to the same pattern of life. . . . Living together means sharing as men, not as beasts, that is, with basic free acceptance, in certain common sufferings and in a certain common task.[20]

Maritain's approach to political institutions, be it noted, always includes a strong emphasis on the inner, free, and self-reflective operation of actual human persons to understand what they are and what they need. Without this internal appreciation of what is happening and of willing it to happen, it is no longer really human and does not reside, as it should, in the active intellect and will of the people who compose any political order, including a proposed international one.

Maritain is at considerable pains to relate a common will to a common good in understanding what a political order entails. Lacking this common good, no doubt, many often heroic people will have to endure suffering and hardship out of a motive of personal love and generosity to make up for what is not there by reason, natural virtue, and intelligent organization. Many problems and sufferings, however, come about because of a lack of a common organization that could place the sufferings in a context wherein they are realized to be part of the common effort to alleviate such sufferings. "Given the human condition, the more significant synonym of *living together is suffering together*. When men form a political society, they do not want to share in common suffering out of love for each other. They want to accept common suffering out of love for the common task and the common good."[21] The latter notion has the connotation of justice and common responsibility. It differs from the also laudable notion of complete generosity whereby the receiver has no direct participation in the project, however much he may need love and aid. Sometimes, perhaps often in human history, this generosity or charity outside the political order or within a corrupt one is all there is when a common good and common organization are lacking or when government officials and ordinary citizens lack the virtue or energy to establish a fully political order.

Maritain could, at times, give examples of what he means that reveal some naïveté or failure on his part—for instance, the understanding of how wealth is best created and distributed. Thus, he writes:

> The very existence of a world-wide society will also inevitably imply a certain relative no doubt, yet quite serious and appreciable— equalization of the standards of life of all individuals. Let me put it in crude terms: perhaps, if the issue were made sufficiently clear to them, people in the Occidental nations would be ready to accept, for the sake of peace and of a world political organization ensuring lasting peace, a serious lowering of their standards of life in order to provide people on the other side of the iron curtain with an equivalent raising of their standards of life.[22]

Maritain thinks this proposal would require a certain "heroism." In retrospect, providing people, on what used to be the other side of the Iron Curtain as well as in other parts of the poor world, with "rising standards of living" needs hypotheses other than those distributionist ideas that Maritain seems to have had in mind here. The real problem, even at the time he made his proposal, is the nature of the regime on the other side of the Iron Curtain, not a lack of generosity in the West. The solution turns out not to be that one part of the world gives up something to distribute to others, as if the problem were a zero-sum world in which the wealth of some indicated its lack in others. Generally, the ideal of "equalization" is one that goes against the possibility of everyone having a sufficiency because of a system of work, profit, and free markets. But these are details that seem more obvious half a century after Maritain wrote.

V.

Is a body politic on a world scale, with a topmost agency called the state rising out of it to deal with a world common good, different because the world body politic is radically different from the national states with which we are familiar? Maritain does not think the problem is exactly analogous to the type of diversity-unity solutions that have been practiced in so-called "federal" polities. On a world scale, the diverse national societies would continue to have a fundamental place. He proposes what he calls "a pluralist unity." The diversity of differing bodies politic would be preserved and fostered as part of the common good. Uniformity is not the mark of common good but a sign of its failure in a political sense. A wide variety and multiplicity of talents, virtues, initiatives, and services seems to be more the mark of a real common good.

Nonetheless, Maritain argues that people will need to become conscious of what they do have in common, and they will need consciously to establish this common good. Returning to the notion of civic friendship (chapter 8), Maritain describes the internal attitude of those individual people in the world body politic:

> Among all peoples the sense of the common good of that *one people* [that is, one people of the world] should develop, and supersede the sense of the common good peculiar to each body politic. A sense of civic friendship as large as that one people should also and simultaneously develop, since civic love of friendship is the very soul or animating form of every political society. To insist that this sense of a worldwide civic friendship and a world-wide common good is a prerequisite condition for the foundation of a world political society would be putting the cart before the horse. Yet some beginning should actually take shape in the peoples; moreover, the sense of the common good

of the community of peoples, with the mood of good will and fellow-feeling it implies, is implicitly and virtually involved in the freely developed will to live together, which is the basic condition prerequired for the formation of a world political society coming into existence by means of freedom.[23]

Civic friendship is not meant to substitute, nor can it, for the higher reaches of personal friendship, on both the human and divine levels, for which human beings exist. What Maritain does imply is a basic philosophical and spiritual orientation that recognizes, until proved otherwise, the basic dignity and good will of others as something that, while including, also transcends the diversity of particular nations and cultures.

Again recalling his insistence that the world political state is a question of political philosophy, Maritain sees that whatever voluntary or governmental agencies and organizations might be required, the "essential part would be played by the will of the people, in every nation, to live together, in the world."[24] This "will" would be informed by a careful argument about why the institution of world order is itself good and therefore to be desired or chosen. But even if it is good in thought, it will not exist unless it is willed and acted upon in a practical fashion. The fact that each person transcends history in the order of his good is the most crucial factor in defining the personal dignity of each human being. It is this dignity that each state, at whatever level, should be conscious of serving. The state is not the highest "being" but an agent of those persons who are directly open to *what is.*

Maritain's recapitulation of what is involved in these distinctions of person, body politic, state, and people serves to recall the principles on which he also bases any international order or society:

> The people are the multitude of human persons who, united under just laws, by mutual friendship, and for the common good of their human existence, constitute a political society or a body politic. The notion of a body politic means the whole unit composed of the people. . . . The people are human persons who not only form a body politic, but who have each one a spiritual soul and a supratemporal destiny. [Thus] the concept of the people is the highest and noblest concept among the basic [political] concepts. . . . The people are the very substance, the living and free substance, of the body politic. The people are above the State, the people are not for the State, the State

is for the people. . . . The people have a special need of the State, precisely because the State is a particular agency specializing in the care of the whole, and thus has normally to defend and protect the people, their rights and the improvement of their lives against the selfishness and particularism of privileged groups and classes.[25]

The essential principles recalled here apply in an even more important way to any international political society. Maritain thinks it is "possible" to follow these principles if we choose to do so even on an international scale. The particular emphasis on the people and on the body politic on a world scale is the theoretical point at which Maritain differs from those governmental notions of a world society that lack any proper grounding. The people are the natural basis of any political society at whatever level. Maritain would not approve a world order that was not based in sound principles and practices. He is not a utopian, but he did recognize the practical worth of sound ideas.

VI.

What of the existing states? Needless to say, Maritain does not envision the disappearance of France, the United States, or Brazil into some kind of world order if it comes to exist. His theory, if anything, would, he thinks, make the French more French and the Brazilians more Brazilian. He does, however, reject any absolute sovereignty that would make the final arbiter of political or moral questions the state apparatus at any level. He has room for both contemplation and church, for voluntary societies and artists of all types. Man understands the reality of politics at all levels but human life is never at any level totally absorbed by it.

The seminal notion of a relatively perfect society or a self-sufficient polity has been the operative notion to identify a political unit since Aristotle. Throughout history various units, most recently what is called the "nation-state," have been the practical embodiment of this organizing concept. Maritain argues essentially that it is no longer possible for any political unit to be "self-sufficient" on less than a world scale, not forgetting all the restrictions that he has put into its realization. What he proposes instead is the concept of the "imperfect society" as a way to deal with the very necessary and real political unities that already exist in the world and whose good is one of the main reasons why we need a more definitive world order.

Indeed, Maritain thinks that the only way to "guarantee" the continued "relative" autonomy and existence of what we call nation-states today is through an international order that makes them more feasible, makes them relatively self-sufficient within their own realm.

> At this point it is advisable for us to elaborate a new concept, the concept of *imperfect* political society—I mean, as *part* of a kind of perfect society that the Ancients did not know, and in which, because of its very extension, the functions and properties inherent in self-sufficiency are divided between a multiplicity of particular bodies and a central common organism. In a world political society the nations would become *by right* and with the guarantees of a supreme juridical order what they already are in fact, but anarchically, namely non-self-sufficient or imperfect bodies politic; and the World State, considered separately from them, and only in its supra-national institutions and life, would also be an imperfect political society. Only the world society taken as a whole both with the supra-national State and the multiplicity of nations, would be a perfect political society.[26]

What is to be noticed is that Maritain keeps the international state and its body politic together and acknowledges the reality and values of lesser societies together with the origin of all in the people. The principle that authority should be kept at the lowest level possible remains operative here, as does the principle that real international problems require an adequate authority to address them.

VII.

Maritain has one final proposal that might also be considered rather impractical. In effect, he modernizes Plato's suggestion at the end of *The Laws* for a Council of the Wise. Whatever it might be called, this council would stand for the contemplative order and for the highest values that need defense and explication but that are, at any given time, insufficiently understood or dealt with. This council implies a conscious recognition on the part of the people and politicians of the relative rarity of wisdom, as well as its freedom and powerlessness in terms of force or actual political authority. On the other hand, Maritain would conceive it to have a certain stature and capacity to look at the international order to state freely what is missing or what might be done. He consciously denies any utopian purpose here. But he does not elaborate in any great detail its composition or method of selection.

Maritain recalls, lest he be accused of overestimating the effectiveness of his proposals, that "I have often expressed the opinion that our major problems cannot be decisively settled before the time of the great crisis and great reconciliation announced by St. Paul."[27] That is, Maritain admits that settling things "indecisively" is still worth doing and part of the core of the human enterprise. Yet true to his philosophical vocation, even here addressing the political order in the name of wisdom, he affirms that this exercise in political philosophy is worth doing.

> I have perhaps yielded to the old temptation of the philosophers, who would have reason, through the instrumentality of certain wise men, to be accepted as an authority in human affairs. After all, this would be less serious an illusion, I suppose—and in any case a less frequent one—than the conviction treasured by so many fatalists, that any reliance on reason has to be carefully avoided in the conduct of *Man and the State*.[28]

These remarkable words are the last ones in Maritain's main book in political philosophy, the ones that conclude also his discussion of an international order that he maintains is not "impossible."

In these words, Maritain simultaneously affirms the primacy of the contemplative order with Aristotle and Aquinas, avoids any radical utopianism often and probably incorrectly associated with Plato, rejects any systematic Machiavellianism, and suggests that "human affairs" are valid but constitute only a part of that to which man is oriented in and through the state. One might ask, in conclusion, whether in these proposals about the world order Maritain is prudent and properly political. No doubt he writes at a time when the need for clear statement of principle is most necessary. Maritain's discussion of Machiavellianism needs more attention to its effects and to the institutional and moral need to counterbalance it on a world scale. As he remarks of himself, perhaps only so much can be expected of a philosopher.[29] Yet I think it is best in concluding to recall again the words of Maritain:

I must confess that in my capacity as an Aristotelian I am not much of an idealist. If the idea of a world political society were only a beautiful idea, I would not care much for it. I hold it to be a great idea, but also a sound and right idea. Yet the greater an idea is with respect to the weakness and entanglements of the human condition, the more cautious one must be in handling it.[30]

In fairness to Maritain, it does seem that he took all sides into consideration. He remains a philosopher in society even in a world order.

NOTES

1. Jacques Maritain, *"Bien Commun National et Bien Commun International,"* discours pronouncé au Palais Taverna, Rome, le 14 juillet 1945, à l'occasion de la Fête Nationale, *OCM,* vol. 8, 1111–12.

2. Jacques Maritain, *The Person and the Common Good,* trans. John J. Fitzgerald (New York: Charles Scribner's Sons, 1947), 43–44.

3. Jacques Maritain, *Man and the State* (Chicago: University of Chicago Press, 1951), 188–216.

4. Ibid., 188.

5. Robert M. Hutchins, *St. Thomas and the World Order* (The Aquinas Lecture, 1949; Milwaukee: Marquette University Press, 1949).

6. Maritain, *Man and the State,* 200.

7. Ibid.

8. See Leo Strauss, "Aristotle," *The City and Man* (Chicago: University of Chicago Press, 1964), 13–49.

9. Maritain, *Man and the State,* 192.

10. Maritain, *The Person and the Common Good,* 7.

11. Maritain, *Man and the State,* 11–12.

12. Ibid., 190.

13. Ibid., 195. Maritain acknowledges that there is a milder and less technical use of the word "sovereign" in which it simply means relatively autonomous.

14. Ibid., 196.

15. Ibid., 198.

16. Ibid., 202.

17. Ibid.

18. Ibid., 204.

19. Ibid., 203.

20. Ibid., 207.

21. Ibid.

22. Ibid., 208.
23. Ibid., 209.
24. Ibid., 210.
25. Ibid., 26.
26. Ibid., 210–11.
27. Ibid., 212.
28. Ibid., 216.
29. Ibid., 201.
30. Ibid., 200–201.

CONCLUSION

The political philosophy of Jacques Maritain concludes where it began. On 4 March 1962, from Toulouse, Maritain wrote to Charles Journet concerning an article by Helmut Gollwitzer on the Christian conscience about the use of atomic weapons. Maritain affirmed in advance the position that came to be the main Western policy position to counteract hostile nuclear or atomic weapons, a policy of deterrence that seems to have worked. The end did not justify the means, but clear thinking about particular means did. His articulation of this position is based on the principle of choosing the lesser evil. This principle permits, when spelled out, making and threatening to use such weapons in circumstances where political institutions of reason to resolve the matter in another manner are lacking.[1] I will not recapitulate Maritain's intricate analysis here. I do emphasize, however, that Maritain's great intellectual strength in politics, something that can be seen throughout these chapters, is his capacity to combine, to recall his marvelous phrase, "justice, brains, and strength" not only at the level of theory but also as a guide for practice.

Maritain habitually identifies himself as a philosopher. A philosopher sees political things not just by themselves but in the overall structure of human thought and experience. Throughout these chapters, I have pointed out an openness of Maritain to all branches of philosophy as well as to revelation as it addresses itself to philosophy. This openness gives his political philosophy a particular character. He remains loyal to the Aristotelian tradition that relates politics to contemplation and the contemplation of *what is* back to politics. Maritain is interesting and exciting not simply because he writes *Man and the State, The Rights of Man and the Natural Law,* and *Scholasticism and Politics,* but also, keeping

221

in mind his political works, because he writes *Art and Scholasticism, A Preface to Metaphysics, The Mystery of Israel,* and *The Degrees of Knowledge.*

Moreover, Maritain does not conceive himself to be a philosopher primarily because he develops some system or insight that no one else ever before concocted. Quite the opposite; he is content if he can lead us back to Aristotle, to Augustine, and, in particular, to Thomas Aquinas. Maritain knows that they remain our fundamental teachers of the highest things. Novelty is not his criterion of truth, which, if we really know it, is as astonishing the hundredth time we discover it as the first. In leading us back to sources of *what is,* he teaches us the importance of what has already been discovered, almost all of which is astonishingly new to an age that has forgotten the wellsprings of truth.

Maritain himself knows Descartes, Rousseau, and Hegel. He tells us of the importance of Henri Bergson in his early studies in Paris. Maritain is grounded in what other philosophers have thought. If we read Maritain's *Notebooks,* we see how much teaching others and being taught by them are part of his life. Indeed, he devotes much attention to education. We would do well to read, in *The Education of Man,* Maritain's two essays, "Moral and Spiritual Values in Education" and "The Education of Women."[2] Yet he knows that education is not itself a "subject" of knowledge but the process by which we come to something else besides education, to the truth itself.

In his obituary of Maritain, John W. Donohue recalls being at a seminar on Thanksgiving weekend at the Anglican-sponsored Kent School in Connecticut in 1955. Maritain, then seventy-two years old, spoke about Christian education. This is how Donohue remembers him that day:

> One sensed that the audience not only admired the thought but cherished the thinker—had, in fact, a special feeling for his slight figure in the dark suit. From one angle, he was the very image of the contemplative philosopher with heavy-lidded eyes under a shock of white hair. But there was also something genial and gentle about him, and for many of his listeners he was a living symbol of ecumenical neighborliness.[3]

In the lectures and addresses of Maritain found in various volumes of his *Oeuvres Complètes,* this combination of contemplative presence and gentle response comes through again and again.

Maritain's life, in one sense, is a life of excited controversy. He is involved in many struggles—over the French Right with Charles Maurras, over whether he was a socialist in *Integral Humanism,* over the Spanish Civil War, over French trauma during World War II, over the natural law and his Democratic Charter, over his praise of America that shocked the European left, and over some of the dangerous movements following Vatican II in *The Peasant of the Garonne.* Eduardo Frei, former president of Chile, goes into politics after reading Maritain. Rafael Caldera in Venezuela is his pupil. Copies of *Christianity and Democracy* are dropped by the RAF over Poland during World War II. Maritain chairs the committee on human rights—other members, Aldous Huxley, E. H. Carr, Benedetto Croce, and Teilhard de Chardin—whose document forms the basis of the United Nations Declaration of Rights in 1948. His influence in Brazil in the 1930s for a democratic movement is decisive. Even as an old man, Maritain reconsiders in *Approches sans entraves,* of all things, a most curious theory to save the devil by putting him in Limbo.[4]

After reading him for a long time, however, my impression is that Maritain was both a gentle man and a lively controversialist. But he was mainly a lover of what is true and what is good. He had the humility and courage to acknowledge the truth found by others with the originality and grace to be genuinely delighted by it. There is a certain serenity and consistency in Maritain. And he can be wrong. What is most striking about him, however, is his capacity to indicate how one thing leads to everything else. He does not discuss art without discussing prudence. He does not tell us to study politics without telling us to study metaphysics. He does not talk about truth without also knowing what St. Paul and St. John said about it.

In reading Maritain, we must be aware of his wife's welcome influence. Raïssa Maritain was a woman who knew of the mystical life itself, theories about which they both studied.[5] Her presence makes Maritain aware of levels of reality that are closed to us if we are not willing to see more than ourselves. "As an atheist, I preferred metaphysics because it is the supreme science, the ultimate crowning of reason," Raïssa Maritain wrote in 1919. "As a Catholic I love it still more because it allows us to have access to theology. . . . It is not enough for me to live, I wanted a reason for living and moral principles which were based on an absolutely certain knowledge."[6] Carefully giving reasons to live and to find the foundations of certain knowledge describes in large part the vocation that Maritain set for himself.

We have seen the influence that the events of his time had on Maritain, in particular the fate of the Jews during World War II. He is not a philosopher who remains indifferent to political affairs because he understands that thought and action are related in the person who is also a citizen. He is quite willing to say the lack of a world political order is an evil that makes the considerations about nuclear weapons so dire and difficult. Men could make what was lacking to be "possible"—a bold affirmation. But not just any solution is proper, even if it is "possible." Maritain's continual efforts to reestablish natural law as a common basis for thinking about human affairs is rooted in his awareness that men do have things in common and that they have to find a means of discourse across cultures and philosophies—another thing to be made "possible." Maritain's grandest claim is that he was a philosopher, not a philosopher against revelation, not a philosopher against science, not a philosopher against politics and art, but a philosopher for whom these fundamental aspects of reality still needed to know and rely on what man's unaided reason, if it might be called that, could know and properly understand.

What might we ask, in conclusion, is the political legacy of Jacques Maritain? In *Christianity and Democracy,* we find a brief chapter entitled "The Tragedy of Democracy." We might say, some half-century or more after Maritain wrote, that the principles that he saw most opposed to democracy have come to be more and more dominant in the very civilization he worked most to save. His view that "true humanism" might find its place after the demise of both forms of totalitarianism, a demise he foresaw, seems misplaced. It is "anthropocentric," not Christian, humanism that has come largely to rule the academic and cultural mind. Maritain thought that the principal reason for the "tragedy" of democracy was "of a spiritual nature."[7] Again recalling words he first learned from Bergson, he writes, that the form and ideal of what "we call democracy, springs in its essentials from the inspiration of the Gospels and cannot subsist without it."[8]

No doubt this position remains the minority position. It is worth reading Jacques Maritain because if democracy is indeed failing along the lines he spelled out, a democracy basing itself on a liberty that knows no norms but itself, his alternative and its philosophic basis become ever more attractive, if not prophetic. Maritain is a philosopher and a political philosopher who does not look for the Kingdom of God in this world. But he does think that it "must be enigmatically prepared in the midst of the pains of earthly history."[9] Maritain ever remains a philosopher of *all that is,* of God and nature, of logic and metaphysics, of mathematics and art, and, yes, of man and the state.

NOTES

1. Jacques Maritain, *"À propos du Moindre Mal en Politique,"* OCM, vol. 12, 1229–33.

2. Jacques Maritain, *The Education of Man: The Educational Philosophy of Jacques Maritain,* ed. Donald and Idella Gallagher (Garden City, N. Y.: Doubleday, 1962), 103–10, 154–58.

3. John W. Donohue, "Jacques Maritain, 1882–1973," *America* 126 (12 May 1973), 436.

4. Jacques Maritain, *"Idées eschatologiques,"* Approches sans entraves, OCM, vol. 13, 441–78.

5. Jacques Maritain, in collaboration with Raïssa Maritain, *Liturgy and Contemplation,* trans. Joseph W. Evans (New York: P. J. Kennedy and Sons, 1960); *Prayer and Intelligence,* trans. Ansgar Thorold (New York: Sheed & Ward, 1929).

6. *Raïssa's Journal,* (Albany, N. Y.: Magi Books, 1974), 110.

7. Jacques Maritain, *Christianity and Democracy,* trans. Doris C. Anson (San Francisco: Ignatius Press, 1986), 19.

8. Ibid., 20.

9. Ibid., 34.

BIBLIOGRAPHY

PRIMARY SOURCES

A. Jacques Maritain:

A Preface to Metaphysics: Seven Lectures on Being. New York: Mentor-Omega, 1962. 142 pp.

Approaches to God. Translated by Peter O'Reilly. New York: Collier, 1962. 125 pp.

Art and Scholasticism and the Frontiers of Poetry. Translated by Joseph W. Evans. Notre Dame: University of Notre Dame Press, 1972. 234 pp.

Challenges and Renewals: Selected Readings. Edited by Joseph W. Evans and Leo R. Ward. Cleveland: World Publishers—Meridian, 1966. 389 pp.

Christianity and Democracy. Translated by Doris C. Anton. San Francisco: Ignatius Press, 1986. 86 pp.

Creative Intuition in Art and Poetry. A. W. Mellon Lectures in the Fine Arts, 1953; New York: Meridian, 1955. 339 pp.

The Education of Man: The Educational Philosophy of Jacques Maritain. Edited by Donald and Idella Gallagher. Garden City, N. Y.: Doubleday, 1962. 191 pp.

An Essay in Christian Philosophy. Translated by Edward H. Flannery. New York: The Philosophical Library, 1955. 116 pp.

Existence and the Existent: An Essay on Christian Existentialism. Translated by Lewis Galantiere and Gerald B. Phelan. Garden City, N. Y.: Doubleday, Image, 1957. 153 pp.

Freedom in the Modern World. Translated by Richard O'Sullivan. New York: Charles Scribner's Sons, 1936. 223 pp.

Integral Humanism: Temporal and Spiritual Problems of a New Christendom. Translated by Joseph W. Evans. Notre Dame: University of Notre Dame Press, 1973. 308 pp.

An Introduction to Philosophy. Translated by E. I. Watkin. London: Sheed & Ward, 1946. 207 pp.

Liturgy and Contemplation. In collaboration with Raïssa Maritain. Translated by Joseph W. Evans. New York: P. J. Kennedy and Sons, 1960. 96 pp.

The Living Thoughts of St. Paul. Texts Selected with Comments by Jacques Maritain. Translated by Harry L. Binsse. New York: Longmans, Green and Co., 1941. 135 pp.

Man and the State. Chicago: University of Chicago Press, 1951. 219 pp.

Notebooks. Translated by Joseph W. Evans. Albany, N. Y.: Magi Books, 1984. 311 pp.

Oeuvres Complètes (Jacques et Raïssa Maritain). 15 vols. Paris: Éditions Saint-Paul; Fribourg, Suisse: Éditions Universitaires, 1982–1991. (*The Collected Works of Jacques Maritain.* Notre Dame: University of Notre Dame Press, 1996 and forthcoming. 20 vols.)

On the Grace and Humanity of Jesus. Translated by Joseph W. Evans. New York: Herder and Herder, 1969. 144 pp.

On the Philosophy of History. Edited by Joseph W. Evans. New York: Charles Scribner's Sons, 1957. 180 pp.

On the Use of Philosophy: Three Essays. New York: Atheneum, 1965. 71 pp.

The Peasant of the Garonne: An Old Layman Questions Himself about the Present Time. Translated by Michael Cuddihy and Elizabeth Hughes. New York: Holt, Rinehart, and Winston, 1968. 277 pp.

The Person and the Common Good. Translated by John J. Fitzgerald. New York: Charles Scribner's Sons, 1947. 98 pp.

Prayer and Intelligence, in collaboration with Raïssa Maritain. Translated by Ansgar Thorold. New York: Sheed & Ward, 1928. 56 pp.

The Range of Reason. New York: Charles Scribner's Sons, 1952. 227 pp.

Reflections on America. New York: Charles Scribner's Sons, 1958. 205 pp.

The Responsibility of the Artist. New York: Charles Scribner's Sons, 1960. 120 pp.

The Rights of Man and Natural Law. Translated by Doris C. Anton. San Francisco: Ingantius Press, 1986. Pp. 87–200.

St. Thomas and the Problem of Evil. The Aquinas Lecture, 1942; Milwaukee: Marquette University Press, 1942. 46 pp.

Science and Wisdom. Translated by Bernard Wall. New York: Charles Scribner's Sons, 1940. 241 pp.

Scholasticism and Politics. Translation edited by Mortimer J. Adler. Garden City, N. Y.: Doubleday, Image, 1960. 230 pp.

Sin of the Angel: An Essay on a Reinterpretation of Some Thomistic Positions. Translated by William Rossner, S. J. Westminster, Md.: The Newman Press, 1959. 106 pp.

The Social and Political Philosophy of Jacques Maritain: Selected Essays. Selected by

Joseph W. Evans and Leo R. Ward. Notre Dame: University of Notre Dame Press, 1976. 348 pp.

Theonas: Conversations of a Sage. Translated by F. J. Sheed. New York: Sheed & Ward, 1933. 200 pp.

Three Reformers: Luther-Descartes-Rousseau. Westport, Conn.: Greenwood, 1970. 234 pp.

Truth and Human Fellowship. Princeton, N. J.: Princeton University Press, 1957. 32 pp.

The Twilight of Civilization. Translated by Lionel Landry. New York: Sheed & Ward, 1943. 65 pp.

B. Raïssa Maritain:

Raïssa's Journal. Presented by Jacques Maritain. Albany, N. Y.: Magi Books, 1974. 404 pp.

We Have Been Friends Together: Memoirs. Translated by Julie Kernan. New York: Longmans, Green and Co., 1943. 208 pp.

"The Maritains Find God." In *The Road to Damascus.* Edited by John A. O'Brien. London: W. W. Allen, 1949. Pp. 116–143.

SECONDARY SOURCES

Books

Etudes Maritainennies—Maritain Studies. 1984–present. The Canadian Maritain Association, the Philosophy Department, University of Ottawa, have published this annual series of books and collected essays on the work of Maritain.

The American Maritain Association has published the proceedings of its annual meetings with the University of Notre Dame Press and currently by the Catholic University of America Press.

The Achievement of Jacques and Raïssa Maritian: A Bibliography. Edited by Donald and Idella Gallagher. Garden City, N. Y.: Doubleday, 1962. 256 pp.

DiJoseph, John. *Jacques Maritain and the Moral Foundations of Democracy.* Lanham, Md.: Rowman & Littlefield, 1996. 173 pp.

Freedom in the Modern World: Jacques Maritain, Yves R. Simon, Mortimer J. Adler. Edited by Michael D. Torre. Notre Dame: University of Notre Dame Press in association with the American Maritain Society, 1989. 289 pp.

Hanke, John W. *Maritain's Ontology of the Work of Art.* The Hague: Martinus Nijhoff, 1973. 131 pp.

Jacques Maritain e la filosofia del'essere. Edited by Vittorio Possenti. Venice: Il Cardo, 1996. 156 pp.

Jacques Maritain: Homage in Words and Pictures. Edited by John Howard Griffin and Yves R. Simon. Albany, N. Y.: Magi Books, 1974. 64 pp.

Lacombe, Oliver. *Jacques Maritain: La génerosité de l'intelligence.* Paris: Pierre Téqui, 1991. 165 pp.

The Maritain Volume of the Thomist. New York: Sheed & Ward, 1943. 374 pp. First published in *The Thomist,* 5 (January 1943).

McInerny, Ralph. *Art and Prudence: Studies in the Thought of Jacques Maritain.* Notre Dame: University of Notre Dame Press, 1988. 205 pp.

Papini, Roberto. *The Christian Democrat International.* Translated by Robert Royal. Lanham, Md.: Rowman & Littlefield, 1997. 289 pp.

Il Pensiero Politico di Jacques Maritain. Edited by Giancarlo Galeazzi. Milano: Massimo, 1974. 404 pp.

Power, M. Susan. *Jacques Maritain (1882–1973): Christian Democrat, and the Quest for a New Commonwealth.* Lewiston, N. Y.: The Edwin Mellen Press, 1992.

Understanding Maritain: Philosopher and Friend. Edited by Deal W. Hudson and Matthew Mancini. Macon, Ga.: Mercer University Press, 1987. 334 pp.

PERIODICALS AND CHAPTERS IN BOOKS

Aron, Raymond. "French Thought in Exile: Jacques Maritain and the Quarrel over Machiavellianism." In *In Defense of Political Reason.* Edited by Daniel J. Mahoney. Lanham, Md.: Rowman & Littlefield, 1994. Pp. 53–66.

Dennehy, Raymond. "The Intellectual Disarming of Freedom." *The New Scholasticism* 64 (Summer 1980): 326–41.

———. "Maritain's Theory of Subsistence: The Basis of His 'Existentialism'." *The Thomist* 39 (July 1973): 542–74.

———. "The Ontological Basis of Human Rights." *The Thomist* 42 (July 1978): 434–63.

———. "Rescuing Natural Law Theory from the Rationalists: Maritain's Restoration of Credibility to Natural Morality and Natural Rights." *Vera Lex* 10 (n. 1 1990): 14–16.

Dougherty, Jude. "Maritain at the Cliff's Edge: From *Antimoderne* to *Le Paysan.*" *Crisis* 12 (November 1994): 40–45.

Evans, Joseph W. "Jacques Maritain and the Problem of Pluralism in Political Life." *Review of Politics* 22 (July 1960): 307–23.

Hittinger, John. "Jacques Maritain and Yves Simon's Use of Thomas Aquinas in their Defense of Liberal Democracy." In *Thomas Aquinas and His Legacy.* Edited by David M. Gallagher. Washington, D. C.: The Catholic University of America Press, 1994. Pp. 119–72.

———. "Maritain and America." *This World* 3 (Fall 1982): 113–23.

———. "Maritain and the Intellectuals." *This World* 5 (Spring 1983): 164–68.

Knasas, John F. X. "Aquinas and Liberationist Critique of Maritain's New Christendom." *The Thomist* 52 (April 1988): 247–67.

La Farge, John. "Maritain in the Americas." *Social Order* 7 (March 1957): 121–25.

Marien, Francis J. "Social and Political Wisdom of Maritain." *Social Order* 5 (November 1955): 386–90.

McCool, Gerald A. "The Jacques Maritain Controversy in Perspective." *Thought* 50 (December 1975): 381–417.

———. "Maritain's Defense of Democracy." *Thought* 54 (June 1979): 133–42.

Schall, James V. "Everything That Can Be Saved Will Be Saved." In *What Is God Like?* Collegeville, Minn.: Michael Glazier/The Liturgical Press, 1992. Pp. 43–63.

———. "Introduction: Calvary or the Slaughterhouse." In *From Twilight to Dawn: The Cultural Vision of Jacques Maritain.* Edited by Peter A. Redpath. Notre Dame: University of Notre Dame Press in association with the American Maritain Association, 1990. Pp. 1–16.

———. "The Law of Superabundance." *Gregorianum* 72 (n. 3 1991): 515–42.

———. "Metaphysics, Theology, and Political Theory" (On Maritain's *Man and the State* and *Scholasticism and Politics.*). *Political Science Reviewer* 11 (Fall 1981): 2–25.

———. "The Mystery of 'The Mystery of Israel.' " In *Jacques Maritain and the Jews.* Edited by Robert Royal. Notre Dame: University of Notre Dame Press in association with the American Maritain Association, 1994. Pp. 51–71.

Ward, Leo R. "Maritain and the Tradition of Natural Law." *Modern Age* 19 (Fall 1975): 375–80.

RELATED BOOKS AND ESSAYS

Arendt, Hannah. *The Human Condition.* Garden City, N. Y.: Doubleday, Anchor, 1959. 385 pp.

Caldera, Rafael. *The Specificity of Christian Democracy.* Caracas: IFEDEC, 1982. 101 pp.

D'Arcy, Martin C. *The Mind and Heart of Love.* New York: Holt, 1947. 333 pp.

De Rougemont, Denis. *Love in the Western World.* Translated by Montgomery Belgion. New York: Schocken, 1983. 393 pp.

Frei, Eduardo and Ismael Bustos. *Maritain entre Nosotros.* Santiago, Chile: Instituto de Educación Politica, 1964.

Gilson, Etienne. *The Unity of Philosophical Experience.* New York: Charles Scribner's Sons, 1937. 329 pp.

Hutchins, Robert M. *St. Thomas and the World Order.* The Aquinas Lecture, 1949; Milwaukee: Marquette University Press, 1949.

Lewis, C. S. *The Four Loves.* New York: Harcourt, 1971. 159 pp.

———. *The Problem of Pain.* New York: Macmillan, 1949. 160 pp.

Machiavelli, Nicolò. *The Prince.* Edited by Leo S. de Alvarez. Irving, Tex.: University of Dallas Press, 1980. 168 pp.

McCoy, Charles N. R. *The Structure of Political Thought.* New York: McGraw-Hill, 1963. 323 pp.

Meilaender, Gilbert C. *Friendship: A Study in Theological Ethics.* Notre Dame: University of Notre Dame Press, 1981. 118 pp.

Midgley, E. B. F. "Concerning the Modernist Subversion of Political Philosophy," *The New Scholasticism* 53 (Spring 1979): 168–90.

———. *The Natural Law Tradition and the Theory of International Relations.* London: Paul Elek, 1975. 588 pp.

Orr, Susan. *Jerusalem and Athens: Reason and Revelation in the Works of Leo Strauss.* Lanham, Md.: Rowman & Littlefield, 1995. 245 pp.

Percy, Walker. "Parting Reflections." *Crisis* 8 (September 1990): 14–19.

Pieper, Josef. *About Love.* Translated by Joseph and Clara Winston. Chicago: Franciscan Herald Press, 1974. 122 pp.

Schall, James V. *At the Limits of Political Philosophy: From "Brilliant Errors" to Things of Uncommon Importance.* Washington: The Catholic University of America Press, 1996. 272 pp.

———. *The Politics of Heaven and Hell: Christian Themes from Classical, Medieval, and Modern Political Philosophy.* Lanham, Md.: University Press of America, 1984. 341 pp.

———. *Reason, Revelation, and the Foundations of Political Philosophy.* Baton Rouge: Louisiana State University Press, 1987. 254 pp.

Simon, Yves. *A General Theory of Authority.* Notre Dame: University of Notre Dame Press, 1980. 172 pp.

———. *Philosophy of Democratic Government.* Chicago: University of Chicago Press, 1951. 324 pp.

Slade, Francis, "Rule of Sovereignty: The Universal and Homogeneous State." In *The Truthful and the Good: Essays in Honor of Robert Sokolowski.* Edited by John J. Drummond and James G. Hart. Dordrecht: Kluwer Academic Publishers, n.d. Pp. 159–80.

Strauss, Leo. *The City and Man.* Chicago: University of Chicago Press, 1964. 245 pp.

————. *Liberalism: Ancient and Modern.* Ithaca: Cornell University Press, 1968. 276 pp.

————. *What Is Political Philosophy? and Other Essays.* Glencoe, Ill.: The Free Press, 1959. 311 pp.

Voegelin, Eric. *Science, Politics, and Gnosticism.* Chicago: Regnery/Gateway, 1968. 114 pp.

Walsh, David. *The Growth of the Liberal Mind.* Columbia: University of Missouri Press, 1997. 386 pp.

Wilson, Catherine. The Foundations of Christian Democracy in Chile. Honor's Thesis, Villanova University, 1994. 123 pp.

Yost, David S. *France and Conventional Defense in Western Europe.* Boulder, Colo.: Westview, 1985. 132 pp.

INDEX

ABOUT THE AUTHOR

James V. Schall is professor of government at Georgetown University. He is the author of numerous books, including *At the Limits of Political Philosophy: From "Brilliant Errors" to Things of Uncommon Importance, Does Catholicism Still Exist?,* and *Reason, Revelation, and the Foundations of Political Philosophy.*